RELIGION, RACE, AND COVID-19

RELIGION AND SOCIAL TRANSFORMATION

General Editors: Anthony B. Pinn and Stacey M. Floyd-Thomas

Religion, Race, and COVID-19

Confronting White Supremacy in the Pandemic

Edited by
Stacey M. Floyd-Thomas

With a foreword by
Michael Eric Dyson

NEW YORK UNIVERSITY PRESS
New York

NEW YORK UNIVERSITY PRESS
New York
www.nyupress.org

References to Internet websites (URLs) were accurate at the time of writing. Neither the author nor New York University Press is responsible for URLs that may have expired or changed since the manuscript was prepared.

Library of Congress Cataloging-in-Publication Data
Names: Floyd-Thomas, Stacey M., 1969– editor.
Title: Religion, race, and COVID-19 : confronting white supremacy in the pandemic / edited by Stacey M. Floyd-Thomas ; with a foreword by Michael Eric Dyson.
Description: New York : New York University Press, [2021] | Series: Religion and social transformation | Includes bibliographical references and index.
Identifiers: LCCN 2021013291 | ISBN 9781479810192 (hardback ; alk. paper) | ISBN 9781479810222 (paperback ; alk. paper) | ISBN 9781479810284 (ebook) | ISBN 9781479810277 (ebook other)
Subjects: LCSH: Social conflict—United States. | Religion and sociology—United States. | COVID-19 (Disease)—Social aspects—United States. | COVID-19 (Disease)—Religious aspects. | Racism—United States. | Discrimination—United States.
Classification: LCC HN90.S62 R45 2021 | DDC 303.60973—dc23
LC record available at https://lccn.loc.gov/2021013291

New York University Press books are printed on acid-free paper, and their binding materials are chosen for strength and durability. We strive to use environmentally responsible suppliers and materials to the greatest extent possible in publishing our books.

Manufactured in the United States of America

10 9 8 7 6 5 4 3 2 1

Also available as an ebook

To Lillian Floyd

the wind beneath my wings

and

Lillian Floyd-Thomas

my sun and shining star

500,000 and counting . . .

The memory of these dead invokes dangerous memories, which protest our forgetfulness of human others, our forgetfulness of what it means to enflesh freedom in our time and place.
—M. Shawn Copeland

CONTENTS

FOREWORD

Breathe Again

MICHAEL ERIC DYSON

Technically, I suppose, every living being dies when we cannot breathe. Our heart stops pumping, our brain's light disappears, our breath, perhaps the most fragile means to sustain our bodies, our very existence, leaves our lungs for the last time. The disappearance of breath marks the end of life in the same way that the presence of breath signals its beginning. James Weldon Johnson, at the end of his immortal poem "The Creation," says that God shaped a lump of clay into the divine image to create human life.

> Then into it he blew the breath of life,
> And man became a living soul.

Most human beings want to keep breathing. Some, in cases of extreme or extended emergency, or in cursed spells of self-destruction, conclude that breathing is no longer worth the effort to keep alive the myth of happiness, or the elusive song of delight that long ago escaped their lips to find no fruitful return in joy or satisfaction. Entire societies fight furiously, even ruthlessly, to get better ways of breathing. They establish political orders to get the better-off people in cleaner and healthier environments. They secure social and economic protections where they and their kind can literally and figuratively breathe easier. But such breathing often comes at the expense of the poor and destitute. The achingly vulnerable can't breathe easy at any time as they are pushed further into precarity, and further away from the safety and stability that the well-off enjoy. For Black folk, breathing has always been biological and metaphoric, both literal and symbolic.

From the start of our forced intimacy with North America, Black folk have been trying to breathe air that is free of the pollution of captivity, of coerced transport, of enslavement, of white supremacy, of social inequality and perennial second-class citizenship. When our captors crashed the shores of Africa to ensnare us, we ceased enjoying the air of freedom. While it is true that our breath had been snatched with bouts of unfreedom in tribal disputes and local seizures, those crucial losses approached nothing like the wholesale rejection of our liberty in chattel slavery. When we were kidnapped from our native haunts, we were denied more than the African air we breathed. We were also deprived of the oxygen of opportunities to deepen our ties to our cruelly estranged motherland. And we had withheld from us the nitrogen of nourishment from the land and limbs of our kin and loved ones.

When we were packed into seafaring vessels of mobile terror for passage to the New World, the air we breathed was polluted by the feces and urine of our fellow captives. We imbibed the stench of vomit from souls who couldn't stomach the sadistic and cruel treatment. We could barely breathe, and many of us gave up the ghost on the perilous journey as we succumbed to sickness and suffering. Some of us had our breath snatched from us at the end of a blunt instrument or by the barrel of a weapon. Some of us stopped breathing as we jumped, or were pushed, overboard. When we arrived at our various ports of call, we were deposited into zones of suffering and grounds of grief to provide relief for the white masses. We could barely breathe free air for centuries afterward. Even when we were finally granted the opportunity to inhale freedom, the relentless spray of contaminants polluted the emancipated air around us.

This backdrop helps to explain a popular saying in Black circles that when America has a cold, Black America has pneumonia. It is no accident that the analogy that best captures the suffering of Black folk in comparison to the ills of white folk has to do in large measure with labored breathing. Even the runner-up analogy shares the same trait. True, it reverses the order of racial citation by arguing that Black folk are the proverbial canary in the coal mine. In short, it suggests that what happens to us first will happen eventually to white folk and the rest of the nation. And that homespun maxim, too, rests on the deadly effect of Black lungs analogously ingesting toxins from the atmosphere.

And neither was it a surprise that those same Black lungs were more likely to quit when hit by the spread of a lethal virus.

The disappearance of Black breath ties together the global outbreak of coronavirus and the ongoing plague of Black oppression into a syndemic, or the convergence of dual pandemics. The fatalities that result from this syndemic are expressed in a common cry: I can't breathe, whether from lungs turned to sponge because of the disease's virulent spread, or, for instance, Black bodies suffocated in the merciless embrace of conscienceless cops. The syndemic reminds us that we must be vigilant in underscoring the poor health care systems that render Black and Brown bodies more vulnerable to dying from COVID-19, all because poor and working people often lack health care insurance that provides them the opportunity to prevent the spread of disease or to reduce its lethal effects. And the plague of racism certainly isn't quarantined to cops: the forty-fifth president of the United States used his bully pulpit to perpetuate legacies of white supremacy, ideas of white nationalism, and practices of xenophobia that aimed contempt at immigrants from Africa, Asia, and South and Central America.

The global pandemic dramatically shifted the way the nation and the world do business. We could no longer go out to eat in packed restaurants, watch live sporting events in person with thousands of others, take in a movie at the local cineplex, or applaud our favorite artists on the concert stage. The separation anxiety engendered by our forced apartness drove us to rely even more heavily on our technology. Whether connected to a smartphone, computer, iPad, or other tablets and devices, screens brought us into unexpected and counterintuitive communion. After all, hadn't we for years been warned of the seductions of gadgets and the distraction of contraptions that rob us of face-to-face experiences? We were thrust into electronic encounters that not a month before we could have never imagined cherishing as much as we do now. Our screens were also salvation and healing when they brought us preachers or physicians or therapists with reassuring words from above or within. Sadly, as the pandemic separated families more dramatically than any force since the Civil War, the afflicted turned to digital surfaces that were the only medium to bring their loved ones within sight for their final good-byes.

At the same time, the pandemic offers us irresistible metaphors for a particular form of Black oppression, the plague of terrorizing policing that not even COVID-19 could eclipse. No masks could hide the fear and hate of Blackness nor stop the spread of viral anti-Blackness. No volume of hand sanitizer could cleanse the grime of diseased Blackness from the hands or knees of loathsome cops. No study of viral ontology could relieve the ontological spite that many cops feel for Black being. No determination to flee the clutches of angry cops could escape the contact trace of bigoted policing. No amount of social distancing—a racially colored idea that sought, more than a century ago, to measure the amount of space that white folk would maintain from Black people in their everyday existence—could keep cops from brutalizing and killing the bodies of Blacks.

All of this came to a fateful head in the killing of George Floyd on May 25, 2020. To witness his killing captured on a mobile phone video was to watch Black breath disappear into the racist ether. It was to watch the plague of poisonous policing play out before our very eyes in the shape of a cop who gave America's racist history a glaring face. Yes, it was the spectacle of a grown Black man begging for his mother that broke the hearts of millions of people the world over. The sounds he made ripped the psychic gestalt of a white society deceitfully premised on the unimpeachable gulf between white supremacy and ordinary whiteness. Floyd's unconscionable death suggested that it was all of a piece. The primal form of violence of kneeling on a man's neck to kill him was so precise and cruelly efficient and tragically ordinary that it revealed the shameless rot at the core of a system that has never valued or loved Black bodies beyond sheer exploitation. Black breath could be squeezed out of Black lungs at will with as little care for Black well-being or worry of moral or legal consequence as Derek Chauvin expressed that fateful day.

Floyd's loss of breath, loss of body, and loss of life fueled social rebellion and historic levels of social protest. The crisis of color forced the nation to reckon with the unaddressed and unrelieved suffering this nation has endured ever since its progenitors decided to kidnap African citizens from their homes and enslave them in the New World. Ever since 1619, the emblematic year the savage theft of Black bodies became visible, to this day, when systemic racism is deeply entrenched in every nook and cranny of the culture, our original sin has continued to lash the national soul. The peril and terror unleashed by the election in 2016 of a president who embraced the spirit and impulse of white nationalists and white supremacy shock and sicken even those who predicted the tragedy of his ascent to power.

Floyd's death happened in the same period as crowds of mostly white folk stormed state capitols with their weapons flashing to protest governors shutting down their states because of the virus. Once it became clear to them that the disproportionate impact of COVID-19 on Black lungs made it a "Black disease," all bets and masks, and in some cases, sheets, were off. Once the preexisting health problems that Black and Brown folk share, from heart disease to diabetes and asthma, came into focus, white rage was sparked. Once it became apparent that Black breath was even more at risk, and that the pandemic endangered Black folk who worked on the front lines, prepared food, and delivered health care, the tolerance for restrictions on mobility collapsed. Once Black and Brown peoples' chronic lack of access to health care, and the crushing economic and social barriers they confront, made the steady evaporation of Black breath a national concern, the performance of white ressentiment was in full gear. All of this was exacerbated by a president who stoked the flames of racism, racial intolerance, and racial bigotry, and who advocated for nationalism and affirmed the virtue of "white power."

Now is the time to rediscover Black love in a time of the coronavirus. Now is the time for the nation to take a hard look at its racist practices, beliefs, ideals, goals, and aspirations. Now is the time to examine its folkways and mores, and also the norms and social and political habits, that have for too long been overlooked, ignored, or denied—or worse yet, accepted as the necessary status quo. The time for racial reckoning is upon us, and we have an incredible opportunity to grapple with our nation's shameful and tragic racial history in meaningful and enlightening ways. It is true that we must move beyond symbolic gestures of racial comity to substantive discussions of genuine equity. We must dig deep and uproot the causes of systemic racism and inequality. And we must recognize the progress betokened in removing statues of Confederate figures and racist political icons that dot our physical and psychological landscapes.

But we must move from statues to statutes, from culture to law. This will ensure that we address draconian measures, like stand-your-ground laws, that put Black and Brown lives at risk. We must also unravel the troubling legal webs that bind local prosecutors and district attorneys to the very law enforcement upon whom they depend to solve cases. These same cops often mistreat, harm, and unjustly kill Black and Brown citizens. The likelihood of those cops being held to account by the same prosecutors and district attorneys is almost nonexistent.

But we must resist racial temptations from within the stream of Black breath too. This is not the time to witch hunt our way across the racial landscape to provide gotcha moments of past racial embarrassment for white "offenders." This is not the time to obsess over their mistakes in racial protocol, or to trigger outrage by focusing exclusively or primarily on what can be heard and read as racially improper. We have bigger fish to fry. The very foundation of deeply entrenched racist practice and behavior, and of profoundly disturbing racist thought and reflection, is finally under pressure. We must keep the pressure up and go after the real culprits of racist culture: the institutional, systemic, and structural dynamics that preserve white racial hierarchies and maintain white racial privilege. These are the forces that routinely and with criminal skillfulness take away Black breath.

A bigger fish we must fry is to have a genuine racial reckoning amid a rash of unjust cop killings of Black folk. The rash has continued, becoming a rush of foul racist behavior and fatal police action that have resulted in a crisis we can no longer ignore. The cop crisis in America is driven in large measure by racial animus, conscious or not, and sustained by other deeply rooted and glaring racial inequalities in our society. We will experience no genuine relief from these plagues until we confront them. If we have not come full circle, we have at least been shown the interrelated character of the crises we confront in our present syndemic: COVID-19 has ravaged the bodies of Black and Brown people, but it has also spread in the broader population in devastating fashion. The racial pandemic began with the enslavement of Black folk, but it soon sunk the entire society with an undertow of racist brutality from which we have yet to escape. While the election of Trump seemed at first only to insult the Brown, Black, immigrant, Muslim, and LGBTQIA communities, the plague of the Trumpian doctrine—which, no matter where it flares, has two basic components of mendacity and mediocrity—swept the entire nation into its traumatizing arc.

This is a book, really a manual, that helps us to brilliantly negotiate the nefarious forces that intersect on Black, Brown, and Indigenous bodies, and that threaten to weaponize a viral pandemic into a willfully racist one. By flushing from our collective system of thought and governance the spiritual, moral, and political detritus of toxic Americanity, this book offers an ennobling and redeeming call to conscience in the age of coronavirus. The book strikes a Whitmanesque note by singing the Body Infected, in all its coarse and vulnerable parts—not to celebrate it but to properly diagnose it in order to bring it to fuller health and better breathing. Systemic racism and social inequity have turned the lungs of American democracy to mush. They must be "Blacksinated" from the further spread of the virus of anti-Blackness. This book is a huge dose of moral medicine for the maladies of our nation.

If the perils of Black breathing show us anything, it is that what happens first to Black folk will eventually happen to the rest of the nation. Yes, we are the canaries in the coal mine of American social and political life. But the good news is that if we solve the persistent problems of Black breath, of Black breathing, of the loss of Black breath, we will, like James Weldon Johnson suggested, breathe new meaning into the lungs of American democracy. If we can turn to Black entertainers and athletes to artistically enliven our national spirit—and often to deepen our collective conscience—we can turn to #BlackLivesMatter and Stacey Abrams and Stacey Floyd-Thomas and others to strengthen our national will and our democratic practice. Blackness has often saved this nation, and if we engage it in our day and time, it may well do it again when we need it most. And then, at long last, we may all be able to breathe a collective sigh of relief.

PREFACE

STACEY M. FLOYD-THOMAS

In her classic novel, *Their Eyes Were Watching God*, celebrated author and patron saint of womanist thought Zora Neale Hurston reminds us, *"There are years that ask questions and years that answer."*[1] Hurston's words speak to our souls, as we consider the epochal, COVID-19 blight that took hold in 2020. There is a fierce urgency to find answers to the questions that these events pose. Not only the death-dealing ravages of COVID-19 but also the deadening blows of police violence and political unrest have created an unrelenting search for clarity and certainty in the midst of the increasing complexity of the world around us. The truth of the matter is we can neither survive nor flourish if many of these questions remain unresolved and the lessons to be drawn from these all-consuming crises go unlearned.

The adage "Hindsight is 20/20" is a hopeful sentiment rather than an established truth. Søren Kierkegaard's theological inflection on this aphorism extols that "life can only be understood backwards; but it must be lived forwards."[2] Predicated on a never-ending future, it presupposes the privileged position that time is always on one's side. This perspective denotes the opportunities afforded to someone who routinely has the luxury of reflecting upon time gone by in an effort to chart one's future. Yet what about those who must incessantly look back and peripherally process, as they are compelled to move forward in real time—particularly in times of devastation, despair, or distress? Those who are trapped day in and day out within the tumult of perilous times most often do not have the option to contemplate what has just occurred, but rather have to figure out ways to discern immediately— sometimes spontaneously—what is the best, most advantageous move to make, lest they suffer even more detrimental consequences not of their own making or choosing. When we consider the widespread devastation caused not only by COVID-19 but also the interlocking systems of oppression that exacerbated the enormous toll it has taken on so many lives, we realize that, for those on the margins of society, "hindsight" does not simply refer to *learning from* one's past but also *living with* one's past in such a way as to gain immediate insight that is crucial for instantaneous foresight.

It is for reasons such as these that this book, by design, has come to fruition with one foot squarely in the midst of the crisis and one foot just a step beyond. It has been envisioned, written, and published while both experiencing the ongoing reality and mounting consequences of the COVID-19 crises and taking the initial steps to reflect upon them from the smallest modicum of temporal distance and perspectival separation—which is to say, this book walks a tightrope, by trying to learn from our current plight while also living so much of it in real time. There is much to be said about engaging the troubles of our current era while also enduring them. Inasmuch as it is a recent work of contemporary lament, at its core this book is intended to lay the groundwork for deeper, long-term historical insight. Indeed, sometimes one can only reflect well when provided with sufficient time and enough contemplative space. But, as suggested above, the motivating force that drove this volume from inception to completion was the premise that, by situating it in both the now and the next, we are doubling down on that most tender and tendentious human endeavor: hope. Nonetheless, as one reflects in real time beyond the numerous horrors and hardships that took hold in 2020, one has to be ever cognizant that there are multiple, clear indications that this "novel" coronavirus is still mutating and people are still dying because of it. Even as I write this preface, therefore, I do so with the haunting realization that the markers of days, months, and even years on a calendar are mere human constructions that feign some modicum of control over natural phenomena that are far more powerful than our ability to comprehend or constrain them.

The COVID-19 pandemic also offers an unprecedented opportunity to explore how religion, race, and civil unrest are interconnected. As a collection of essays, this book reveals the intense necessity to collaborate, both as people and as a nation, in creating alternatives to dehumanizing systems. This volume is founded upon the conviction that such an enterprise requires an intersectional as well as a multidisciplinary analysis.

Most importantly, it demonstrates how deep solidarity, coupled with a compassionate critique rooted in the best virtues and values bestowed by religious imperatives, can help us bring our country into better view. Several critical insights have emerged, because of what COVID-19 has revealed about the United States. Some lessons are crystal clear, while others might be somewhat more obscure, as exemplified by the manner in which citizens who typically went largely unnoticed and undervalued suddenly came into focus as "essential workers" risking their lives during the crisis to keep fellow Americans alive and the entire nation moving forward. But there are many other lessons, once overlooked, that are now starting to come into sharper focus as they are now determined to be "essential" in more than name only. We are writing this volume, therefore, in large part for those who in this moment find their only hope resides in trying to discern a way forward for positive life while facing such death-dealing odds.

As a final note, although the subject of this volume is fraught with the multiple diseases—physical, social, and spiritual—that afflict our nation, the process of creating this anthology has been life-giving for all of us who contributed to its creation. In a moment marked by paralysis, turmoil, and death, it was critical for us to hold on to hope and wrest a win in a year marked largely by loss. Most of us have family members, friends, or colleagues who have fallen prey to the virus, and several of us had the COVID-19 virus raging through our bodies. And each of us suffered the residual effects and incalculable losses that the year had in store for all of us, whether burying loved ones from a distance, engaging in scholarly activism, or being overtaxed by our respective institutions that were striving to save souls, minds, and lives, while doing the work of religion and education. In hindsight, this volume provided us a greater witness and heightened resolve to strive and search for the attainment of greater meaning. We promised not to give up on this project, each other, or searching for answers, despite the travesties of the various circumstances at hand. We remained patient and continued to search for meaning in things both physical and spiritual. Indeed, there are years in which resolutions are never realized and hope is lost, because what are imagined to be road signs leading to new destinations instead become obstacles to the journey itself. Nonetheless, the promise of a future and new possibilities beyond 2020 makes clear to us that whatever lies ahead necessitates urgency rather than complacency, endurance rather than escape, and action rather than ambivalence. This volume seeks both to make plain the clarifying questions that have gone unanswered and to foment the courage to interrogate the answers that eventually will materialize.

S.M.F.T.
Nashville, Tennessee
February 14, 2021

NOTES

1 Zora Neale Hurston, *Their Eyes Were Watching God* (New York: Harper Perennial, 1999), 21.
2 Søren Kierkegaard, *Søren Kierkegaards Skrifter* (Copenhagen: Søren Kierkegaard Research Center, 1997), 18:306.

Introduction

The Evidence of Things Not Seen: The Twin Viruses of Blind Faith and Color Blindness

STACEY M. FLOYD-THOMAS

The COVID-19 crisis that arose in 2020 marked more than a moment in time. The particular dynamics emerging from the coronavirus pandemic and its effects have been felt most intensely by America's most vulnerable populations, many of whom are disproportionately people of color and the working poor, and they have thrown into sharp relief the health and economic disparities that have long affected these populations. In this respect, the pandemic offers the possibility for a pragmatic and prescient analysis of the American experiment of democracy and freedom with regard to race and religion.

It is quite fitting that COVID-19 arrived on the world stage at the start of both a new year and a new decade. As one of the worst, most widespread pandemics in a century, the resultant crisis represents a world-historical event that will leave its imprint on lives and cultures for decades to come. In a matter of months, the disease rapidly swept around the globe, ravaging the resources as well as the resolve of nations believed to be untouchable, unflappable, and impenetrable. It forced people and nations to hit the ground running to make sense of life and death in the face of this global existential threat. Having perennially and flagrantly touted their first-world power and privileged status as those living in the land of the free and home of the brave, Americans particularly experienced humility and vulnerability in the face of this devastating disease. Indeed, at the height of the pandemic, the nation experienced loss of life on a daily basis that rivaled that of September 11, 2001; by any measure, 2020 was deadly and daunting. At its close nearly four hundred thousand Americans had died from COVID-19.

The rampant spread of the pandemic resulted in the grim realization that this virus has neither special regard nor respect for race, class, or country. In COVID-19, the extraordinary power of American exceptionalism met its match. Even so, by and large, the Black community suffered in a disproportionate way, with Black people approximately three times more likely to die from COVID-19 compared to their white counterparts. And even as the pandemic raged, the nation was still grappling with its ongoing racial crisis; within the months of February and March 2020 alone, over two hundred Black people died from police brutality.

Indeed, it is noteworthy that the COVID-19 pandemic occurred simultaneously with two crucially impactful social events: a series of anti-Black homicides that reached a tipping point in May 25, 2020, with the homicidal asphyxiation by a Minneapolis police officer of forty-six-year-old George Floyd, who at the time was himself recovering from COVID-19, and the subsequent response and reemergence of the #BlackLivesMatter movement, a rapidly growing social protest movement comprising people from a spectrum of racial backgrounds and walks of life. The systemic anti-Black bias and state-sanctioned violence among law enforcement against people of color is itself a ravaging pathogen within the body politic of American society—a virulent host upon which the coronavirus has attached itself and found ample sustenance and weakened immunity. Conversely, #BlackLivesMatter can be conceptualized as a sort of social vaccination of care and concern—one that works to fight racist social ills in tandem with medicinal vaccines as they combat the COVID-19 virus.

The United States exhibited a frail and fractured body politic that offered little more than a handful of haphazard options and makeshift half-measures on local, state, and federal levels. Political leadership across the board seemed unable to counter or nullify the invidious and injurious right-wing culture of white supremacy expressed at the highest echelons of the federal government. As a result, discourse concerning the virus must seriously engage the constraints faced by those members of society deemed "the least of these." Today's rhetoric of "essential workers," "frontline heroes," and "the common good" constitutes a gentler, more euphemistic language, while still being ensnared by the abrasive and abusive right-wing ideology undergirding some of the worst contemporary social policies and practices. These paltry yet palliative efforts ultimately serve only to mask an otherwise indefensible system. Moreover, a truly twisted and intertwined sociological and theological structure supports our current social order: working people everywhere—most especially women, immigrants, and people of color—are ruthlessly dominated by a sociopolitical, cultural, economic, and religious hierarchy that prioritizes the wishes and whims of an elite few who benefit most from systemic white male privilege.

The crisis both captures the zeitgeist of the Trump era in a nutshell, and begs an assessment in light of the broader social, political, cultural, and religious factors that have shaped racial realities in American life and US religious responses to the pandemic. The chapters in this book respond to this mandate. Written by a wide, diverse range of religious scholars—anthropologists, ethicists, historians, legal experts, rhetoricians, sociologists, and theologians—they collectively analyze the coronavirus at the intersection of race and religion to reveal how it will reshape for years to come the broad contours of political, economic, institutional, and spiritual concerns within American society and culture. The explorations of these issues shed light on various dimensions of trauma, outrage, grief, and loss, while also exposing the fissures revealed by COVID-19's lethality and illuminating how the racial realities and religious significance associated with the virus might inform our understanding of a postpandemic future in new ways.

This volume, thus, focuses on religion, race, and COVID-19, highlighting how the dynamics emerging from the virus are affecting our most vulnerable populations and shaping a new religious landscape. The book makes the case that the pandemic is not just a medical, economic, or social phenomenon but also a religious one. Religious practice has been altered in profound ways. Issues of religious freedom were reignited over debates concerning whether government can restrict church services. Christian white supremacists not only defied shelter-in-place orders, but also found new ways to propagate racist attacks, with their white Christian identity seeming to fuel these reactions to the pandemic. Some religious leaders—including among communities of color—saw the virus as an indicator of God's wrath or as a divine test, such that altering traditional practices to mitigate the virus's spread was perceived to indicate a weakening of faith.

This book looks to illuminate the religious significance of the virus, particularly the ways in which a theological structure supports our current social order, in which essential workers tend to be among society's most vulnerable and our social and religious hierarchies prioritize those who benefit from white male privilege. The authors also show how the marginalized in society draw on theological and religious resources to deal with these existential threats. While not comprehensive, the volume analyzes many of the challenges, changes, and contours that demonstrate how religion informs social transformation, but it does not always presume or automatically predict a positive outcome. In the wake of this pandemic, and the larger Pandora's box that it has uncovered, the book offers insight into the saliency and lasting impact of religiosity within human culture, both for America and around the world.

Each of the chapters contends with an issue relating to religion, race, and the fallout from the virus, exploring alternatives to the contemporary status quo and grappling with the issues that the threats of both the coronavirus and systemic racism have made all the more obvious. Additionally, they examine the collective failure of the national imagination to fully grasp the roots of American inequalities that the uncontrolled outbreak and spread of COVID-19 have exposed in various sectors of our society and culture. These resounding inequalities and resulting injustices lie behind the massive wave of sprawling lines outside food banks, polling centers, COVID-19 testing sites, and state unemployment offices, as well as ever expanding protests against racial violence. While COVID-19 does not discriminate according to racial and ethnic differences, the virus did an astonishing job adapting to America's long-standing legacies of social stigmas and structural inequality, especially the country's inhumane disregard of marginalized communities and oppressed peoples. This stark reality limits historical possibilities to seemingly draconian options, often presented as if they represent the only alternatives to combat a rising tide of infections and related deaths.

Yet alternatives to the contemporary status quo are not only possible but also necessary in order to illustrate emergent forms of intersectional solidarity that expand the vision of life and liberation beyond the threats posed by both the coronavirus and systemic racism. People of faith possess not only theological prerogatives but also political, cultural, and economic imperatives requiring them to deal with the idolatry of vicious and virulent white supremacy in tandem with the existential menace posed by the COVID-19 pandemic. While diverse in their personas and perspectives, the contributors to this volume share a common concern to reveal the intense urgency behind demands to collaborate, as people and as a nation, in creating alternatives to dehumanizing systems, by suggesting that such an enterprise requires an intersectional and interdisciplinary approach as well as a multidisciplinary analysis. Most importantly, they demonstrate how deep solidarity and a compassionate critique, both rooted in the best virtues and values bestowed by religious imperatives, can help us meet what Martin Luther King Jr. once called "the fierce urgency of now."

Several critical insights have emerged because of what COVID-19 has revealed about the United States. Some lessons are crystal clear. Many citizens who typically go unnoticed, undervalued, undercompensated, and unprotected have risked their lives during this crisis to save others. Whether they are serving as grocery clerks, fast-food employees, mail carriers and package deliverers, cleaners, janitors, trash collectors, or frontline health care providers, their labor has been essential not only in keeping America moving forward but also literally in keeping Americans alive even as they themselves often face precarious economic and health situations. But other lessons, once denied, are also starting to come into sharper focus. With this in mind, we are determined to reciprocate and be essential for those who struggle to discern a way forward for positive life while facing such death-dealing odds.

Scholars have long wrestled with the value of knowledge production in the midst of fleeting yet prescient events. This book intends to engage the "transvaluation" of American understandings of faith in the midst of fear, in order to show how social transformation actually occurs when creative and illuminating, albeit inchoate, faith is both formed and informed during crises. An analysis of this transformation of faith amid fear will help us to understand and catalog the creation of new forms of religion seeking to inform the process of meaning-making in the midst of the multiple crises of this historic era. This effort explores this phenomenon while illustrating how scholarship itself becomes primary source material whenever it seeks to provide scholarly accuracy in media res.

Chapter Outline

The book begins with "'First Natural, Then Spiritual': The Context and Contours of Black Faith in the COVID-19 Era," by Stacey Floyd-Thomas, in which she considers how the multiple, yet merged, COVID-19 crises have reawakened the activist vision of the sanctuary movement. Much like hush harbors, the Underground Railroad, and other historic segregated and subversive endeavors brought together spiritual courage and secular concerns, this modern-day sanctuary movement once again relies upon the spirituality of an invisible institution in order to save Black lives. It aims to wrest Black faith from shallow, sterile, and stultifying religion that emulates mainline ecclesiastical bodies while undermining social cohesion and self-definition based on Black racial identity as much as shared religious heritage. This new, impromptu sanctuary movement emerged as a rapid response to stay-at-home mandates and racial hostility as the faith of Black people resurfaced in live-streaming spaces, providing both asylum and amelioration in the face of a nation exhibiting an appalling response to a lethal virus and systemic racism in a society that, by all indications, affirms that Black lives don't matter. Through a combination of media analysis and case studies of clergy and congregations located in hotspots, Floyd-Thomas examines those who experienced deadly stress when a pandemic and violent racism collided. In so doing, she explores the unique ways in which the pandemic has compelled the pragmatic saliency of Black faith to strip away all pretenses about the current state of our society and proclaim what matters most in saving Black lives without losing their souls in the process.

In chapter 2, "Who's Saving Whom?: Black Millennials and the Revivification of Religious Communities," Melanie C. Jones notes that the COVID-19 pandemic marked a viral crisis of faith as shelter-in-place mandates forced faith communities to shift from institutional edifices to streaming websites to remain spiritually vibrant, socially relevant, and economically solvent. In their hopes of staying afloat, many Black ministries, ranging from makeshift storefront churches to megaministries, turned to millennials—people born between 1980 and 2000—in order to help save the day. Millennials not only represent the largest, most educated generation in the United States but also serve as the digital natives responsible for the rise and promulgation of social media (Facebook, Instagram, Snapchat, etc.). Prior to the pandemic, however, Jones contends that a generation gap existed within the Black Church tradition. On the one hand, many elders previously held fast to pejorative assumptions about the young adults in their midst as either irreverent or irrelevant to the perceived viability of the tradition. On the other hand, this prevalent narrative ignored the 65 percent of the less popularized majority of Black millennials who still belong to traditional faith communities, as well as those who value religious experience garnered through nontraditional pathways. This chapter examines how, at the height of the global COVID-19 outbreak, countless clergy were hailing millennials as champions for the ways they have advanced the church into the furthest reaches of the online arena. In this time of crisis, Black churches are now looking to these young, gifted, and Black digital natives to help them potentially transform these virtual realms into sacred spaces dedicated to social change and prophetic ministry. The very generation indicted for abandoning faith is now, amid the COVID-19 pandemic, called to save faith communities from the depths of decline, despair, and dis-ease.

In "Live and Let Die: Spirits of White Christian Male Defiance in the Age of COVID-19," Christopher M. Driscoll asserts that the COVID-19 pandemic has been characterized by a pattern of white Christian men defying state and federal law, particularly by holding worship and funeral services. Additionally, a new, yet not-so-new kind of racist and misogynistic violence has emerged in the phenomenon of "Zoom bombing," which follows tactics of individual vigilantism and anonymous acts of violence at work historically among white Christian supremacists. This defiance also includes more general forms of bucking of social decorum and best health practices, exemplified well by the former president's refusal to wear face coverings when in public spaces. While such behavior is neither new nor sporadic, the pandemic offers a certain and revealing clarity to this behavior. Driscoll historicizes and contextualizes white US Christian male defiance in the midst of COVID-19, a defiance with roots both in a white Western Christian heritage of religious sanctioning and justification for social atrocities, and in the tactics of a specific frontier faith that developed *as* white American Christianity. In fact, these broad behavioral trends can be explored with specific attention to white Christian men and their historic reliance on pandemic and disease. Driscoll's chapter addresses the following questions: How and why have white Christian men defied social distancing orders, engaging in racist rhetoric and even physical attacks? Did something about white Christian social identity and heritage fuel this reaction to the pandemic?

Chapter 4, "Where There Are No Answers: Reflecting on Theological Claims in the Age of COVID-19," by Anthony B. Pinn, argues that Christian communities have not been without a response to these challenging times and are attempting to make religious sense of circumstances that target some fundamental assumptions regarding collective life. They do this by using theology as a language meant to offer stability and comfort by pointing out the basic problem at work and the resolution available. While this phenomenon is a general effort within Christian circles, it is most graphically present in the rhetoric and actions of religious leaders in general and religious leaders of color in particular. Pinn explores how challenges to this particular theologized response—of Christian business as usual—are viewed as an attack on Christians, for whom this virus is something of a test of faith and altering traditional practices are viewed as a weakening of faith. Others see the virus as pointing to an existing moral failure, not simply of Christian communities but of the nation as a whole, that resulted in God's wrath. In a word, it is a consequence of sinfulness instead of a consideration of sickness. Pinn makes the case that a rigid commitment to religious business as usual expressed as an act of religious commitment ignores threats to physical life, most particularly for the most vulnerable and essential among us.

In "The Corons and American Indian Genocide: Weaponizing Infectious Disease as the Continuation of a eurochristian Religious Project," Tink Tinker (wazhazhe / Osage Nation) addresses how American Indians view the coronavirus through the prism of the history of genocide against Native peoples and as the continuation of a Eurochristian religious project. More than five hundred years ago, when Eurochristian diseases became genocidal pandemics among Indian communities, the earliest Eurochristian colonizers rejoiced, and later chronicled them politically, theologically, and legally. As Indian peoples became increasingly infected by the coronavirus and began dying in Indian communities across Turtle Island in early 2020, Indian memories of the earlier biological genocide leapt back to life. Tinker's chapter contends that from the symbolic imagery and sacred rhetoric of the New Israel to Manifest Destiny to American exceptionalism, Eurochristian colonialism has continually given political legitimation and religious motivation to the natural disasters and other catastrophic moments that have befallen American Indians throughout their history.

In "Love Crafts Countries: Loving beyond the White Divide—A Story of Blackness, Korea, and Transformative Power on the Damascus Road," Blanche Bong Cook explores a transformational consciousness rooted in intersectionality as an antidote to white heteropatriarchy. Using the acclaimed novel and HBO television series *Lovecraft Country* as a source of inspiration and interpretation, Cook offers in chapter 6 intersectional consciousness and redemptive love as a prototype of solidarity among subaltern occupants of the Lovecraft Countries, places of endless precarity. It is a love story set in the Korean War and the Black working-class South Side of Chicago with two protagonists who love beyond the white heteropatriarchal divide, finding a redemptive love that endures beyond the grave. It is a love story of choice: we can emerge from COVID-19 and live together, or we can continue our treachery in silos and die.

In his chapter, "Insure Domestic Tranquility: The Uncivil, Un-Christian and Unconstitutional Crisis in a COVID-19-Era America," Miguel A. De La Torre focuses on the fact that the preamble of the US Constitution calls for the government to *insure domestic tranquility*. The founders of the American Republic constructed a political state that, during times of social strife and uncertainty, would ensure peace—peace on the streets and peace of mind from whatever chaos the nation would have to face. But De La Torre emphasizes that those who ratified the Constitution originally intended domestic tranquility to only apply to whites, to the exclusion of those who were not considered and never could be deemed fully human. He argues in chapter 7 that this particular sociopolitical foundation of the United States best explains the current disproportionate impact that COVID-19 is having upon disenfranchised communities of color. Thus, US citizens, residents, and migrants of color are left out of the *domestic tranquility* safeguard as they face higher death tolls and greater levels of financial ruin. The violence resulting from the coronavirus is exacerbated by the consequences of centuries of institutionalized violence caused by US racism and ethnic discrimination. As both a Christian social ethicist and Latinx studies scholar, De La Torre questions: How is the Christian concept of hope to be defined in the midst of the hopelessness that COVID-19 brings to those disinherited communities relegated to the underside of US history and society? What becomes the Christian ethical response? In response, he explores how to respond to COVID-19 through the motif of *jodiendo* to arrive at a more liberationist approach to the postmodern angst in which Latinx find themselves.

In chapter 8, "Deep in the Heart of Texas: Race, Religion, and Rights in the COVID-19 Era," Juan M. Floyd-Thomas offers a microhistorical study of Texas that focuses on how influential conservative political figures in the Lone Star State demonstrated a lethal blend of neoliberalism, nihilism, and necropolitics to spur a frenetic rush to "re-open America" while much of the United States was still in the throes of widespread viral infection. Such activity, Floyd-Thomas argues, throws into sharp relief a wide array of previously ignored, yet persistent social inequalities. He utilizes sociological data, public policy papers, economic indicators, and other sources in order to show how the poorly planned and badly botched attempts to revive the US economy most negatively impacted the most vulnerable demographics of our society: the working poor, women, people of color, immigrants, and the elderly. He concludes his chapter by highlighting the key concern of finding both the meaning of life and resources for hope in the midst of a global pandemic.

Conā S. M. Marshall, in her chapter "Dying Laughing: Comedic Relief and Redemption in the Time of COVID-19," explores the manners in which comedians in general, and Black comedians in particular, have filled a quasi-religious leadership role during the pandemic. Marshall focuses on the nuanced relationship that Black American comedians and their audiences have had with laughter as a means of interpreting humanity, injustices, and liberation during this pandemic. She argues that in the context of comedy people of color specifically have repositioned themselves for the task of finding faith in the face of terrifying circumstances as they grapple with accepting the absurd as they "die" with laughter. Within Black comedy, Marshall contends, there typically are interworking systems of ideologies and activities by which people not only engage the absurd but also claim comedy's salvific or redemptive properties, which explicitly or implicitly utilize religious rhetoric.

While many have been consumed with death at the hands of COVID-19, as the so-called invisible disease, Marshall displays how comedians and laughter have served as conduits for processing pain and translating absurdity in order to decipher the current pandemic reality more faithfully.

David P. Gushee argues in chapter 10, "Toxic Religion, Toxic Churches, and Toxic Policies: Evangelicals, 'White Blessing,' and COVID-19," that COVID-19 is a ferocious enemy to human life that presents a difficult challenge to every religion, government, and nation in its path. However, the virus found the United States uniquely and desperately vulnerable, in part because of inherent and incessant built-in problems in the nation's very large white evangelical subculture. At its worst, this subculture tends toward an insular, antiscience, antielite, anti–mainstream media, anti–common sense, anticommunitarian, antiliberal, anti–social justice, conspiracy-oriented, theologically vapid, paranoid-populist way of engaging the world. While serious debates need to take place at the intersection of religion, ethics, and COVID-19—including religious freedom versus public safety as well as the question of whose needs must be sacrificed for the greater good—Gushee contends that the bigger story is the utter inability of white evangelicals to deal with COVID-19 on the terms required for the social good.

The volume concludes with "I Know Why the Culture War Stings: Racial Realities and Political Realignment in the 'Religious Freedom' Debate," by Marla F. Frederick. Her chapter focuses on the debate over "religious freedom"—a debate that, she notes, rages as cities across the country literally burn. From debates over baking wedding cakes to wearing face masks and worshiping together, the "religious freedom" argument in the United States has been foundational to white evangelicals' political grievance against what they have described as the "radical left." These debates, however, take place within a larger US context wherein white evangelicals often see themselves as victims who are losing ground as a cultural majority to a perceived non-Christian, multicultural mass of noncitizen socialists. The pandemic's capacity to amplify these fears through necessary limitations on cross-border travel and public gatherings, including worship services, raises important questions about how religious freedom operates as a weapon in a larger historic culture-war tool kit that is both raced and classed. Frederick questions: Do Black religionists feel that their religious freedoms are equally under assault?

If so, why, and if not, why not? In what ways might Black religionists understand the religious freedom argument as a distraction from larger, immediate, existential threats to Black freedom in the United States: COVID-19 and extrajudicial violence? Through reviews of religious media (e.g., sermons, news stories, and viral videos), Frederick explores Black religionists' understanding of religious freedom in light of those expounded in mainstream evangelical debates.

Religion, Race, and COVID-19: Confronting White Supremacy in the Pandemic is not merely about one moment in time; rather, it addresses the lasting effects of some of the United States' most persistent social ailments. The virulent impact of COVID-19 was accompanied by the vitriol that spewed from the poisonous politics produced by the nation's forty-fifth president and taken up as both rallying cry and cause by his political cronies and citizen zealots. The combination of the two—Trump's outrageous political machinations and the perils of the coronavirus crisis—created a particularly deleterious dynamic, spurred on by the Trump administration's willful disregard of the health crisis, which caused the situation to worsen exponentially. At the onset of the COVID-19 crisis, Trump had already dismantled the pandemic plans and preparations that his predecessor put into place. In its earliest stages, Trump disregarded multiple, classified warnings of the US intelligence community, scientific expertise on the rapid spread of the virus, and its impending arrival on American shores. Throughout the crisis, Trump insisted on playing down both its threat and effects. The particular political climate produced in these respects by the Trump presidency can very well be referred to as "COVID-45."

COVID-45 played no small part in the tumultuous manner in which 2020 came to its conclusion and 2021 began, in that it was combined with the manufactured angst and baseless conspiracies about the undisputable results of the 2020 presidential election. It is safe to propose that COVID-45 also directly affected the outcomes of both the presidential election (of an Irish Catholic and a Black–Southeast Asian woman) and the two senatorial elections (of a Black Christian minister and a white Jewish millennial) that unexpectedly turned Georgia, one of the country's most solid red (Republican) states into a nascent blue (Democratic) state. Put another way, in addition to their many disastrous outcomes, the confluence of the invisible virus (COVID-19) and the virulent

Trump political virus (COVID-45) also manufactured antibodies and agents of social change.

The religious significance of these events cannot go missing, as reflected in a number of chapters that address Trump's antics and his deliberate misleading and manipulation of his largely white, evangelical Christian base (see the contributions by Miguel De La Torre, Christopher Driscoll, Juan Floyd-Thomas, and David Gushee). For this base, the results of the 2020 presidential election were disconcerting to the point of being existentially dissonant, culminating in the violent insurrection by white supremacists, at Trump's behest, on January 6, 2021—designed to attack and overtake the US Capitol, overthrow the government, and overturn the results of the election. Forms of faithful tradition, coupled with modes of social resistance to the totalizing, pervasive notion that whiteness is normative or sovereign, responded to and met this crisis head on. Stacey Floyd-Thomas, Melanie Jones, Conā Marshall, Blanche Cooke, and Anthony Pinn explore the resistance and freedom found in the traditions of the Black Church, Black culture, or Black humanism that have served as the antidote to the combined COVID-19 and COVID-45 crises.

With the dawn of COVID-19, Black ministers and theologians hearkened to the deadly virus called racism that immediately reached pandemic proportions on American soil in 1619, or after, as Tink Tinker demystifies in his chapter, initially beginning to mutate from 1492 until today. The regenerative forms of American-racism-turned-genocide mimic a virus and has many people facing and fighting off three lethal pandemics. One is COVID-19, which began devastating the United States in 2020, and the second is COVID-45 that took up residence for a presidential term, both of which have claimed the lives of people of color in America at an accelerating rate. The third—racism—is a five-hundred-year-old virus that affects the soul of America, taking its toll while holding the lives of people of color in its balance. Acutely named "COVID-1619," the year when enslaved Africans arrived to North America, pastor and public theologian Otis Moss states that in 2020,

[We] encountered two men who tested positive for Confederate COVID-1619. . . . The disease is often asymptomatic and spreads through human contact, rhetoric, ignorance, and family relationship. Ahmaud

Arbery, a man of potential, was attacked and killed by men infected with America's most common and potent viral agent. This virus alters the eyesight of the attacker, weaponizing the body, giving the illusion of blackness as a threat, making melanin appear as a weapon and any movement as potential danger. It took ten weeks for an arrest to be made due to the potency of this viral agent.[1]

Whereas all the chapters in this volume bring to the forefront the racial realization and religious significance of the COVID-19 era, the various manners in which the virus of white supremacy and sovereignty, emboldened by Trumpism, fostered political turmoil do not go unacknowledged. From the constant refrain of "Make America Great Again," to June 1, 2020, when peaceful protesters in Washington, DC, were dispersed with violence and tear gas so that Trump could be photographed holding a Bible (upside-down, an apt metaphor for his presidency) while standing in front of the historic St. John's Episcopal Church, to the "United States Epiphany" on January 6, 2021 (the religious Day of Epiphany), when a crisis of whiteness was evidenced by an attack on the US Capitol, this political virus is an embedded and vital part of the interwoven historical account of the multilayered, biopolitical, and necropolitical coronavirus that ran rampant throughout 2020. Each contributor provides salient insight into how white political grievance and white political violence are problems of religion and how they were operative during the COVID-19 crisis. This saliency provides immediate insight and lasting hindsight on the unforgettable year that was 2020—a year that closed with the voting out of a presidential tyrant, the ushering in of hope via a vaccine to COVID-19, and an ongoing reckoning with the fact that, as a society, we still await a vaccine for COVID-1619.

NOTE
1 Otis Moss, "The Cross and the Lynching Tree: A Requiem for Ahmaud Arbery," streamed live on May 31, 2020, retrieved on January 10, 2021, www.youtube.com /watch?reload=9&v=vkJlToooonrA&feature=youtu.be.

1

"First Natural, Then Spiritual"

The Context and Contours of Black Faith in the COVID-19 Era

STACEY M. FLOYD-THOMAS

In 2020, some nineteen weeks into the COVID-19 crisis, during a Facebook Live broadcast titled "Pastoring during a Pandemic," renowned biblical scholar and womanist preacher Renita Weems confessed that she had crashed against the proverbial coronavirus wall.[1] She had begun the year with high hopes and great expectations in her role as copastor of a "small great church" in Nashville. However, her beloved town had become a target for torrential tornados, terrifying power outages, and tumultuous racial unrest that brought blackouts of all sorts on her and the church congregation. Weems declared to her Facebook audience that she was feeling as if she was "flying a plane while building it in mid-air."

Weems admitted with great vulnerability that she found it challenging to persist in the face of the insurmountable odds, while also ministering to people both locally and beyond via live-streaming platforms. The latter is certainly not new to Weems, who has maintained a far-reaching and celebrated social media presence for almost twenty years. That notwithstanding, she admitted that she found herself "adrift" by being restricted from physically going to her church. A self-avowed introvert, Weems acknowledged that going to church, which she had at times regarded as a burden, was now what she desperately yearned for, at the same time her presence was desperately needed. She realized that her church, the Ray of Hope, was not only a congregation but also a haven of hope for spiritual nourishment, social connection, and community organizing for a ransacked Black community disproportionately reeling from incalculable loss, including the loss of pastors and a (physically present) faith community. Giving serious thought and reflection to both her ministerial call and the seed of her own faith, Weems recognized the significance of gathering for in-person worship in terms of the mindfulness, preparation, and experiential dimensions of being two or three gathered in the presence of God. The absence of this practice brings into sharp relief the biblical admonition to not forsake the assembling of ourselves together (Hebrews 10:25). Moving through the world along a Sunday-to-Sunday orientation prepared her to physically align and socially incline herself to the spirit of God embodied in the presence and form of Black people gathered together for congregational worship. She understood her role as one of guiding the form and function of how to be hopeful in the face of death-dealing circumstances that continually tested the church's resolve.

Weems's account has been a common refrain among Black Church leaders during the COVID-19 pandemic, a widespread reality that compels consideration and appreciation of the forms and functions that Black faith took in this challenging experience. At their root is how the stay-in-place mandates imposed for safety from the societal and physical ravages of the disease either frustrated or furthered spiritual growth. When thinking about the tension between form and function in the Black Church in this unprecedented time, the biblical maxim "first natural, then spiritual" from 1 Corinthians 15:46 seems fitting. The ravages and devastation that have metastasized from the physical to the spiritual through the vicissitudes of the COVID-19 pandemic are undeniable, as are the exacerbated comorbidities of racial violence. The crises accompanying the COVID-19 pandemic have reinforced the fact that the context and contours of the Black Church have been the functioning of its faith beyond the form that it takes. As womanist ethicist Barbara Holmes observes,

> The Black church has an actual and a meta-actual form. It inhabits the imagination of its people in ways that far exceed its reach. Although it is no longer a truly invisible institution, it will always be invisible to some extent because it embodies a spiritual idea. This idea is grounded not only in history but also in the narratives and myths of an oppressed people.[2]

There is a functionality that will not concern itself with the form of Black faith. The deliberate actions and divine activity of Black faith move from freedom of religion toward freedom *as* religion. COVID-19 compelled the Black faithful to repackage an old question, "What does it mean to be Black and Christian?" to "Can you be Black and Christian virtually?" As Black people fought off racial animus and police brutality on the one hand, and staved off the deadly coronavirus on the other, many found themselves forced to flee their churches and forge their faith on the run. Many practiced a faith revealed at its core as a fugitive faith marked by the sanctity of Black life, the sanctuary movement of social justice, and the serendipitous spirit of its leaders.

Circumstances surrounding the COVID-19 pandemic have raised some interesting questions related to understanding the function that drives the various forms of the Black Church in different contexts. "Showing and proving," "making a way out of no way," "a place to be somebody"—these simple words attempt to define the essence, people, and purpose of the Black Church in America. This complex entity, as Henry Louis Gates attests, is something that Karl Marx could neither imagine nor validly critique, because he "lacked the tools to see beyond its surface levels of meaning."[3] Instead, Gates invokes James Weldon Johnson to convey about the Black Church what science and philosophy could not:

> What merely living clod, what captive thing,
> Could up toward God through all its darkness grope,
> And find within its deadened heart to sing
> These songs of sorrow, love and faith, and hope?
> How did it catch that subtle undertone,
> That note in music heard not with the ears.[4]

Functions are invisible until they are given form; the form that lacks a function serves no purpose. Owing a debt to Aristotle and Hegel, modern philosophy reminds us to regard form and function not as a duality but as a unity. For the architect, form and function are central to his or her profession. The architect maintains that the purpose of a building is its true foundation, rather than the concrete and structure upon which the building is erected. In fact, Frank Lloyd Wright is credited with expanding his mentor Louis Sullivan's notion that "form follows function" to another level, by asserting that "form and function are one."[5] The notion of a "sacred canopy" (a term made popular by sociologist of religion Peter Berger) may best describe the value of having a place and making it your own—the act of making a world for oneself without being a product of another.[6] To demarcate a physical manifestation within which one houses one's faith and which provides shelter for one's community literally creates a connection to time and place that is grounded, contextualized, and immanent.

However, once the Black Church became enshrined as such, it wrestled with conforming. The construction of an edifice in some ways represents a surrender to form at the expense of purpose. As historian of religion Charles Long reminds us, the form and function of religion signify the ultimate orientation of human beings to the world and their sense of it. Throughout its history, the Black Church's "extra-church orientations" have stemmed from a faith-filled yearning to find "someplace to be somebody" so as to make "a way out of no way":

To be sure, the church is one place one looks for religion. Given the situation of Americans of African descent, their churches were always somewhat different from the other churches of the United States. But even more than this, the church was not the only context for the meaning of religion. For my purposes, religion will mean orientation—orientation in the ultimate sense, that is, how one comes to terms with the ultimate significance of one's place in the world. The Christian faith provided a language for the meaning of religion, but not all the religious meanings of the black communities were encompassed by the Christian forms of religion. [There are] other forms of religion in the history of black communities—as those forms are contained in their folklore, music, style of life, and so on. Some tensions have existed between these forms of orientation and those of the [white] Christian churches, but some of these extra-church orientations have had great critical and creative power. They have often touched deeper religious issues regarding the true situation of black communities than those of the church leaders of their time.

The religion of any people is more than their structure of thought; it is experience, expression, motivations, intentions, behaviors, styles, and rhythms. Its first and fundamental expression is not on the level of thought. It gives rise to thought, but a *form* of thought that embodies the precision and nuances of that source. This is especially true of Afro

American religion. Americans of African descent have been forced to deal with several heritages—those of Africa, those of the New World in the *form* of the cultural and political situation of the United States, and the heritage of a distinctive culture created in this country from this amalgam. And they have had to deal with these realities always under a situation of oppression and duress.[7] (Emphasis added)

The Black Church has often wrestled with a faith that follows form, at times prioritizing form over function. In *The Souls of Black Folk* (1903), W. E. B. Du Bois writes that Black churches "are differentiating now into groups of cold, fashionable devotees, in no way distinguishable from similar white groups save in color of skin; now into large social and business institutions catering to the desire for information and amusement of their members, warily avoiding unpleasant questions both within and without the black world, and preaching in effect if not in word."[8] Du Bois prophesied a century ago about the societal as well as spiritual crises awaiting Black women, men, and children whose supplication to a colonizing, whitewashed religiosity potentially left them prone to the erasure of their own bodies, minds, and souls. This struggle has been part of the toil and turmoil of Black faith, as it has strived to form a Black Church in the midst of a world that devalues Black people. The Black Church has always faced pressure to model "respectability" while aspiring to change the very categories that define such respectability. Along the way, the old wooden church became the brick-and-mortar building, which then morphed into steel and glass, a process that has shared some ignoble characteristics with the biblical attempt to build the Tower of Babel. Yet when a crisis like the one occasioned by COVID-19 arises and hinders or prevents your ability literally to go back either to the place that formed you or that you are responsible for shaping, then you find yourself breaking down at the same time you are most needed for the task of building up those around you.

The Sanctity of Black Life

The conjoined realities of the history of racism in America and the formation of Black faith bring into sharp focus the issue of the sanctity of life. The introduction of American Christianity to Black people, whether in the plundering vessels of slave ships called *Jesus* off the coasts of West Africa or in the plantation churches of slaveholders, was generated by a religious impulse that inextricably linked, on the one hand, the horrific reality of soul murder and an unrelenting, death-dealing, dehumanizing mission to, on the other hand, the quest for soul salvation and freedom.[9] These practices shored up white privilege as much as they justified enslavement and persecution of Black people. Indeed, slave masters often provided divine names for these ships and churches to justify slavery as something God had ordained. The social control of enslaved Black people and the preservation of white privilege and power necessitated white spaces that kept Black bodies under strict surveillance. These spaces were infused with a spirituality that served social control by pairing obedience to white masters to a palpable sense of resignation to suffering as their divinely ordained lot in life. No one questioned slaveholding, and the practice seemed universal; most white Christians saw virtually no incongruity between slavocracy and salvation. Preaching among slaveholders trumpeted a biblical mythology of Black servitude that mandated slavery, whether stemming from the Hamitic curse of the Old Testament or the reality of slavery evidenced in the Epistle to Philemon in the New Testament. Christian scripture was perverted to teach that Black bodies could not contain the image of God, in that they were infected with sin and animated with savage proclivities.[10] Thus, greater beings, contained in white bodies and made in the image of God, had been given dominion over Black bodies.

The dominant theological postulation was that God had ordained and mandated that particular people could be treated as property. The fear of animals roaming free who required both shelter and surveillance provided a justification for chattel slavery in the same way that Plato reasoned, as the basis of ancient Greek civilization, that philosopher-kings needed to lord over women, children, and other savages.[11] Faith shaped by and perpetuated in slaveholding Christianity and the slaveholders' fear of insurrection led to the civilizing of a white supremacy with a coercive and destructive power that prohibited the assembly of Black worship or the autonomy of Black church meetings. Nonetheless, Black faith reinterpreted the preached redemption of suffering for the enslaved subversively as a promise of freedom. The exodus narrative took on new meaning for Black faith as a means for enslaved Black people to achieve liberation. As a result, Black faith had to be hidden in plain sight. These insurgent, independent interpretations cultivated a drive for secret, concealed gatherings where the outright preaching of freedom combined with coded messages in worship, songs, and dance that carried with them first a physical, then a spiritual means of escape.

Yet, despite the inability to read sacred texts for themselves and the prohibition against their own church meetings, the faithful impulse for physical freedom and spiritual salvation gave rise to the invisible institution of the Black Church—dubbed "hush harbors" and "brush arbors"—wherein Black people, free from the menacing surveillance of slave masters, worshiped a God who not only offered salvation but the blessed assurance and promise of freedom. Although the enslaved knew no shelter, they knew that to forsake the assembly of themselves, one with another, constituted a life-or-death matter. For those enslaved, Black bodies and Black life assumed sacred status. Historians remind us that the Black Church as an invisible institution has long been "an agency of social control, a source of economic cooperation, an arena for political activity, a sponsor of education, and a refuge in a hostile white world."[12] Both naturally and spiritually, the sanctity of Black life necessitated principles and practices that protected Black people in such a way that souls could be saved without lives and minds being lost in the process. Thus, the Black Church's role, through its revelatory message and its rituals, through its worship and its witness, repeatedly sounded the refrain that Black lives matter. Though invisible, the Black Church assumed its rightful value as a holy and sacred entity.

Sanctuary Movement

From the days of enslavement to the securing of civil rights, the Black Church has served as both the symbolic and physical shelter of the vital resources and succession of human rights for Black people. By preaching, teaching, hosting, serving, rallying, redeeming, and prophesying, the Black Church has provided the physical, emotional, moral, and spiritual support necessary for Black survival and flourishing in what Maya Angelou calls "these yet-to-be United States."[13] Indeed, as historian Vincent Harding reminds us, the Black Church has long been a sanctuary movement of sorts. Serving as a "sanctuary network" and freedom movement since the indefatigable antebellum leadership of Harriet Tubman's Underground Railroad, Black faith has been a veritable inspiration for the multiracial struggles for justice, liberation, human rights, and peace. Black faith has even provided an essential force for the spread and realization of democracy in the United States from the 1960s onward.[14] The profundity and the performance of Black faith in the face of real death has mattered in ways previously known, but now is being rediscovered as Black faith finds its place in a context where no safe space exists.

What happens when what was once an invisible institution now, centuries later, has to contend with an invisible threat? Arguably, the COVID-19 pandemic is an opportunity to reconsider the relevance that Black faith in particular has played in the spiritual, physical, and psychological health of the American experiment. The threat and throes of this COVID-19 pandemic have Black Americans envisioning themselves as refugees of both church and state. On the one hand, they are being forced to leave the fortification and fellowship of their sanctuaries while fleeing to a more profound sense of faith, due not only to the life-threatening consequences of the coronavirus but also the heightened deadly conditions brought on by racial animus: Black people are caught in the crosshairs of the pandemic and racial conflict. In both contexts, clergy are mounting ministerial movements by seeking to link divine justice to social justice. This time of pandemonium is an opportunity to look not simply externally but more constructively internally at how Black lives matter with regard to Black prosperity, posterity, and progeny. As Christian social ethicist Robert M. Franklin states,

> When we entered the extended family compound, we felt that we were in the safest place on earth, a place where all sorts of goods and services were shared, where no one went hungry, where everyone knew our name, and where we all encouraged one another to face another day. It was this sense of deep security provided by so many working-class and poor black families that kept black youths from realizing that we were poor, if measured by the standards of the government or the sociologists.[15]

Thus, we need to consider how the multiple crises of this COVID-19 period have reawakened the activist vision of the Black Church as a sanctuary movement. Much as hush harbors, the Underground Railroad, and other historic, subversive endeavors brought together spiritual courage and secular concerns, this modern-day sanctuary movement once again relies upon the spirituality of an invisible institution to save Black lives. Yet there are challenges. African American studies and religion scholar Eddie Glaude frames the issue in his provocative article "Is the Black Church Dead?":

> We have witnessed *the routinization of black prophetic witness.* Too often the prophetic energies of black churches are represented as something inherent to the institution, and we need only point to past deeds for evidence of this fact. Sentences like, "The black church has always stood for. . . ." "The black church was our rock. . . ." "Without the black church, we would have not. . . ." In each instance, a backward glance defines the content of the church's stance in the present—justifying its continued relevance and authorizing its voice. Its task, because it has become alienated from the moment in which it lives, is to make us venerate and conform to it. But such a church loses its power. Memory becomes its currency. Its soul withers from neglect. The result is all too often church services and liturgies that entertain, but lack a spirit that transforms, and preachers who deign for followers instead of fellow travelers in God.[16]

The coronavirus cleared out schools, shopping malls, sports arenas, and sanctuaries due to state-mandated stay-in-place or shelter-in-place orders. On the one hand, pastors—mindful of the physical as well as spiritual well-being of their congregations—used the internet to overcome the barriers of social distancing in order to preach from vacant sanctuaries or their own homes. On the other hand, many clergy not only found themselves unexpectedly without the brick and mortar of stained-glass windows, pulpits, and pews but also found their congregants online yearning for pastoral care and spiritual witness in response to the apparent omnipotence, omniscience, and omnipresence of COVID-19. Religious leaders discovered that their sermons and services must rise to the occasion to effectuate what they always claim to do: subdue the worries of the day with the serenity of scripture and scripted rituals, but in a way that had to address what King called "the fierce urgency of now."[17] For as Howard Thurman's query poses, "What good or use is religion to those who find their 'backs against the wall'?"[18]

The COVID-19 pandemic has made evident that a new and different kind of sanctuary movement is afoot, particularly for the Black faith community—a movement that serves and saves naturally and spiritually through social, economic, political, and religious ways that, more recently, Black faith has not engaged much as a church tradition. What was once considered insignificant or ignored is now at the forefront; while it might be "hidden" from public discourse, it contains resurrecting power for the Black faithful. The merged crises prompted by COVID-19 have led to a search for sanctuary framed by critically considering the pragmatic value of mounting a religious campaign in the United States to provide safe haven for Black people with resources to overcome the disempowering, disquieting, and devastating circumstances accompanying our current social and spiritual conflicts. Wading through the murky waters of separation of church and state, the role of religion as the moral consciousness of a nation and the appraisal of what was once sacred (e.g., the rites of communion, confession, or membership) seems meaningless in the presence of a death-dealing virus.

Whether through the phantom menace of anti-Black violence or through a global viral outbreak that is disproportionately killing people of color, Black people once again are being forced out of view as lives worth saving. Once again, the role of the Black Church beyond the confines of a building is to address the fine line between the preciousness and precarity of Black life. As historian Juan Floyd-Thomas points out,

Keeping the faith means more than just maintaining the consistency and constancy of one's prayer life and devotional practices but also holding a deep conviction that through God's grace, love, and mercy, tomorrow can be better than yesterday. . . . Historically, Black churches have been a place to which African Americans could escape from their oppression and dehumanization by white people. In these sacred houses of worship, it has been preached, prayed, and sung that "everybody is somebody in God's eyes even if you're considered nobody here on Earth!" . . . But even when the theological message has been focused on otherworldly escape with a fixation on the heavenly promise of freedom in the afterlife more than struggling for freedom in the earthly realm, the church has been a refuge and safe haven for healing.[19]

Historian Jon Meacham argues that "leaders are far more often mirrors of who we are rather than makers of who we are, and that's an uncomfortable reality."[20] More often than not, Black religious leaders have been poignantly represented or, conversely, made into a mockery for how Black lives matter in the midst of death-dealing realities. When portrayals of Black churches appear in popular media or as an online phenomenon, they have ignored the power of Black Church tradition. These media prefer to incite controversy and promote conspiracy theories (most notably, conservative news loops of Jeremiah Wright's soundbites and more recent attacks on Raphael Warnock) or manipulate through cultural appropriation and comic relief (Nike's King James basketball ads or gospel choirs in Popeye's Fried Chicken commercials). These diametrically opposed stereotypes are a far cry from the vision of Black Church leadership described by Du Bois: "The [Black] Preacher is the most unique personality developed by [African Americans] on American soil. A leader, a politician, an orator, a 'boss,' an intriguer, an idealist—all these [they are], and ever, too, the centre of a group. . . . The combination of a certain adroitness with deep-seated earnestness, of tact with consummate ability, gave [them] preeminence, and helps [them] maintain it. The type, of course, varies according to time and place."[21]

During this moment, religious leaders with spiritual responsibilities and social justice missions seek to explore what it means to transfer the impact of "stay-at-home" and "shelter-in-place" directives on hollowed-out Black church sanctuaries, by transforming homes into literal and figurative "houses of the holy." At a conceptual level, they must confront head on the reality that their parishioners and the public may experience great difficulty in conjuring some sense of the sacred in their own mundane dwelling places. Their congregants are confronting the dilemma of attempting to turn their residential space into a place where the spiritual and the secular can effectively coexist. They video stream on a small screen yet still must grapple with existential matters that are larger than life. Additionally, Black religious leaders seek to navigate the politics, practices, and pragmatic concerns of the largely secular #BlackLivesMatter movement—about which they have been largely silent or nonresponsive, in spite of the fact that the Black Church has historically been the primary, if not the only, locale within which the value and sanctity of Black lives has been consistently preached.[22] In the midst of such threats, a *kairos* moment avails itself to the Black Church to redeem time, recover history, restore right relationship, and reconcile itself to its origins, by providing sanctuary once again. In its attempts to save others, the Black Church has an opportunity to resurrect itself from an otherwise certain death.

Serendipitous Spirit of Black Religious Leadership

If any church has proven to be alive and well during the coronavirus crisis, it is Friendship West Baptist Church (FWBC) in Dallas, Texas. A megachurch that fulfills a corresponding megaministry in one of the nation's COVID-19 hotbed zones, FWBC claims that Jesus is synonymous with justice.[23] In his role for the past thirty-seven years as FWBC's senior pastor and "drum major for justice," Rev. Dr. Frederick Douglass Haynes III certainly emulates the fiery advocacy of the legendary Frederick Douglass,[24] preaching from his pulpit to a flock of over eight thousand, traveling the world speaking truth to power, proclaiming liberty to the captive and freedom to the oppressed, giving voice to the voiceless, and providing hope and help to those in need. FWBC advertises that it is in its "DNA to fight for justice, with a focus on social, economic, gender, food, and environmental justice for everyone."[25]

Like many other churches, beginning in March 2020 FWBC followed the state mandate to refrain from assembling for its weekly worship services or its scheduled ministry meetings. However, FWBC also conveyed overtly that, although its facilities and staff were limited, COVID-19 would not prevent its ministry. The church hung two banners, prominently affixed to its edifice, visible to anyone driving past on Interstate 20: "Black Lives Matter" and "Church is not closed, we have been redeployed." During the COVID-19 shutdown, FWBC discovered itself not only to be a source of protection, support, and justice but also to be a church called to make a difference. FWBC's ability to address social justice concerns during the coronavirus crisis rallied its congregants and others to support the church. From the beginning of the stay-at-home mandate through the close of 2020, FWBC (1) served as one of the first COVID-19 testing sites in Dallas County, in the midst of a community that tested the least while dying the most; (2) continually fed and clothed over two thousand–plus families through the congregation's Faith Formula ministry; (3) kept hundreds of people sheltered by finding housing for homeless families and keeping families housed who were unable to pay rent and mortgage due to COVID-19-related unemployment; and (4) served as a supersite for the 2020 presidential elections, providing space for more voting machines than any other facility in Dallas County, other than the American Airlines Center, and offered a trusted and safe site free from the voter suppression and intimidation efforts of many who pursued a white supremacist agenda.

The reality of a 150,000-square-foot church emptied of its congregants and experiencing a 50 percent reduction of its offerings created a fiscal fear and physical anxiety for Haynes, his ministerial staff of more than thirty people, and a megaministry that required $850,000 monthly to stay afloat. Nevertheless, in opposition to the common-sense strategy of many staffed churches, Haynes refused to furlough staff and, instead, ramped up the church's megaministry. He declared the megachurch a refuge center to fight for the rights of those who were navigating the rising waive of necropolitics.[26] FWBC proclaimed this commitment at the beginning of the first week of the state mandate—on a Sunday with the lowest church giving. By the Friday of the same week, church donations and offerings poured in from virtually everywhere—congregants, community members, colleagues, and others from around the globe—resulting in a total offering that exceeded any previously received, followed by subsequent strong weeks of donations.

The impact of FWBC's difference-making responses to the coronavirus crisis did not go unnoticed beyond its membership; the church attracted the attention of both the upright and unchurched in the greater Dallas region. Church members and other community folk both rose in response when the church grounds were infiltrated by an "all-White group driving about a thousand jeeps, pickups and motorcycles flying 'Back the Blue' banners and at least one Confederate battle flag."[27] Community members, the vast majority of whom were not necessarily members of FWBC, saw it as an opportunity to "have the back of the church who always has the back of the people," because "when it comes to doing the work of justice, FWBC shows up to the scene of the crime."[28]

Whereas COVID-19 may have posed a possible death sentence for the church, it also provided it with a renewed lease on life. The congregation's response provided a megaministry through which hurt people could heal, build, and be restored in a nation that owes a debt of justice to the people Jesus understood to be the least of these in need of liberty and life. Here, Black faith gives one a greater sense of discernment to help people find their next move, or as the song says, "keep your eyes on the prize." Some ministers and ministries lacking FWBC's resources and recognition nevertheless have mastered a similar spirit of serendipity. This is not a championing of redemptive suffering, but as Haynes preached in the midst of the shutdown,

> Black people's God makes providential moves serendipitously and sovereignly, setting up our come up even through our set back. Serendipity, by way of my old definition, is a disappointment that becomes a divine appointment with something good that you never saw coming out of something bad that you were already dealing with . . . but another definition of serendipity is when God surprises you with the unexpected and the unimaginable, especially in the space of the unlikely. It means that God shows up in a way that surprises you. You didn't expect it. You didn't see it coming, but God serendipitously blesses you out of something that was burdening you. God serendipitously lifts you up through something that was trying to tear you down. God serendipitously opens up a door for you that you didn't even knock on after another door had been shut to you.[29]

Black congregations and leaders provided ministries not only by walking through doors that had once been shut but also by using their God-given strength to carve out a doorway through which they and the entire race could pass. The best example of serendipitous leadership within Black faith in recent decades appeared among Black women who have forged a theological response to the centers of power attempting to keep them in their subjugated spaces. In the same manner that the enslaved and illiterate found a way to free themselves from the illogical, immoral rhetoric of a slaveholding Christianity in order to hone a liberating theology for their own freedom, Black women, compelled by conscience, have sought to undo the damage and impact of misogyny and miseducation. Carter G. Woodson, historian and founder of Black History Month, stated,

> When you control a man's thinking you do not have to worry about his actions. You do not have to tell him not to stand here or go yonder. He will find his "proper place" and will stay in it. You do not need to send him to the back door. He will go without being told. In fact, if there is no back door, he will cut one for his special benefit. His education makes it necessary.[30]

Knowing this, Black women have realized that both the uncritical use of the Bible and patriarchal theology are not exclusive to white Christian supremacy. They also exist in the same African American denominational churches where Black women make up an invisible, often suppressed and silenced, majority who are routinely denied full access to the truth that can set them free. Like the slave masters who denied the autonomy of enslaved Africans, Black churches have refused Black women the ability to serve as religious leaders. Black women's oppression has been equally yoked to an unquestioned divine authority claimed by both white supremacy and Black misogyny, all the while relying on the might of Black women to support and reinforce the male claim to sovereignty both naturally and spiritually. Realizing the epistemic shift that seeking truth and speaking truth to power mandated, Black women have sought both theological correctives and moral exemplars capable of moving Black women from the margins of servitude to the center of their faith. In her classic text *Sisters in the Wilderness*, theologian Delores Williams states that "the corrective—emerging among Black female theologians, ethicists, biblical scholars, ministers, and laywomen—is called womanist theology."[31]

This womanist theology is infused with a spiritual intent and negotiated with ethical tenets. In the same way that the strength of the Black Church as the invisible institution has always been its pragmatic ability to link divine justice to social justice, its power to do so can be attributed to its liberationist theological intents, which are multidialogical, liturgical, and didactic. These intents are committed to the interpretation and imagery I have defined elsewhere as the four tenets of womanism: radical subjectivity, traditional communalism, redemptive self-love, and critical engagement.[32]

To tap the wellspring of womanist theology is to know not only its intentions but its moral praxis, all of which culminate from the traditional communalism of Black women who are left largely invisible. Traditional communalism conveys the moral principles and cultivates practices of Black women living in solidarity with and in support of those with whom they share a common heritage and contextual language of oppression. It expresses a preferential option for Black women's culture that espouses both an epistemological privilege of "making a way out of no way" and constructive criticism forged in the "in/visible dignity," "un/shouted courage," and "quiet grace" that promote the survival and liberation of *all* Black women and their communities.[33] As womanist sociologist of religion Cheryl Townsend Gilkes has made clear, "If it wasn't for the women, we wouldn't have a Black Church."[34] While the Black Church has been the home base of Black social and spiritual empowerment, Black women have made up 66 to 88 percent of its congregants and have been its veritable backbone.[35]

Whereas the Black Church's popular preachers and public theologians have been largely represented as male, its moral compass and mass movement both reside in the Black women who have been its most essential workers. Despite encountering the unrelenting threats and burdens of triple jeopardy in terms of race, gender, and class oppression, Black women have provided radical wisdom, critical voices, and transformative direction within some of the most consequential moments in American history. Significant and landmark movements such as the suffragist and abolitionist movements, and the civil rights and women's rights movements—not to mention many educational and, most especially, religious institutions—would not have been as efficient or effective, let alone exist, without the essential and excellent work of Black women. As inheritors of an immense legacy that includes an epistemological lectionary for real insight for faith seeking understanding, Black women live in the serendipitous nature (often misnamed and stereotypically touted as "Black girl magic") of their triple consciousness. This prism enables Black women not only to comprehend what Williams names as "demonarchy" but also to conjure the means of saving their community spiritually and physically by "creatively wrestling with the demonic and interlocking forces of white racism, male superiority, and economic disenfranchisement that convey that black women's subordination" is to be accepted, reinforced, and regarded simply as both the way of the world and the will of God.[36] Black women's creative wrestling is the constructive charge of traditional communalism, within which they adeptly read their social context and the sacred text guided by, as ethicist Eboni Marshall Turman states, an "impulse and theological crafting, [which] is [a] Sister's fulcrum, giving profound and corporeal meaning to the Pauline declaration, 'For we wrestle . . . against powers and principalities' (Eph. 6:12) in the wilderness of triangulated antiblack woman oppressions."[37]

The nation's experience with COVID-19 has been tragic and traumatizing. Yet the virus represents just another way station in the wilderness of oppression that is better known as "misogynoir."[38] Survival in this hostile terrain demands reckoning with the vise grip of racist-sexist-classist-xenophobic oppression that imposes binary thinking as a counter to Black women's traditional communalism. As their pioneering predecessors before them, they too have now risen to the occasion in both ability and agility to address and redress the crisis they confront in their wilderness wanderings. Even as they journey through the valley of the shadow of death, womanists deconstruct and reconstruct while simultaneously subverting the forces that demonize communities and devalue the lives within them.[39] Black women, who comprise the overwhelming majority of Black Church congregants, serve as prophetic voices who remind the Black Church of its mission to seek justice and give voice to all people.

Such a development has taken Black women from the underground, by moving them from the margins to the center and beyond to the front lines, as they have gone online to facilitate their ministries worldwide. In the face of COVID-19 and at a social distance, womanist religious leaders who are used to being shut out and without the surety of sanctuary have consistently mounted virtual pulpits both before and throughout the COVID-19 crisis. Whether by social media, streaming platforms, or supporting their own podcasts and websites,[40] these Black women are doing essential work for their souls and their communities by creating digital hush harbors. This has resulted in corrective, courageous spaces neither intended to dismantle the master's house nor break the stained-glass ceilings of the Black Church, but rather to do the liberating, life-affirming labor of Black faith by embodying the serendipitous spirit of sustainability in the midst of devastation.

In this spirit, this online sanctuary movement is rooted in and catalyzed by womanism' traditional communalism. While the American slavocracy forced the creation of the invisible institution that gathered Black bodies in hush harbors away from brick-and-mortar church structures, the COVID-19 pandemic demanded a similar reconfiguration into what I would call an "intangible institution." With state-mandated prohibitions against large, in-person gatherings for worship and fellowship due to the coronavirus, Black pastoral leadership found itself at a critical juncture for reimagining and redefining what church looks like—not only without face-to-face gatherings but also given this previously unexpected foray into a digital world. Black, theologically trained female pastors and self-avowed womanists have been pivotal virtual pioneers in this regard. Their gifted grasp of theory, theology, and technology has been integral for extolling womanism from the classroom to the church for the entire community, male and female. These thinking women of faith have taken seriously the sanctity of Black lives and also have challenged the presumed universality of the dominant ethical systems to identify a substantial wealth of moral resources and Christian teachings to address the challenges of people oppressed by race, sex, and class. Their vocational journeys also demonstrate their aptitude, attitude, and ability to transgress, transcend, and tear down racial, gender, and class boundaries. Therefore, this serendipitous gift and opportunity of an online sanctuary movement in this new context revealed the workings of a womanist theological intentionality infused with the ethical tenet of traditional communalism. When brought into sharper view, this unique, digitized embodiment of the remaining womanist tenets of radical subjectivity, critical engagement, and redemptive self-love serves to give definition and direction to Black faith as it enters a new domain.

The Radical Subjectivity of Digital Hush Harbors— Pink Robe Chronicles

As I have explored elsewhere, radical subjectivity is the womanist tenet that emerges as Black women come into the fullness of their identity development by refusing normative notions of being Black and female, and being brave in a context where all the Blacks are men and all women are white.[41] Here, womanists reject numbing up and dumbing down as a guide to survival by defying a forced naiveté as a form of acceptance. Instead, radical subjectivity is the conscientious effort to resist silence and marginality through power analysis, biotextual specificity, and embodied mediated knowledge as the measure of wisdom and intelligence. It is the audacious act of naming oneself, claiming voice, space, and knowledge as a divine posture and form of Black female identity politics. It is not a tangible, static identity, but rather a channeling of the call to divine activity, or what womanist minister and poet Raedorah Stewart Dodd calls "feeling a whole lot like God."[42]

But what does it mean for Black women to bear witness via worship on the web? "Something happens when Black women are in a digital space," says Rev. Dr. Melva Sampson, practical theologian and homiletics professor at Wake Forest University Divinity School. "When we go live, we create spaces of safety that we are not always able to do in brick and mortar."[43] Akin to a superhero, on Sunday mornings before donning church clothes, Sampson becomes an oracular prophet, visibly adorned in her pink robe and spiritually clothed in her womanist radical subjectivity. She curates a digital space that takes seriously those womanists and allies "who are willing to affirm the audacious act of naming and claiming voice, space, and knowledge."[44] In 2016, Sampson created Pink Robe Chronicles (PRC) as an online Facebook community, and it steadily evolved into an online virtual sanctuary movement. On any given Sunday, countless web-based worshipers make their way to PRC out of curiosity and resistance to oppressive, offline religious spaces. Moreover, many of the virtual visitors to PRC show up in order to reject fiercely the tendency of the Black Church to use the bodies of Black women and queer people while rendering invisible their actual lived identities and spiritual yearnings. As a result, PRC became a digital clearing crafted "to moan, protest, and affirm the sound of her own voice,"[45] while enabling Sampson to pursue her vocation more fully. Meeting every Sunday at 8 a.m. on Facebook and YouTube, Sampson grapples with theodicy, soteriology, aliveness, power, intersectionality, and respectability politics.[46]

Pink Robe Chronicles is a manifestation of radical subjectivity; this online gathering is not simply a digital experiment but instead is a divine experience. Streaming from her kitchen or home office, with secular music or spirituals playing and with the fluidity with which Black faith ushers in African traditional religion, it is diasporic Black Christian inculturation. Sampson cultivates a diasporic digital hush harbor as a communal gathering from her domestic dwelling. She employs the term "digital hush harbor" for all of the characteristics and activities that might take place in a historic hush harbor.

For Sampson, the hush harbor is a clandestine place where one can steal away, a place where enslaved Africans historically would go for cathartic release. Whether through swaying or dancing the ring shout, singing or wailing, the hush harbor was able to contain all that was them as all that was good. As a Black preaching woman who is professionally trained, politically progressive, and unashamedly shaped by popular culture, Sampson's sense of space and pace of worship—while intentionally yet nonchalantly wearing a well-loved house robe—signifies that liberation is a call to "come as you are"—the ultimate expression of radical subjectivity in its indefatigable self-determination and self-possession.

Such a gesture is not only womanist but also Afrocentric and Afrofuturist, in that it constitutes a veritable Sankofa moment in action, going back to reach and reconnect with those cultural and spiritual traditions that have been rendered invisible and blocked from cultural memory. (*Sankofa* is a Ghanaian term that means "going back and getting what you left behind.") This radically subjective and Afrocentric posture breaks up the shallow ground of a colonized consciousness and pushes her diasporic community to move beyond what they were told was "good" and "Godly," so as to experience new ways and create new spaces in a cyberspace hush harbor. This posture has been embraced and reified in similar digital hush harbors such as Pastor Danny's UnfitChristian,[47] Pastor Bae's Proverbial Experience,[48] Whitney Bond's Still Saved,[49] and Iya Funlayo-Wood-Menzies's community Ase Ire, which is a live digital Ifa-Orisa community.[50] As a web of mutuality, online hush harbor communities come together without the need of covering, supervision, or permission or approval from a governing church board.

Pink Robe Chronicles acts as an exemplary case of radical subjectivity, as it audaciously self-determines that the sanctuary movement can and must exist beyond the restrictions of brick and mortar as it settles into a new normal. Defying traditionalist constraints of Black churches' male-centered pastoral leadership, governing boards, textual liturgies, and orders of service, Pink Robe Chronicles reenvisions the gathering of church as a digitized hush harbor that is a multireligious, racially, gendering, and sexually affirming and inclusive; spiritually transformative sacred cyberspace. Spiritual leadership is re-imagined with the centralization of Black preaching women engaging in acts of Sankofa as central to their homiletic pursuits. As a result, Sampson's efforts are disrupting exclusionary, oppressive practices of white supremacy and the institutional Black Church so as to reconnect with the cultural and spiritual traditions of brush harbors. This radically subjective shift to streaming Black faith equally disrupts the notion of sanctuary, by acknowledging that for such a space to be safe, faith must be fluid and social change must be a constant perspective rooted in Black women's spontaneous, supernatural, extraordinary, yet everyday methods of problem solving. For many, Sampson becomes Pastor Melva because she channels a radical subjectivity that is committed to the reason and representation that her ministry evokes in a way that is consistent with goodness and God's incarnation, making her listeners feel a whole lot like God too.

The Redemptive Self-Love of The Gathering

Inspired by womanist visions of ministries like Pink Robe Chronicles, and economically and spiritually empowered by womanist allies like Dr. Haynes and Friendship West Baptist Church, The Gathering is not only the first self-identified womanist church but also is supported by a mainline white denomination: Disciples of Christ. Cofounded and copastored by two Black women who are self-avowed womanists, Rev. Dr. Irie Lynne Session and Rev. Kamilah Sharp, The Gathering "exists to create worship experiences that address social justice issues through womanist preaching and action" that can be transported anywhere. As such, its mission is "to welcome people into community to follow Jesus, partner in ministry to transform our lives together, and to go create an equitable world."[51] As a result, The Gathering has become an atypical faith community: a racially diverse, gender nonconforming, open and affirming womanist congregation comprising Black, white, Latinx, lesbian, gay, straight, and nonbinary people. They are not called "members" but rather "ministry partners," because they are forging a womanist ethic of traditional communalism and redemptive self-love in an effort to bring about something new—an indelible imprint of what the image, idea, and incarnation of God look like when Black women's ecclesial leadership clears the way.

The Gathering radically shifts the social and theological nature of the Black Church by displaying both offline and online the future possibilities of its centralization of all four of the womanist ethical tenets, but particularly its exemplification of redemptive self-love, which Session reiterates as

> Black women who love themselves. Regardless. Redemptive self-love emphasizes that irrespective of what others say, do, or how they are treated, black women will commit to love themselves. Redemptive self-love is cultivated in many ways. It is handed down through moral wisdom from mother to daughter, mirrored in the literary tradition, and it is situated in the lived experiences of contemporary black women. Redemptive self-love informs womanist preaching. It maintains love as a virtue.[52]

At The Gathering, Black women's ways of knowing are valid and their being is seen as virtuous. Departing from its physical context in Dallas, Texas, a bastion of biblical conservatism, the copastors employ a womanist biblical interpretation and liberationist theology that is in contradistinction and absolute defiance to misogynoir. Additionally, as a physical entity, The Gathering actively rejects the ecclesial hierarchy and manufactured patriarchy that typify Bible Belt churches and are often replicated in both the Black Church writ large and local area churches in particular. The Gathering's spiritual embrace of nonhierarchical leadership, however, is poignantly womanist. Redemptive self-love is evident in that they strive to reconcile and minister to those who have been objectified, battered, exploited, trafficked, marginalized, or prostituted, so as to restore them to their first creation as beloved children of God, rather than seen only in their condition of being crucified by social stereotypes or silenced and made submissive by the preaching and proof-texting of scripture.

The Gathering's redemptive self-love is equally invested in the formation of other womanist religious leaders across the nation—in its service as a spiritual laboratory and professional workshop for womanist preachers who are seeking ways to disrupt heteronormativity and dismantle white supremacist patriarchy. By situating itself within an edifice and electing membership within a mainline denomination, while simultaneously streaming all their services online and extending invitations to those outside the Disciples of Christ denomination, these womanist copastors claim space and position for a place of womanist faith and a primer for womanist leadership without giving up their own power and perspective. This radically subjective intervention is The Gathering's goal and vision for "anointed women to know that their voice as preachers and ministers was also a divine call from God."[53] It does so in a range of ways, such as using communal language like "ministry partners" to include their congregants as active participants in the ministry of the church and society; building a social media network of Womanist Wednesdays; inaugurating the Teresa Fry Brown Institute (named for the nation's leading womanist homiletician and executive leader of the African Methodist Episcopal Church); providing pastoral care and practical theological tools and insight for women "to help them be more successful in following their divine call"; and by giving explicit instructions in their publications about how to plant and fund a womanist church of one's own.[54]

At The Gathering, the entire community—male, female, or non-gender-conforming—do not keep silent. They preach and teach that to be spiritually censored is a sin. Likewise, these womanist copastors help other womanists who either are discerning their call or already practicing it to refrain from seeing their call as an effort to "usurp authority over a man" or to "submit to the authority of husbands." Instead they lead who comes to be the subject of their own salvation. Through lessons and liturgy, The Gathering acknowledges and affirms the very embodiment of those who are marginalized as being fearfully and wonderfully made. Further, The Gathering produces segments of "Talk Back to the Text"—an online and in-person call-and-response engagement that devises moments of reflection from ministry partners to question if the sermons resonate with their own embodiment. Hashtags like "#WeGather" have become a communicative device to call the like-minded to steal away to The Gathering's digital hush harbors. Breaking the stained-glass ceiling of religious patriarchy, extending beyond the pews within its building, and claiming a womanist pulpit that extends the divine affirmation of redemptive self-love, The Gathering's online religious presence via Switcher Studio and Facebook Live reaches beyond the building to gather digitally and amass a far larger congregation than its edifice could hold or its staff could support. According to psychologist and womanist practical theologian Phillis Sheppard, The Gathering

> takes seriously the need to dismantle the idea that the faith community is to be found solely within the four walls of a building. A womanist's public theology stretches itself into the local community and beyond— indeed, into the reaches of cyberspace. [The Gathering] is a gift for those who take womanist theology and womanist care seriously. Their commitment to careful theological reflection and a welcoming ecclesiology is evident in their worship and their writing. They have made the vision of womanist church an embodied reality and, therefore, invite others to do the same.[55]

By repudiating the perceptions of Black women's bodies, ways, and loves as inherently vile, these womanist copastors take up the mantle of leadership as they embrace the role of caregiver for the least of these. Simultaneously, they refute the normalization of patriarchal authority. Engendered toward a public theology and empowered by pastoral expertise, these womanist copastors exercise the full spectrum of their experience of oppression alongside their scholarly preparation as religious leaders. As such, The Gathering is an outer space that has put womanism into practice beyond the limiting effects of stereotypes or social or physical location, by channeling a spirit at work that embodies public presence, pastoral care, and liberation theology in both a prophetic stance and a hospitality of protest online and on the front lines. By stepping in and stepping up with divine authority and a virtual omnipresence, The Gathering affirms and promotes that

> Womanism, [which] centers Black women's experience, is essential to the wholeness of church and society. . . . Womanism is not only what the Black Church needs but what America needs if we're truly going to embrace the best of who we are as a people. . . . The mission of womanism is

to make the church whole again and to bring the wisdom that is necessary for us all to be liberated and for none of us to be left behind.[56]

Like many other churches, The Gathering found ways to meet obvious physical needs in response to the COVID-19 crisis. Expanding ministries assisted with housing and provided personal protective equipment (PPE) and clothes to families around the Dallas–Fort Worth metroplex. A new Fish & Loaves Ministry provided home-cooked meals to people who were food insecure. The copastors knew they needed more attentive services in order to maintain a spiritually uplifting ministry. They also sought to create a level of intimacy with people that could facilitate resilience in the midst of crisis. Since people faced COVID-19 as a day-by-day and moment-by-moment reality, they needed reliable contact with others to gather strength for themselves and their families.

Prior to COVID-19, The Gathering did not have a prayer ministry. When the virus began to affect everyday life, leaders created a new ministry and began to call their ministry partners to extend prayer and pastoral care as a way to demonstrate that social distancing cannot eclipse connecting with others or the nurturing of personal relationships. They also started a texting ministry that included the entire congregation: community members who are elderly, alone, and isolated, and those who are essential workers, underresourced, or otherwise vulnerable. For The Gathering, a texting ministry extended the twentieth-century telephone call tree—which had played an important role in providing communication and coordinating recovery during difficult times—into the twenty-first century. Ministering in real time provides an opportunity to share physical, social, or spiritual concerns with those who might provide immediate insight or resources that might help. Life's transitions flow more smoothly when shared with a caring community. The community shared in the fluidity of faith that flowed from grief groups in response to death, support groups among those caring for elders or spouses, celebrations of new births, or networks simply sharing job tips. The Gathering became a web of connections facilitating spontaneous recovery in the midst of immediate crises. The community shared in grief, faced challenging questions, navigated health challenges, and found spiritual support among those engaged in prayer for one another.

While these kinds of support structures are essential for many churches in general and Black churches in particular, the unique spontaneous efforts that arose during the COVID-19 crisis also gave rise to a fulfillment of The Gathering's vision to celebrate Black women preachers. In this way, leaders offered a womanist twist. Although they began streaming their worship services before COVID-19, the crisis created the opportunity for The Gathering to expose its congregation to the preaching style and scholarship of womanist preachers from all over the United States, and to support, financially and spiritually, these women whom the Black Church have overtaxed, underpaid, and undervalued. In offering a forum that provided professional development for and the prophetic witness of other womanist preachers, The Gathering's internet outreach dramatically expanded even though it had long been online.

The Critical Engagement of the Late, the Lost, and the Left Out

Ultimately, the social and spiritual mandate to follow Jesus, as The Gathering reminds us, is not about merely having an edifice, ecclesial authority, or educational training:

> Following Jesus means responding to the least, last, and the lost, and being intentional in ministry to the marginalized, oppressed, and downtrodden . . . to do the deeper work of seeing the healing, restorative justice, and liberation . . . in a way that raises prophetic voices and issues a rallying cry, speaking truth to power.[57]

This following of Jesus requires critical engagement, that is, the deft ability to critique religion *and* society in such a way as to "make plenty good room," even at the risk of "making good trouble," in order to clear the way for the least, last, and the lost. In her text *The Womanist Preacher*, communication scholar and rhetorician Kimberly Johnson states that womanist preachers are especially adept at employing the womanist tenet of critical engagement:

> Critical engagement sermons seek to culturally critique society's oppressive forces, by challenging the ways in which we view people's problems and by forcing us to confront our own internal system of beliefs, so that

we can collectively combat external systems of belief. The preacher must offer a perspectival corrective that moves people toward partnership and inspires them to collectively change their thoughts and behavioral practices. The preacher must also devise a plan on how we can fix/eliminate the problem. Critical engagement reflects a cultural critique of society's cultural norms.[58]

Here there is an unequivocal and unshakable belief that Black women's epistemology of oppression and lexicon of survival strategies are replete with resources for true liberation. This involves a multidialogical intent that is reflected in a purpose-driven perspective to advocate for and participate with multiple communities on behalf of their liberation. It also exhibits a didactic intent demonstrated in the pragmatic ability to teach and make the way plain so the truth that is empowering and life giving can help the oppressed get free. As such, critical engagement calls forth inexhaustible courage and communication that is characterized by Black women's intellectual positioning, investment, and integrity.[59] This positioning requires that womanist religious leaders, in the church and society at large, possess a keen sense of what freedom is. As victim and visionary, as well as participant and observer, a womanist's critical engagement requires navigating the path to freedom with great wisdom and finesse—she must be radical *but also* traditional, self-loving *but also* engaged, subjective *but* communal, and redemptive *but also* critical. The emphasis here on "but" signifies a positioning that veers away from mutual exclusivity toward maximal complexity.

Rev. Dr. Jacqui Lewis is a legendary and visionary womanist preacher and pastor of Middle Collegiate Church (Middle Church), a Reformed Protestant congregation in New York City. When she assumed leadership, the congregation was particularly proud of its church edifice, which predated the American Revolution and was adorned with vintage Tiffany stained-glass windows. In 2012, Rev. Lewis was celebrated for her years of leadership and ability to transform Middle Church into a radically different multiracial, multicultural congregation, a success she attributed to her "womanist sensibility" that is indelibly linked to "always thinking about how to story the gospel by any means necessary . . . on all kinds of nuances . . . as loving all people . . . think[ing] about rehearsing the reign of God here on earth."[60] While such achievement was no small feat, little did Lewis know that eight years later she was going to have to provide previously unimaginable levels of pastoral leadership seemingly overnight, as New York City became a hotspot for COVID-19, police brutality, economic instability, racial animus, and culture wars.

As part of its mission, Middle Church aspires to serve as the bridge between the now and the not yet:

> Inspired by the prophets and Jesus, who taught us to love God with everything we have, and to love our neighbor as ourselves, we live our faith out loud as we work for justice. At Black Lives Matter protests, LGBQTIA+ rallies, the Women's March, Climate Change events, and activism around gun violence, prison reform, the rights of immigrants, and a living wage, we are there. We affirm the transformative power of moral imagination to create a more just society.[61]

Based on such a vision, it is not surprising that the church rose to the occasion of addressing the perils of 2020. Driven by the foresight of its mission, the depths of the resources of its predominantly wealthy and white congregation, and the eschatological hope of its leader's womanist vision, Middle Church became a supersite for advocacy and resourcefulness. Much like FWBC, it assured its members and the surrounding community that "needing care is not a sign of weakness. God doesn't want you to white-knuckle it alone."[62] The church provided resources for those who asked what they could do in the midst of the national COVID-19 crisis that put New York City into lockdown, leaving many of its most vulnerable citizens bereft and alone. Middle Church and its ministerial team readily devised and implemented key and clear ways to practice "Revolutionary Love" and "The Courage to Imagine," ranging from rent and mortgage grants to help people stay in their homes to mounting various policy-driven and educational initiatives that address issues such as voter reform, immigration police reform, criminal justice reform, and allocating 10 percent of its budget for the #BlackLivesMatter movement.[63] Once again, Middle Church made a way through, under the vision and guidance of the pastor who saw over the rising tide of much that was troubling the most vulnerable in the congregation and city.

However, just when it seemed that hope was on the horizon— COVID-19 cases were abating to some degree, people were going back to work, kids were going back to school, and Trump had lost the election—December 5, 2020, became a tragic day on which Middle Church was seemingly no more, due to an electrical fire that entirely burned down its cherished edifice. Upon viewing the total devastation, Lewis said, "I see a gutted building full of smoke. The sanctuary is gone, absolutely gone."[64] In a calendar year such as 2020, already saturated by tragic and traumatic events, the psychological and spiritual toll experienced by Middle Church's faithful members and casual onlookers alike was incalculable. On a subconscious level, the shock, surprise, and sadness of a Black pastor's church on fire still triggers deeply seated memories of this nation's past.[65]

That notwithstanding, Middle Church's congregation immediately experienced the provision of womanist traditional communalism from fellow Black woman ministers Traci Blackmon and Lisa Hammonds, both of whom had recently experienced their own struggles and loss at the hands of police brutality or natural disasters.[66] Within a week, Blackmon's initiative resulted in two hundred thousand dollars raised on behalf of Middle Church through a nationwide fundraising campaign, while Hammonds reached out to Lewis personally to provide her with crucial guidance and wisdom as to how to recover not only spiritually but *fiscally*, affirming for Lewis that "no fire can stop Revolutionary Love."[67] That being the case, the loss of Middle Church's edifice raised the larger question of what happens when you can't go back to church? With the Black Church losing its facilities as sites of fellowship, Black Church leadership must engage in redrafting the historic nature of hush harbors that critically engaged with crisis and systems of oppression in the wee hours of the night through Black embodied spiritual conventions—in this case, however, in cyberspace.

Many womanist religious leaders know that there must be intentional effort to engage critically current events and crises, in order to mine the mother lode of those protowomanists who rest in power (R.I.P.). They must unearth social teachings of fortitude and perseverance of the invisible institution, but also need to find the safe haven and spiritual discipline of self-care, so that they will have the stamina to rise up from the ashes of immeasurable loss, surging disease, and raging evil that confront them at every turn. Serendipitously transforming social media platforms into the equivalent of twenty-first-century Underground

Railroad stations, the Womanist Salon Podcast (WSP)[68] and the Wee-Hr (The Women's Education Healing Retreat),[69] both formed by womanist religious leaders and theologians, create virtual space and implement code-switching so as to direct the essential agents and caretaking conductors toward respites to steal away and rest up as they risk their lives to engender justice and race toward freedom.

Since the first week of the stay-at-home mandate in March 2020, the Wee-Hr has become a late-night collective on Facebook Live around 10 p.m. every Friday for over a thousand digital viewers to address invisible wounds and teach people how to get well. As the brainchild of Rev. Dr. Claudette Copeland, the Wee-Hr is regarded as a branch of her overarching ministry and has become a safe haven during COVID-19 by focusing on the wellness of individual bodies—particularly Black women who have been overtaxed in community service, underpaid at work, and overworked in their careers and in caring for family, church, and community. Copeland cried out, "God help us. We are the caregivers. And we sorely need CARE. Not just prayer. Care. God help."[70] The Wee-Hr is Copeland answering her own call by creating a platform that cultivates intimacy with and for women like her, by creating retreat-like digital spaces to process reflectively social injustices and other traumas, all the while nourishing relationships and counterbalancing social distancing through dialogue and learning via technology. Through spiritual direction on Friday nights, Copeland provides escape routes to, and rest stops on, the Underground Railroad for the "vast group of under-appreciated, silent individuals who need time, environmental safety, professional spiritual support and unhurried space to do the unfinished business of Inner Healing."[71]

As a pastor, spiritual director, and one of the most celebrated Black female preachers, Copeland charitably provided care and cover during the COVID-19 crisis by "helping professionals, first responders, medical personnel, clergy, clergy spouses, military and former personnel, wounded spouses, relationally traumatized singles," along with those who are "sexually questioning, sexually injured, [those with] parental grief, chronic illness, the bereaved and grieving."[72] Late at night, often into the wee hours, Copeland counsels, sometimes sings and prays, but all the while creatively engages and cares for the lost and left out, who nevertheless are expected to lead the way toward freedom. Copeland transports her listeners into her living room by virtually "creating a cloistered physical space of exquisite beauty, confidentiality, nourishment, safety and uninterrupted serenity. . . . To work, learn, rest and play . . . [under the virtual care of a] competent and caring credentialed helper."[73]

Likewise is the case with the Womanist Salon Podcast (WSP). Cohosted by intergenerational womanist scholars, public theologians, and ordained clergywomen, Rev. Dr. Renita Weems, Dr. Stacey Floyd-Thomas, and Rev. Melanie Jones—also known as the "Hair Docs"—WSP critically engages listeners in dialogue regarding the political, popular, practical, and prophetic. Launched October 25, 2020 (in commemoration of the date of the 1997 Million Woman March),[74] and released at midnight on Saturday nights, the podcast and IG Live sessions metaphorically digitize a steal-away by hiding in plain sight a virtual, remote hub exclusive to Black women's experiences. Much like actual Black women's beauty salons, WSP is a space for women to tend to their ultimate concerns, affirming that sayings and rituals like "taking your hair down," "snatching edges," and "scratching your head out" are sacred, because, as sociologist Ingrid Banks notes, "hair matters."[75] WSP is also a fictive oasis, in that it has become a place for "the left out" to meet up and hang out. The salon is perhaps the only place within a postmodern era that the full range and diversity of Black women, regardless of age, aesthetic, profession, or confession of faith, exclusively gather without the presence of whiteness and the surveillance of men.

In an effort to make it plain by cultivating vulnerability and thick solidarity, the Hair Docs abscond their roles as scholars and preachers and leave the creature comforts of the professional class to engage Black women. While there is nothing ostensibly religious about the Womanist Salon Podcast in and of itself, many listeners attest to investing levels of affinity and affection often reserved for how many folks regard church matters. As one WSP listener exclaimed,

> When I listen to the Hair Docs, I really feel the spirit at work—moving you to be more, do more, and claim more because you're with sistahs who are encouraging you to be your best because they make you see yourself through their own eyes while making you braver, smarter, and more

beautiful. They are different people, with different lives but their voices and perspectives are in sync and harmony with wide range of sistahs I know in New York, Texas, California, or Georgia . . . singing along and saving our lives looking for a miracle, expecting the impossible, feeling the intangible, seeing the invisible . . . finding God in ourselves and loving her fiercely.[76]

The WSP challenges traditional ways of experiencing church and metaphorically creates alternative ways to encounter the gospel, divine wisdom, and spiritual formations, whether the physical church doors are open or not. In both oral and aural fashions, listeners embrace the Hair Docs faithfully, because they appreciate hearing culturally and spiritually rounded dialogue among people who care more about what is in their heads rather than how they style their hair.

The Womanist Salon and the Wee-Hr have been instrumental in envisioning the possibility of spontaneously caring for the sanctity of life and offering safe haven as "religious surrogates that provide users with access to community healing."[77] For the social media hosts, it became clear that because of COVID-19, Black women could be headed for mental health crises—as they and their loved ones were forced into quarantine and were stricken with COVID-19, as they had to relinquish their loved ones to emergency rooms, and as they were increasingly bereaved, all without presence of pastoral care, personal touch, or professional support. As a digital underground untethered to a physical building, these virtual womanist harbors present a vision that has gone just as viral as the coronavirus and have critically positioned the sanctuary movement as antibodies to both the effects of COVID-19 and virulent intersectional oppression.

Conclusion

The global pandemic required us to abandon the prospect of assembly within the physical church, demanding that Black Church leadership critically engage with the functionality and operations of the Black Church as people adjusted to new ways of being. Online ministry that purposely is not named as "church" has been offered late Friday nights for insomniacs, lonely hearts, and those who do their best thinking and working at night. Likewise podcasts that drop Saturdays at midnight and feature interactive shop-talk on Sunday evenings serve as surrogate holy spaces during hellish times for those who feel alone, need dialogue, and acutely feel invisible, isolated, and detached from their local church, family, or society in general.

The Black faithful—be they drum majors for justice or essential womanist waymakers—have always risked death for resurrection through their ministries of intervention and insurrection. Toward this end, Black faith illustrates that, whereas some notions or forms of the Black Church are dead or have fallen prey to the consequences and crises posed by COVID-19, the work, worth, and word of Black faith are nonetheless what matters. As the conduit of the sanctity of life, and given strength vis-à-vis a sanctuary network, Black faith moves from freedom *of* religion toward freedom *as* religion. These drum majors for justice and womanist wonders and allies have sustained sites of service and streams of opportunity to rid themselves and their communities of the trappings of edifices and events that locked them into peril and performances of an irreverent or irrelevant past. They have implemented new forms of creative activity that wrested from a pandemic an opportunity to prepare the way for a new mind-set and mission and to create a real future and a newfound faith that addressed the everyday areas and realities of life.

These examples, though few in number, illustrate the power that is at work in the midst of peril. They display how the vision of the sanctuary network of ministers—one detached from physical sanctuaries—has streamed faith in such a way that it has gone viral in expanding the reach of its traditional communalism by reinterpreting the kin-dom of God and reconciling itself to missions with integrity. It has also gained access to new ideas and new resources, supporting the experience of a new spiritual attribute that otherwise might have remained dormant. These examples of the Black Church transformed into intangible institutions reveal a functionality at work for those people who are not concerned with the formalistic trappings of Black faith. Instead, those bold and brave believers make their trek from the physical to the virtual world to seek what their souls must have. Along the way, beyond the apparent danger and despair of the world, and even beyond the confines of the church, they claim religious agency and the attunement of Black religious leadership to the spirit that enables a clarity of call and a sense of purpose that bears witness to divine serendipity.

NOTES

1 "Pastoring during the Pandemic," *Pastors Sunday Evening Chat*, Ray of Hope Community Church, Facebook Live, August 9, 2020, www.facebook.com/watch /live/?v=626553147976058&ref=watch_permalink.

2 Barbara Ann Holmes, *Joy Unspeakable: Contemplative Practices of the Black Church* (Minneapolis: Fortress, 2004), 5.

3 Henry Louis Gates Jr., *The Black Church: This Is Our Story, This Is Our Song* (New York: Penguin, 2021), xvi.

4 Ibid. The quotation is an excerpt from the poem "O Black and Unknown Bards" written by James Weldon Johnson and first published in James Weldon Johnson. ed., The Book of American Negro Poetry (New York: Harcourt, Brace, and Company, 1922).

5 See Horatio Greenough, *Form and Function: Remarks on Art, Design, and Architecture* (Los Angeles: University of California Press, 1969).

6 Peter Berger, *The Sacred Canopy: Elements of a Sociological Theory of Religion* (New York: Anchor, 1967).

7 Charles Long, *Significations: Sign, Symbols, and Images in the Interpretation of Religion* (Aurora, CO: Davis Group, 1995), 7.

8 W. E. B. Du Bois, *The Souls of Black Folks* (New York: W. W. Norton, 1999), 120.

9 For further exploration of the concept of "soul murder," see Nell Painter, *Soul Murder and Slavery (Fifteenth Charles Edmondson Historical Lectures)* (Waco, TX: Baylor University Press, 1995).

10 Derived from Genesis 9 in the Hebrew Bible, the "curse of Ham" or the "Hamitic curse" narrates how Noah cursed the descendants of his son Ham, the Canaanites who are depicted as dark, with servitude. It remains a way not only to explore the complex origins of the concept of race but also to validate racism, caste, and slavocracy throughout the modern world from Africa to the Americas. Two other verses from Paul in the New Testament—Ephesians 6:5 and Colossians 3:22—call on slaves to be obedient to their masters. "Slaves, obey your earthly masters with fear and trembling, in singleness of heart, as you obey Christ; Slaves, obey your earthly masters in everything, not only while being watched and in order to please them, but wholeheartedly, fearing the Lord." For further discussion of how racist biblical interpretation inspired white supremacy and the story of slavery in America, see Katie G. Cannon, "Slave Ideology and Biblical Interpretation," in *Katie's Canon: Womanism and the Soul of the Black Community* (New York: Continuum, 1995), 47–56; Sylvester A. Johnson, *The Myth of Ham in Nineteenth-Century American Christianity: Race, Heathens, and the People of God* (New York: Palgrave Macmillan, 2004); Stephen Haynes, *Noah's Curse: The Biblical Justification of American Slavery* (New York: Oxford University Press, 2007); and Colin Kidd,

The Forging of Races: Race and Scripture in the Protestant Atlantic World, 1600–2000 (New York: Cambridge University Press, 2006).

11 For an examination of the pretense of enlightenment and the problem of embodiment that Platonic philosophy poses for underrepresented groups, see Stacey Floyd-Thomas, "Plato on Reason," in Stacey M. Floyd-Thomas and Miguel A. De La Torre, eds., *Beyond the Pale: Reading Ethics from the Margins* (Louisville, KY: Westminster John Knox, 2011), 3–14.

12 Albert J. Raboteau, *Slave Religion: The "Invisible Institution" in the Antebellum South* (1978; New York: Oxford University Press, 2004), ix. For further discussion of the "invisible institution," see John W. Blassingame, *The Slave Community: Plantation Life in the Antebellum South* (New York: Oxford University Press, 1972); Eugene Fox-Genovese, *Roll Jordan Roll: The World the Slaves Made* (New York: Pantheon, 1974); Cain Hope Felder, ed., *Stony the Road We Trod: African American Biblical Interpretation* (Minneapolis: Fortress, 1991); Herbert G. Gutman, *The Black Family in Slavery and Freedom, 1750–1925* (New York: Pantheon, 1976); Charles W. Joyner, *Down by the Riverside: A South Carolina Slave Community* (Urbana: University of Illinois Press, 1985); and John Lofton, *Denmark Vesey's Revolt: the Slave Plot That Lit a Fuse to Fort Sumter* (Kent, OH: Kent State University Press, 1983).

13 Maya Angelou, "These Yet-to-Be-United States," *Los Angeles Times*, June 3, 1990, www.latimes.com.

14 Vincent Harding, "In Search of African Liberation Pedagogy: Multiple Contexts of Education and Struggle," *Journal of Education* 172, no. 2 (1990): 37.

15 Robert M. Franklin, *Another Day's Journey: Black Churches Confronting the American Crisis* (Minneapolis: Fortress, 1997), 7.

16 Eddie Glaude Jr., "The Black Church Is Dead," Huffington Post, April 26, 2010, www.huffpost.com.

17 King employed the phrase "the fierce urgency of now" on at least two memorable occasions: his "I Have a Dream" speech delivered on August 28, 1963, at the Lincoln Memorial on the Washington, DC, National Mall, and his "Beyond Vietnam" sermon of April 1967, given at Riverside Church in New York City.

18 Howard Thurman, *Jesus and the Disinherited*, reprint ed. (Boston: Beacon, 1996), 7.

19 Juan Floyd-Thomas, *Making It Plain: Liberating Black Church History* (Nashville: Abingdon, 2014), 7.

20 Jon Meacham, *The Soul of America: The Battle for Our Better Angels* (New York: Random House, 2019), 266.

21 Du Bois, *Souls of Black Folk*, 120.

22 See Josiah U. Young III, "Do Black Lives Matter to 'God'?" *Black Theology* 13, no. 3 (2015): 210–18; Lawrence T. Brown, "The Movement for Black Lives vs. the Black Church," *KALFOU: A Journal of Comparative and Relational Ethnic Studies* 4, no. 1 (2017): 7–17; Johari Jabir, "The Black Church: A Tree with Many Branches," *KALFOU: A Journal of Comparative and Relational Ethnic Studies* 4, no. 1 (2017):

18–29; Juan Floyd-Thomas, "'A Relatively New Discovery in the Modern West': #BlackLivesMatter and the Evolution of Black Humanism," *KALFOU: A Journal of Comparative and Relational Ethnic Studies* 4, no. 1 (2017): 30–39; George Lipsitz, "Making Black Lives Matter: Conjuring and Creative Place-Making in an Age of Austerity," *KALFOU: A Journal of Comparative and Relational Ethnic Studies* 4, no. 1 (2017): 40–58; Keeanga-Yamahtta Taylor, *From #BlackLivesMatter to Black Liberation* (Chicago: Haymarket, 2016); Anthony B. Pinn, "In the Wake of Obama's Hope: Thoughts on Black Lives Matter, Moralism, and Re-Imaging Race Struggle," in Juan M. Floyd-Thomas and Anthony B. Pinn, eds., *Religion in the Age of Obama* (London: Bloomsbury, 2018), 142–51; and "Black Lives Matter" cover story and symposium, *Christian Century*, March 8, 2016, www.christiancentury .org.

23 Generally speaking, the term "megachurch" refers to high-attendance churches with very large facilities.

24 "Black Lives Matter Ride in for Justice Tomorrow," *Focus Daily News*, August 8, 2020, www.focusdailynews.com.

25 Friendship West Baptist Church, "Church and Conference Center," accessed October 27, 2020, www.friendshipwest.org.

26 A term informed by the works of philosopher and father of postmodernism, Michel Foucault, and Achille Mbembe, "necropolitics" refers to the way in which Foucault's notion of "biopower" and Mbembe's notion of "sovereignty" repre- sent the conjoined forces of social and political power that control people's lives in such a way that it simultaneously protects the privileges of the powerful and necessitates the subjugation of the marginalized population. See Michel Foucault, *The Will to Knowledge: The History of Sexuality, Volume I* (London: Penguin, 1976), and Achille Mbembé, "Necropolitics," trans. Libby Meintjes *Public Culture* 15, no. 1 (Winter 2003): 11.

27 "Black Lives Matter Ride in for Justice Tomorrow."

28 "Controversy Erupts after 'Back the Blue Cruise' Makes Uninvited Stop at Friendship West Baptist Church," August 20, 2020, www.youtube.com /watch?v=JVXw7B_6ENg.

29 Frederick D. Haynes III, "God Is Making Moves (Ezra 1:1–5 NRSV)," Sermon, Friendship West Baptist Church, Dallas, Texas, January 10, 2021.

30 Carter G. Woodson, *Miseducation of the Negro* (1933; Trenton, NJ: Africa World Press 1990), 40.

31 Delores S. Williams, "Womanist Theology: Black Women's Voices," *Christianity and Crisis* 47, no. 3 (March 2, 1987): 67. Also see Delores S. Williams, *Sisters in the Wilderness: The Challenge of Womanist God-Talk* (Maryknoll, NY: Orbis, 1993), xiii.

32 The four womanist theological intents can be found in Delores S. Williams, "Womanist Theology: Black Women's Voices," and at Delores S. Williams, "Womanist Theology: Black Women's Voices," Religion Online, accessed February 1, 2021, www.religion-online.org/article/womanist-theology-black-womens-voices/.

For the four tenets of womanism, see Stacey Floyd-Thomas, ed., *Deeper Shades of Purple: Womanism in Religion and Society* (New York: NYU Press, 2006), 16.

33 Womanist ethics progenitor Katie Cannon developed a womanist virtue ethics characterized by "invisible dignity, quiet grace, and unshouted courage" based on the moral wisdom of Black women's experience of oppression since slavery and narrated as sacred in Black women's literature. See Katie Cannon, *Black Womanist Ethics* (Atlanta: Scholars, 1988).

34 Cheryl Townsend-Gilkes, "If It Wasn't for the Women . . . ,'" in *Black Women's Experience and Womanist Culture in Church and Community* (Maryknoll, NY: Orbis, 2001). See also Rosetta E. Ross, *Witnessing and Testifying: Black Women, Religion, and Civil Rights* (Minneapolis: Fortress, 2003); Richard Newman and Judith Weisenfeld, eds., *This Far by Faith: Readings in African American Women's Religious Biography* (New York: Routledge, 1996).

35 Sandra L. Barnes, "Whosoever Will Let Her Come: Social Activism and Gender Inclusivity in the Black Church," *Journal for the Scientific Study of Religion* 45 (2006): 371–87. See also C. Jones and K. Shorter-Gooden, *Shifting: The Double Lives of Black Women in America* (New York: HarperCollins, 2003).

36 Eboni Marshall Turman, "Powers and Principalities: A Black Womanist Interrogation of Demonarchy 25 Years Hence," *Black Theology Papers Project* 4, no. 1 (2018): 1.

37 Ibid.

38 Coined by Moya Bailey, "misogynoir" was developed to describe the targeted hatred, disdain distrust, and discrimination directed toward Black women. See Moya Bailey, *Misogynoir Transformed: Black Women's Digital Resistance* (New York: NYU Press, 2021).

39 See Bettye Collier-Thomas, *Jesus, Jobs, and Justice: African American Women and Religion* (New York: Knopf, 2010); Kelly Brown Douglas, *What's Faith Got to Do With It?: Black Bodies / Christian Souls* (Maryknoll, NY: Orbis, 2005); Kelly Brown Douglas, *Stand Your Ground: Black Bodies and the Justice of God* (Maryknoll, NY: Orbis, 2015); Floyd-Thomas, ed., *Deeper Shades of Purple*; Marcia Y. Riggs, *Plenty Good Room: Women versus Male Power in the Black Church* (Cleveland: Pilgrim, 2003); Marla Fredrick, *Between Sundays: Black Women and Everyday Struggles of Faith* (Berkeley: University of California Press, 2003); Eboni Marshall Turman, *Toward a Womanist Ethic of Incarnation: Black Bodies, the Black Church, and the Council of Chalcedon* (New York: Palgrave Macmillan, 2013); Renita J. Weems, *Just a Sister Away: Understanding the Timeless Connection between Women of Today and Women in the Bible* (West Bloomfield, MI: Walk Worthy Press, 2007), Daphne Wiggins, *Righteous Content: Black Women's Perspectives of Church and Faith* (New York: NYU Press, 2004).

40 Candice Benbow, "While More Black Churches Come Online Due to Coronavirus, Black Women Faith Leaders Have Always Been Here," *Essence*, March 24, 2020, 7, www.essence.com.

41 Floyd-Thomas, ed. *Deeper Shades of Purple*, 16. The term "all the women are white and all the Blacks are men" is a womanist and Black feminist refrain taken

from the classic text by Patricia Bell Scott et al, *But Some of Us Are Brave: All the Women Are White, All the Blacks Are Men: Black Women's Studies* (New York: Feminist Press at CUNY, 1993).

42 Raedorah Stewart Dodd, "When Mama Was God," in Floyd-Thomas, ed., *Deeper Shades of Purple*, 17.

43 Melva Sampson, "Pink Robe Chronicles," *Dr. Melva Sampson*, January 8, 2021, www.drmelvasampson.com/.

44 Ibid.

45 Melva L. Sampson, "Digital Hush Harbors," *Fire!!!* 6, no. 1 (2020): 60.

46 Ibid.

47 Danyelle Thomas, *Unfit Christian*, www.unfitchristian.com/.

48 Lyvonne Proverbs, (@weresurthrivors), 2021, Instagram, January 2021, lyvonne. podia.com/healing.

49 Whitney Bond, (@stillsaved), 2021, Instagram, January 2021, linktr.ee/ WhitneyBond.

50 Iya Funlayo, "About Iya Funlayo," *Ase Ire*, accessed February 1, 2021, https://aseire .com/funlayo/.

51 Irie Lynne Session et al., *The Gathering, A Womanist Church: Origins, Stories, Sermons, and Litanies* (Eugene, OR: Wipf and Stock, 2020), 7.

52 Irie Lynne Session, *Murdered Souls, Resurrected Lives: Postmodern Womanist Thought in Ministry with Women Prostituted and Marginalized by Commercial Sexual Exploitation* (Charleston, SC: CreateSpace, 2015), 77.

53 Session, *The Gathering*, 32.

54 Ibid., 11–65.

55 Ibid., xiv.

56 Ibid., 3.

57 Ibid., 7.

58 Kimberly P. Johnson, *The Womanist Preacher: Proclaiming Womanist Rhetoric from the Pulpit* (Lantham, MD: Lexington, 2017), 79.

59 Floyd-Thomas, ed., *Deeper Shades of Purple*, 208.

60 Session, *The Gathering*, 3–4.

61 "Our Vision," Middle Church, accessed February 1, 2021, www.middlechurch.org.

62 "Financial Assistance," Middle Church, accessed February 1, 2021, www.middle church.org.

63 "Love & Justice," Middle Church, accessed February 1, 2021, www.middlechurch.org.

64 Maria Cramer and Edgar Sandoval, "East Village Fire Damages 128-Year-Old Church," *New York Times*, December 5, 2020, www.nytimes.com.

65 Jerrolyn Eulinberg, "Black Wall Street and the 1921 Tulsa Race Massacre: Remembering 100 Years in 2021," Relevant Religion Series, the Public Theology and Racial Justice Collaborative Martin L. King Jr. Lecture, Vanderbilt Divinity School, Nashville, Tennessee, January 14, 2021.

66 Besides donations from numerous members and city residents, Middle Church received its first fruits from a Facebook fundraiser set up for Lewis by her

womanist friend Rev. Traci Blackmon (#BLM advocate and a United Church of
Christ pastor in St. Louis, Missouri) who announced that the money was pledged
in what she called "the resurrection number" of three days. Keeping in stride
with a generosity of experience, Rev. Lisa Hammonds, pastor of St. John's African
Methodist Episcopal Church, which was recovering from a tornado that hit
Nashville at the beginning of the stay-at-home mandate in March, advised Lewis,
"Document everything. Cross every T. Dot every I." Hammonds added that
"clergy should publicly grieve their loss to help give their congregants permission
to mourn as well." But she said they also have to cope with the taxing and daunt-
ing work of dealing with government, disaster relief, and insurance officials. See
"After Middle Church Fire, Advice from Houses of Worship That Have Survived
Disaster," *Religion News Services*, December 15, 2020, https://religionnews.com.

67 "Historic New York City Church Gutted by Massive Fire," *11 Alive*, December 5,
2020, www.11alive.com.
68 Stacey Floyd-Thomas, Melanie Jones, and Renita Weems, *The Womanist Salon
Podcast*, linktr.ee/thewomanistsalon.
69 Claudette Copeland, "Wee-Hr," Facebook, Claudette Copeland Ministries,
January 9, 2021, www.facebook.com.
70 Claudette Copeland, "Wee-Hr," Facebook post, Claudette Copeland, February 8,
2021, www.facebook.com.
71 Claudette Copeland, Claudette Copeland Ministries, www.claudetteacopeland.org/.
72 Ibid.
73 Ibid.
74 The Million Woman March was a protest march organized on October 25, 1997,
comprising roughly five hundred thousand people on Benjamin Franklin Parkway
in Philadelphia, Pennsylvania. A major theme of the march was family unity and
what it means to be an African American woman in America. See Bobbi Booker,
"Million Woman March: 1997 Philly Event Equally Significant," *Philadelphia
Tribune*, October 2, 2015, www.phillytrib.com.
75 Ingrid Banks, *Hair Matters: Beauty, Power, and Black Women's Consciousness*
(New York: NYU Press, 2000).
76 Sew Sew Designs, October 25, 2020, Instagram (IG) Live, the Womanist Salon
Podcast AfterGlow with Hair Doc Dr. Floyd-Thomas.
77 Carla Jean-McNeil Jackson, "Hashtags and Hallelujahs." *Fire!!!* 6, no. 1 (2020):
98–131.

2

Who's Saving Whom?

Black Millennials and the Revivification of Religious Communities

MELANIE C. JONES

The COVID-19 pandemic has marked a viral crisis of faith, as shelter–in-place mandates forced faith communities to shift from institutional edifices to streaming websites to remain spiritually vibrant, socially relevant, and economically solvent. In their hopes of staying afloat, many Black religious communities (ranging from makeshift store-front churches to megaministries) turned to millennials—people born between 1980 and 2000—to shift modes of connectivity to virtual platforms. Millennials not only represent the largest, most educated generation in the United States but they are also digital natives responsible for the rise and promulgation of social media (Facebook, Instagram, Twitter, etc.). The pandemic unveils a glaring generation gap within the Black Church tradition. On the one hand, elder generations, prompted by the myth that living while Black is better for millennials, misunderstand millennial presence as either irreverent or irrelevant to the perceived viability of the tradition.[1] The 2014 Pew Research Center report, "The Religious Landscape," supported the reality of negative perceptions of religion when it revealed that 35 percent of millennials identified as "nones," those who do not identify with any religious group.[2] On the other hand, this narrative ignores the 65 percent of the less popularized majority of Black millennials who belong to faith communities and those who value religious experience garnered through nontraditional pathways. Contrary to most anecdotal accounts, a large cross-section of Black millennials has launched into the digital deep to revive faith communities in the United States.

In *Black Millennials and the Church*, Black practical theologian Joshua Mitchell chronicles how Black millennials in a pre-COVID-19 era made demands for churches, in their words and deeds, to embrace relevant technology and a renewed commitment to social justice. For instance, the Black Youth Project reports that millennials are calling for the Black Church, which has lost its seat as the center of radical Black social movements in a post–civil rights era, to become more politically engaged and reconnected with African-centered spiritualities.[3] Millennials represent the champions who have advanced Black faith into the furthest reaches of the online arena. For example, millennial Black clergywomen, most typically marginalized by sexism with little to no access to many Black Church pulpits, have led the way in extending ministerial platforms to digital domains before and during the COVID-19 lockdown. During the COVID crisis, Black churches were spurred to look to these young, gifted, and Black digital natives to help transform virtual realms into sacred space dedicated to social change and prophetic ministry. The very generation indicted for abandoning faith was now, amid the COVID-19 pandemic, called to save faith communities from the depths of decline, despair, and dis-ease and show the way toward a digital awakening. This chapter interrogates the politics of redemption as it exists between Black millennials and the Black Church seized in a moment of truth and transformation.

COVID-19 and the Crisis to Keep the Faith

Though the early occurrence of the novel coronavirus (COVID-19) traces back to early winter 2019, the White House declared the outbreak a national emergency and global pandemic on March 13, 2020, with more than 1,645 people infected in 47 states. Federal, state, and local governments moved swiftly to close schools, institutions, retail stores, restaurants, physical plants, and places of worship to contain the virus. For many, March 13 was a day of reckoning, in that a national shutdown could no longer be evaded as stay-at-home orders loomed, and public health warnings intensified with over 118,000 cases in 110 countries. For Breonna Taylor, a twenty-six-year-old Black millennial woman, March 13, 2020, marked a fatal ending as Louisville police barged into her home under a no-knock warrant and fired several rounds that resulted in her untimely death. Seemingly, Americans were caught in the crosshairs of multiple pandemics—an unholy trinity of COVID-19, COVID-1619, and what womanist ethicist Stacey Floyd-Thomas names as "COVID-45"—that revealed devastating consequences for Black lives in America that have been 400 years in the making.[4] COVID-19 names a deadly virus strand exponentially more dangerous than the common cold and flu, more deadly than today's living generations have ever seen. American greed and an untouchable sense of entitlement differentiated COVID-19 as "their" problem (e.g., President Trump calling the coronavirus the "Chinese virus") and not "our" problem, a statement intended to diminish its impact on American soil. The coronavirus's disproportionate effects and the climbing death toll for people of color in this nation revealed the death-dealing, daily attacks against Black life. COVID-19 exposed that the world was already in crisis and America was never great before the pandemic, with devastating realities of food insecurity and scarcity, unequal access to health care, inadequate care for trauma and violence, rising unemployment, the collapse of small businesses, unfair wages ensuring that "the majority" can barely make ends meet to sustain basic needs, skyrocketing homelessness, debilitating student debt, an economic bailout for the rich coupled with economic hardship for the poor, criminalizing of the impoverished, unjust treatment toward the incarcerated, and most significantly, increasing awareness of poor governance and leadership as high as the occupant at 1600 Pennsylvania Avenue in the nation's capital. Historians will remember 2020 as the year of global pandemic and protest. Millions of protesters in the summer of 2020 flooded the streets of major cities around the globe, risking their health and safety to contest the deaths of fallen Black bodies and making a millennial-led #BlackLivesMatter one of the largest social movements in history.[5]

COVID-19 changed everything, especially the technologies of Black faith. Due to the pandemic, Black churches shifted their worship services and gathering online not by choice but by force. State and local shelter-in-place mandates that allowed only nonessential work and requirements of social distancing meant compliant churches needed to employ online media to convene congregants, shepherd disenfranchised people, and survive a crucial turning point. Though some churches—Black and otherwise—rejected the warning and held in-person worship services and gatherings, the effects of these decisions were not without fatal consequences for the assembled. On the one hand, Black churches that had dismissed digital technologies—with no prior church website, social media pages, or access to streaming capacity—had to make immediate adjustments to connect congregants and hold worship services via conference calls, Zoom, or other virtual means. On the other hand, Black churches equipped with vibrant, high-level streaming capabilities confronted a different growing edge with recording worship moments and restaging virtual interaction often with a few participants gathered in physical space. Regardless, creativity and digital innovation were essential for all Black churches confronting the crisis to keep the faith during COVID-19. Not only were millennials correct that Black churches need to engage digital technologies to remain relevant for today's people and times, but the pandemic impelled Black churches to heed their call.

Mapping Millennial Markers

On any given day, a Google search that begins with "Millennials are" may populate the results with frequently used keywords that indicate common misconceptions and negative generational portrayals—lazy, killing a struggling business industry (e.g., the napkin industry), stupid, idiots, what age, the worst, entitled, and screwed. The popularity of the term "millennial" does not correlate with common knowledge about the experiences of millennials themselves. I identify millennials as a generational cohort of persons born between 1980 and 2000.[6] Millennial is not a catchphrase for youth and young adults or the recognition of a particular life stage, but a generational marker that characterizes today's largest population cohort.[7] Although 60 percent of millennials resist the label itself, "Millennials surpass the Baby Boomers as the largest living generation in this nation (72.2 million in 2019) and surpass GenX'ers as the largest share in today's workforce."[8] Recent US Census reports reveal "more than half of the nation's total population are now members of the millennial generation or younger."[9] Alongside GenZ's, millennials represent one of the most racially diverse generations in America, with nearly half belonging to nonwhite racial or ethnic groups.

The majority of scholarship addressing millennials fails to engage adequately the complex social realities facing nonwhite racial groups. The Black Youth Project released a 2015 report titled "Black Millennials in America," outlining particular factors of the Black millennial experience.[10] In addition to racial diversity, Black millennials are more likely than older generations to name their sexual and gender diversity and identify as LGBT at younger ages: eighteen to twenty-nine (6.4 percent) and thirty to forty-four (3.2 percent). Though mostly educated, Black millennials are not above the poverty line, with the millennial median household income approximately $35,300, compared to $43,900 for GenX'ers at the same age in 2001. Millennials lag in heading households compared to GenX'ers and Boomers and hold the highest number for racially diverse households and single-mother heads of households.[11] The economic challenges may correlate to millennials marrying at a lower and slower rate than previous generations. In addition to the institution of marriage, millennials are less connected to other institutions than their predecessors. Black millennial political involvement holds political leaders more accountable for addressing social issues and mitigating social problems facing marginalized communities.

To be a millennial is to be marked by crisis. The last twenty years capture Black millennials coming of age during critical points in time such as September 11 (2001), America's global war on terror (2003–present), Hurricane Katrina (2005), Hurricane Rita (2005), the Great Recession (2007–2010), the killing of Trayvon Martin and emergence of #BlackLivesMatter (2012), the death of Michael Brown and the protests in Ferguson (2014), the Emmanuel Nine Massacre in South Carolina (2015), the mass shooting spree at Pulse nightclub in Orlando (2016), the election and presidency of Donald J. Trump (2016–2021), and most recently, the COVID-19 pandemic and the summer of reckoning in the aftermath of the deaths of Ahmaud Arbery, Breonna Taylor, George Floyd, and Black transpersons (2020). In the face of multiple pandemics in 2020, millennials continue to endure pivotal historical moments that alter the way humans live, travel, work, learn, gather, connect, and dream. In numerous ways, the impacts of these social ruptures threaten millennials' economic stability, mental health, livelihood, and quality of life during their early adult years.[12] Named the "do-gooders," it makes sense that millennials persist, often relentlessly, in pursuit of social transformation and remain at the forefront of creative maneuvering in the face of compounding adversity. Three significant factors mark the millennial generation: digital technology, rising educational advancement coupled with economic instability, and shifting religious trends.

First, millennials and younger generations are digital natives; born in a digital, media-saturated world, they cannot fathom a life without the internet, email, computers, cell phones, and gaming. Though not all millennials had personal access to expensive technological equipment in their earlier years because of unequal access and turbulent economic conditions, the term "digital native," coined by educational analyst Marc Prensky in his 2001 article "Digital Natives, Digital Immigrants," speaks to different analytical wiring given constant exposure to digital inter-faces and stimuli. Millennials think and process differently about how to approach problems and create solutions.[13] Most millennials possess high-level talents, skills, and abilities to develop, operate, and master digital technologies. Millennials thrive on "fast access to information, high-quality graphics over content, instant gratification, frequent re-wards, and the benefits of a networked society,"[14] which are hallmarks and pitfalls of social media.[15] Crisis evokes radical creativity when con-sidering that millennials are also responsible for the invention and rise of social media. Today, Facebook is the largest social media platform in the world. Most Facebook public users are unaware that it started in 2003 on the campus of Harvard University as the brainchild of mil-lennial college students Mark Zuckerberg, Eduardo Saverin, Dustin Moskovitz, and Chris Hughes, seeking social transparency among col-lege users in its early iterations before welcoming public adult users. Facebook is one of many social media inventions and innovations de-veloped and curated by millennial leaders and interests later distributed for public consumption. The origins of Facebook mirror the larger tech empire as white, elitist, capitalist, and heteronormative. Though sites like BlackPlanet.com were developed and organized for Black audiences in 1999 before Facebook and MySpace, even in the world of tech, it is clear who ultimately gets the credit and rises to the top. Black millennials navigating the digital world illustrates their digital literacies and vibrant technocultures as employing technologies of resistance against death-dealing mechanized odds.

Second, millennials are the most educated and least compensated generation in human history. Millennials came of age during the dra-matic economic downturn of 2007–2010, known as the Great Recession. According to the Pew Research Center, four in ten millennial workers or 46 percent of millennial women ages twenty-five to twenty-nine have a bachelor's degree or more, which is higher than the 32 percent of Gen X'ers in 2000, 26 percent of Boomers in 1985, and 16 percent of Silents in 1964.[16] While millennials represent higher educational attainment levels with more college graduates than preceding generations, Black and Hispanic millennials still fall behind white and Asian millennials in postsecondary education. Millennial women are more likely than their male counterparts to complete college degrees, which may increase economic payoffs for college graduates.[17]

Despite higher education, the employment cutbacks and collapsing of entry-level positions during the Great Recession and now the COVID-19 pandemic have emboldened a gig economy, spreading millennials across multiple smaller jobs with unreliable benefits and unstable incomes. Employers and organizations crave millennial ingenuity, but they are not always willing to pay their worth. Every major corporation, organization, business, and institution faces the current conundrum of how to harness millennial genius while retaining millennial participation. In other words, institutions are always pondering, "How do we employ millennials for strategic advancement while keeping millennials active in the establishment?" Unfortunately, the church and religious communities struggle with this question the most.

Third, millennials represent the largest generational faction that does not identify with a religious group.[18] The 2014 Pew Research study identified 35 percent of millennials as identifying as "nones," defined as individuals belonging to the category of atheists, agnostics, or those with little emphasis on a religious identity. The religious landscape of Black millennials is missing from the BYP report, which scripts a false narrative that religion is a nonfactor for this demographic. Though 18 percent of Black millennials identified as unaffiliated with a religious group in the Pew study, this number is lower than 24 percent of their white counterparts in this same category. Black millennials tend to be more religious than other millennials but less religious than older cohorts of Black people.[19] An ongoing buzz question of Christian communities in North America is, "Why are millennials leaving the Church?" Faith communities and denominations have used the 18 percent unaffiliated amount to perpetuate a narrative of millennial disinterest in matters of faith. Yet what about the 82 percent of Black millennials or 65 percent of all millennials calling for faith communities to revive their social witness and renew their modes of engagement to digital platforms? The truth is that millennial faith looks different, with less emphasis on building religious institutions and greater interest in social change that inspires individual and communal liberation. Perhaps the more urgent question is, "Why are faith communities failing millennials?"

Death, Dying, and the Black Church

The Black Church is the principal social and religious institution of the Black community. The authors of *Black Church Studies: An Introduction* describe the Black Church as "the single most autonomous Black institution in North America."[20] The origin of the Black Church traces back to the antebellum South, where enslaved Africans gathered in free worship in the hush harbors and brush arbors as an invisible institution. The Black Church was formed as a resistance movement in "the clearing" where the enslaved sought to escape a vicious American slaveocracy cradled in white supremacist ideology and Christian complicity. Spirituals like "Steal Away to Jesus" and "Go in de Wilderness" represent the signal songs used by the enslaved to escape to a carved-out freedom dwelling to meet the divine in the wilderness and gather with kinfolk in the wind. By the late eighteenth and early nineteenth centuries, the exodus of Black Christians out of segregated white Christian churches and into public Black worship dwellings illustrates the Black Church becoming a visible institution. In their classic 1990 volume, *The Black Church in the African American Experience*, sociologists C. Eric Lincoln and Lawrence Mamiya assert, "The Black Church has no challenger as the cultural womb of the Black community," which gave birth to numerous social organizations and cultural traditions from music to food to fashion to film.[21] Though Christianity is not the sole center of the Black sacred cosmos, the "religious worldview of African Americans is related both to their African heritage, which envisaged the whole universe as sacred, and to their conversion to Christianity during slavery and its aftermath."[22] From the antebellum to the postbellum, any historical narration of the Black Church cannot be understood without valuing younger generations as revolutionaries in Zion who have led the Black Church to the edges of its prophetic witness in word and deed. One significant example is the Black southern preacher Martin Luther King

Jr.'s rise to national prominence as a leader of a nonviolent civil rights movement who propelled the Black Church to the center of the freedom struggle at the tender age of twenty-six.[23]

There is scholarly tension about whether the nomenclature of "Black Church"[24] may simply refer to African American denominational churches or congregations. Lincoln and Mamiya identify the Black Church by the historically Black mainline denominational churches (National Baptist Convention U.S.A., National Baptist Convention of America, Progressive National Baptist Convention, African Methodist Episcopal Church, African Methodist Episcopal Zion Church, Christian Methodist Episcopal Church, and Church of God in Christ) and the rising tide of numerous independent African American denominational groups across Baptist, Methodist, and Pentecostal lines. Some Black religious scholars understand the Black Church to comprise African American congregations within historically white denominations (e.g., Catholics, Episcopalians, Presbyterians, and Congregationalists). Others recognize nondenominational churches that are "Black" in nature concerning leadership, aesthetics, worship style, preaching, spiritual formation, and cultural traditions as also belonging to the Black Church. Lawrence and Mamiya argue a dialectal model of the Black Church to speak of its character and functions between the "priestly and prophetic, otherworldly and this-worldly, universalism and particularism, communal and the privatistic, charismatic and bureaucratic, and resistance and accommodation."[25] In *Sisters in the Wilderness: The Challenge of Womanist God-Talk*, womanist theologian Delores S. Williams contends that the Black Church "is invisible, but we know when we see, hear and feel it quickening the heart, measuring the soul and bathing life with the spirit in time. . . . To speak of the African-American denominational churches as the black church suggests a unity among the denominations that does not exist."[26] In Williams's view, merging the Black Church with African American denominational churches and congregations enables the hiding of a multitude of sins, especially at the intersections of age, gender, sexuality, and class. Affirming the historical Black Church as the center of meaning making and liberation for Black people eclipses the numerous ways African American denominational churches and congregations remain violent to the most vulnerable in their midst, including but not limited to women, children, youth, LGBTQ persons, and the poor.

Black religious studies scholar Eddie Glaude spawned rattling controversy with his provocative 2010 *Huffington Post* article asserting the
death of the Black Church. According to Glaude,

> The Black Church, as we've known it or imagined it, is dead. Of course,
> many African Americans still go to church. According to the Pew
> Research Center's Forum on Religion and Public Life, 87 percent of
> African Americans identify with a religious group and 79 percent say
> that religion is very important in their lives. But the idea of this venerable
> institution as central to black life and as a repository for the social and
> moral conscience of the nation has all but disappeared.[27]

Glaude points to three central indicators to illuminate the death of
the Black Church. First, *"black churches have always been complicated spaces."*[28] Glaude demystifies the Black Church as a prophetic
and progressive incubator and exposes the increasing conservatism
of Black churches that further reveals "a conservative dimension of
Black Christian life."[29] To this point, Black feminist historian Evelyn
Brooks Higginbotham, in her classic text *Righteous Discontent: The
Women's Movement in the Black Baptist Church, 1880–1920*, unveils the
Black Church as an institutional locus for the emergence and evolution
of respectability politics and other confining social practices that limited and restricted the freedom of Black Baptist women at the turn of
the twentieth century while increasing conservative ideals.[30] Second,
Glaude argues, *"African American communities are much more differentiated"* with less reliance on the Black Church to serve as "all things" to
Black people. The history of the Black Church or Black clergy serving
as the public mainstay or center of personal, political, social, spiritual,
moral, and educational development has diminished as more Black
institutions have become "distinct and specialized."[31] Moreover, the
increasing populations of Black Christians attending popular white congregations, especially in evangelical churches, shrinks Black Christian
reliance on the Black Church for spiritual formation and sustenance.
Third, Glaude maintains the death of the Black Church at the hand
of *"the routinization of black prophetic witness."*[32] Glaude laments the
Black Church that speaks of its prophetic witness as past rather than
present. For Glaude, "The question becomes: what will be the role of

prophetic black churches on the national stage under these conditions? Any church as an institution ought to call us to be our best selves—not to be slaves to doctrine or mere puppets for profit. Within its walls, our faith should be renewed and refreshed. We should be open to experiencing God's revelation anew."[33] The ongoing work to uplift, support, and advocate for the Black community's needs requires Black churches to play a role in the here and now rather than resting on a past legacy. The failure of the Black Church to energize, mobilize, and revitalize Black faith reveals if not an immediate death of the Black Church, then a dying Black Church.

Meet Millennials or Miss Millennials?

Mitchell frames Black churches facing the ugly truth of decline as straddled between conventional grief and anticipatory grief. Mitchell writes, "Can our church survive and thrive for the next 60 years, or have we already become the walking dead?"[34] Conventional grief identifies Black churches that are mourning the loss of what has passed. These churches were once booming with vibrant youth and young adult ministries that ensured a leadership and membership pipeline as congregants matured through the life stages. Anticipatory grief points to Black churches recognizing that their churches are "ghost towns" with an aging membership that anticipates that their church will soon die. To answer the question "Why are millennials leaving religion or the Black Church in particular?," one response from Mitchell's analysis is that millennials have inherited dying Black churches with declining memberships, outdated technologies, and ways of celebrating a glorious past with little to no relevance for the present. Drawing on the Matthean text when Jesus goes to meet Peter who has stepped out of the boat, Mitchell empowers Black churches to meet millennials where they are—without gimmicks and through efforts of greater "transparency, relevant programming, communal and social engagement, user-friendly websites, mobile giving, active social media, and streaming capacity (choose wisely)."[35] Here, Mitchell clarifies that the Black Church will lose the millennial generation's interest if it fails to reexamine hierarchal practices of communication, outreach, and social engagement, and use of digital technologies. Either the Black Church will launch into the unknown deep to meet millennials where they are or watch millennials shake the dust off their feet as they leave churches behind for a brave new digital world.

Black millennial faith blogger and founder of the Unfit Christian, a millennial-led online community of self-identified misfit Christians and seekers, Danyelle Thomas describes the millennial exodus from traditional Black churches prior to COVID-19 as rooted in a loss of connection, a need for faithful rather than fraudulent leadership, an absence of fulfillment in outmoded worship styles and spiritual practices, missing parallels with millennial experiences and biblical interpretation, a desire for cultural disruption over assimilation, an interest in expansive sexual ethics, dismissal of hell-and-brimstone rhetoric, a quest for social change, and an urgent call for politics to return to the pulpit. Thomas posits, "Black Millennials are also unwilling to commit themselves to a stagnant, stale church. Many of us feel disconnected from churches that have not grown and matured with us from our youth into our young adulthood. With many churches showing open hostility and disdain for the movements that matter to the youngest demographic within church congregations, Black Millennials feel no need to connect to churches that do not support them or their needs."[36] The millennial command for social transformation and the undoing of a politically neutral Black Church is resounding among the churched and unchurched. In *What Google Can't Give: The Relevancy of the Church for Black Millennials in the Tech Age*, Black millennial entrepreneur and data analyst Brianna Parker asserts,

> Social justice is the top concern millennials believe churches should address. This is predictable for Black millennials in this day of body cameras that record police officers murdering and abusing unarmed citizens with no guilty verdicts delivered. Millennials will not operate as woke citizens throughout the week and take a nap when they enter church on Sunday morning. In fact, I'd trust that millennials would rather not enter the church than to enter a fantasy world when they go to worship. It is important to look at social injustices and find a way to impact the actions or policies in a way that either diminishes imperial power or impacts policies.[37]

Black millennials are disinterested in sustaining traditional institutions, especially the Black Church, that do not offer a word against systemic, intersectional oppressions. Millennials lament Black churches and faith communities that have lost touch with the social pulse of a contemporary era. Relevance for the Black Church in the digital age means more than flashy ads and glitzy promotional flyers, but this is a cry for a "now" word that, in Thomas's framing, "equips millennials with how to take on a society that hates us."[38]

The diminishing power of the pulpit may be related to the rise of millennial-led activism through digital platforms. #BlackLivesMatter emerged first as a protest hashtag developed by three Black queer millennial women, Alicia Garza, Opal Tameti, and Patrisse Cullors, in 2012 initially as a knee-jerk response to the killing of seventeen-year-old Trayvon Martin in Florida and the troubling acquittal of George Zimmerman. The deaths of Trayvon Martin, Michael Brown, Eric Garner, Renisha McBride, Sandra Bland, Tamir Rice, and countless other fallen Black bodies to police brutality and their contested grand jury decisions for almost a decade has reignited a radical Black resistance movement with a blending of innovative cyber and concrete demonstrations employing the body as a means of protest to make Black lives matter in America. Thousands of local and global protesters and activists, under the banner of #BlackLivesMatter across numerous grassroots coalitions, have organized, galvanized, and radicalized against the ugly, terrorizing, and dehumanizing realities facing Black folx—men, women, trans, gender nonconforming—in life and death.[39] While numerous Black clergy leaders participate in movement demonstrations, today's millennial activists remain vocal about the Black Church's missteps. Black Youth Project contributing writer Maya King makes the case that "the Black church can engage more Black millennials by bringing politics back into the pulpit." King proffers,

> Today, the Sunday morning charge to take action in the face of injustice does not carry the same power it once did. Black clergy have entered a new era of social change alongside their congregations, forcing them to consider their responsibilities to those they serve outside of spiritual guidance. It has ushered in an identity crisis of sorts among a number of Black church leaders as they determine the role fellowship will play in social movements, especially for those in search of more strategy than faith.[40]

Black churches will need to find value in the power of the pews and welcome activists working alongside (not behind) Black religious leaders to enliven social change. The Black Church pulpit devoid of an inclusive gospel that embraces Black people of all walks of life with a seat at the table has no word for Black millennials.

Digital technologies have also weakened the power of the pulpit. For millennial activists, "The Black church is losing relevance among social justice advocates, in part, because they now have access to a wider array of options to explore. Moreover, the rapid rise of mobile technology contrasts sharply with what could be perceived as a general unwillingness among churches to keep up with the change. The power of the pulpit now pales in comparison to that of a tweet or a Facebook post in sending messages."[41] Why wait until Sunday for spiritual inspiration and strategies for liberation when sharing information and rallying like-minded global resisters can happen in a single minute online any day or night through one hashtag? While the Black pulpit's political message needs attention, technology also plays a vital role in the accessibility of the prophetic witness of the Black Church.

The 2008 election of Barack Hussein Obama—a significant presidential voting election for many millennials—unraveled the ties between the Black Church and Black political progress that many Americans saw manifested in multimedia news and online platforms in living color. Renowned Black leaders—from Adam Clayton Powell Jr., Ambassador Suzan Johnson Cook, and Floyd H. Flake of New York to James T. Meeks and Bobby Rush of Chicago to Dwight Jones of Virginia to Clementa C. Pickney of South Carolina to Raphael Warnock of Atlanta and countless others throughout history—have sought and held elected political offices while also serving as religious leaders of major faith communities. Most notably, the ordained Baptist minister Rev. Jesse Jackson Sr. became the second Black candidate to run for president as a Democrat in 1984 and 1988, which made the paths straight for President Obama to run and win just twenty years later. While not all Black political leaders were expected to identify as clergypersons, validation from Black Church leaders and churchgoers was essential for winning a political office before 2008.

Barack Obama's rise to the highest office in the land, however, came with the cost of rejecting his longtime pastor and spiritual adviser, and one of the nation's most influential prophetic preachers, Jeremiah A. Wright Jr., and the Trinity United Church of Chicago (TUCC) that nurtured his spirituality and the faith of his family for more than twenty years. Efforts to delegitimize Senator Obama in 2008 led to a national witch hunt by the media to demonize the witness of Jeremiah Wright, whereby soundbites of Wright's sermons were clipped to distort meaning and manipulated to indict his rhetoric as antipatriotic. For example, a malicious media seeking to stifle Obama's presidential campaign recovered Wright's five-year-old sermon to "put him on blast" and deauthorize Black prophetic witness. Wright's April 2003 sermon "Confusing God and Government" interprets America's heinous moral situation alongside the fallen empires narrated by the biblical prophets. Rev. Wright as a contemporary prophet heralds, "God damn America for treating our citizens as less than human. God damn America for as long as she acts like she is God and she is supreme."[42] Renamed by media as "God *damn* America," the words of Wright's sermon become inflammatory rather than remaining on their intent: focusing on America's vicious attacks against the poor, foreign, incarcerated, addicted, innocent, and vulnerable.

To add insult to injury, Obama's "A More Perfect Union" campaign speech, also known as the "race speech," delivered in 2008, was successful in clarifying his position for American ideals of liberty and justice for all while simultaneously delegitimizing the Black Church prophetic tradition that shaped his spiritual formation and racial identity as a Black man. Obama declared "unyielding faith in the decency and generosity of the American people," while "condemning, in unequivocal terms, the statements of Reverend Wright that have caused such controversy, and in some cases, pain."[43] Memoir accounts written by former First Lady Michelle Obama and President Barack Obama even after the presidency continue to cast incendiary assaults on Jeremiah Wright. Obama's recent publication, *A Promised Land*, insists on making the case that Wright's sermons more than a decade later were rants that were "a little over the top" and "usually grounded in fact but bereft of context."[44]

While Black churches (from small to mega) and prominent televangelists have historically broadcasted worship services and sermons on radio and television for more than fifty years, the 2008 inquisition of Wright's Black prophetic rhetoric motivated a fear of "going viral," signaling an inward turn or "digital retreat" by some Black churches to reduce scandal and overexposure of the Black religious experience to ignorant nonwhite audiences and sinister purveyors. Some Black churches that witnessed the Obama-Wright saga turned away from public-facing technologies in efforts to mitigate mainstream surveillance of Black prophetic speech and charismatic worship. The media firestorm, clickbait trolling, and explosive memes of Wright's sermonic corpus are inextricably linked to the social media innovations of the digital age. Here we see the emergence of a Black Church "hyper public" whereby Black churches face the inescapable reality of hypervisibility in the public square and digital cybersphere. With Glaude in mind, naming the challenges of hypervisibility confronting the Black Church in the twenty-first century is not a move to glorify a prophetic nostalgia or lament a riveting Black prophetic preaching tradition of the Black Church weakened by scandal. The backdrop of the Obama-Wright episode marks unique connections between the convergences of millennials moving into their adult years with developing political interests and some Black churches resisting digital technologies in attempts to evade political censure. On the one hand, Obama won the 2008 and 2012 presidential elections because of his ability to tap into millennials' and minorities' deepening interest in making a difference ("Yes We Can") with grassroots solutions to looming challenges. On the other hand, Obama's election signaled the possibility for social transformation in the sociopolitical arena without strong ties to the Black Church tradition, as evidenced by his severed relationship with Jeremiah Wright. Moreover, both of these striking realities played out for millennials online.

The Dawn of a Digital Awakening of the Black Church

In the early 2000s, during the first emergence of public access to the internet, some Black institutions including Black churches held a technological faith that ascribed theological language to digital innovations and cyber inventions with a sort of Utopian "this-worldly salvation," which "assumes humans will make ethical decisions about technology and science based on global human needs, not solely on personal gain or market demand."[45] One example is a *Black Enterprise* ad in a March 2002 issue that addressed technology as a "great equalizer."[46] While digital technologies may be a source for fostering sustainability and connectivity, Black religious scholar Elonda Clay disturbs the notion that technology is value-neutral and reveals its economic engine, social abuses, and moral dangers that impact the Black Church. Clay writes, "The subtle impact of technology on society changes everything. We are now experiencing three paradigm shifts that affect the mission of the Black Church: changes in the way we experience church, redesigns of the global context for ministry, and challenges to our spiritual beliefs."[47] Clay exposes the problem of the "digital divide," which provides unequal access to information technology and refers to technological illiteracy of people of color across age, class, and geographical lines. Clay unmasks "Techno-Crow" akin to Jim and Jane Crow to name the "systemic exclusion of people from participation in democratic processes based on their technological literacy, verification by an automated system, or access to new, functional technology. 'Techno-Crow' also excludes people through the architecture of the Internet or 'code' (software, hardware, and programming language)."[48]

Quite frankly, accessibility and employment represent two other reasons some Black churches have been left behind in the Digital Age. The increasing expenses of technological enhancements for small to medium-size Black churches present a burden that these churches often forgo when seeking to keep the doors open, pay clergy salaries, and repair aging and dilapidated buildings. The market-driven forces that enable vibrant social media, high-resolution streaming capacity, advanced production equipment, and skilled technicians are by and large exclusive to medium-size to mega Black churches with expansive budgets and growing membership. In line with Clay, digital technology for Black churches means more than who has it and who does not; the challenges connect to who knows how to use it. Black churches need competent personnel for installation, operation, and maintenance to keep up with ever-shifting technological codes and discoveries. Moreover, there is an ongoing learning curve for engineers behind the screen, performance coaching for worship leaders and preachers onscreen, and a need for education and literacy training for parishioners who are watching their screens as the primary consumers. Black churches need millennials who possess generational expertise to usher in the digital dawn of a new day.

Diverse approaches to digital technology vary across Christian churches and range within and beyond Christian ethicist H. Richard Niebuhr's *Christ and Culture* typologies, such as antagonistic, accommodationist, architectonic, paradoxical, and conversionist.[49] In a recent journal article, "My People Are Free! Theorizing the Digital Black Church," Africana studies scholar Erika Gault maintains,

> The digital Black Church exists wherever Black technologists employ *spiritual coding*, a unique way of communicating divine presence in Black gatherings; *breaking*, introducing communal and Black epistemological strategies of combating or breaking up structures of inequality; and *networking*, creating links between Black people, Blackness, and the spirit world. In the hypermediated context, these processes occur in non-sequential order and are often created or curated by Black Church outliers.[50]

Is the embracing of digital technologies marking a new awakening for the Black Church? Does the Black Church's technological shift in the digital age represent more than a subtle but substantial translocation from a seventeenth- and eighteenth-century invisible institution and a nineteenth- and twentieth-century visible institution to a hypervisible institution in the current twenty-first century? Gault confirms, "The current pandemic throws into sharp focus the *physical-to-digital migration* as yet another major shift in the life of the Black Church."[51]

The Smithsonian National Museum for African American History and Culture's Center for the Study of African American Religious Life (CSAARL) curates "gOD-TALK: A Black Millennials and Faith Conversation"—a multicity tour hosted by Assistant Curator of Religion Teddy Reeves. This project collects oral histories of Black millennials and their shifting interests around organized religion through panel conversations and digital programming.[52] The provocative in-person conversations feature and attract wide audiences both onsite and online, including Black millennials from diverse faith traditions and nonreligious identities (e.g., agnostics, atheists, humanists). On October 27, 2020, CSAARL premiered a fully virtual panel featuring intergenerational, multifaith voices entitled "gOD-TALK 2.0: Digital #Black Faith" to discuss Black religion in the digital age. According to

CSAARL's curator of religion Eric Williams, "Black millennials represent, perhaps, the most understudied and creative sector of Black religious life. Black millennials have much to teach the larger tradition of Black religion about navigating religion in digital spaces."[53] Before COVID-19, the Black digital religious spaces' resident leaders and agents included those whom the Black Church dismissed and ignored. In Gault's view, "Those who have been marginalized, those who have been ostracized from our traditional religious institutions and have already been making a home on the Internet. They have been the leaders."[54] I contend that numerous Black millennial women, whether deemed Black Church insiders or outliers, lead the way as models for digital Black faith. Black millennial pastor Sarah Jakes Roberts curates talk shows, podcasts, conferences, book clubs, and worship services to empower Black millennial women of faith under the Woman Evolve brand. Black data analyst and entrepreneur Brianna K. Parker admits she "still believes in the Black Church" and consults through Black Millennial Cafe to support Black churches navigating virtual worship with strategy and intention. Neichelle R. Guidry, dean of Sisters Chapel at Spelman College and founder of ShePreaches, gives spiritual nourishment to the churched and unchurched as the "pastor in your pocket" through her Modern Faith podcast. Lyvonne Proverbs Briggs, "known as Pastor Bae," offers weekly vlogs to followers that integrate Christian spirituality with African-centered practices under a weekly banner of the Proverbial Experience. These examples represent a small subset of numerous Black millennial clergywomen owning digital faith and curating weekly faith-based content at every corner of the virtual world before and amid COVID-19.

In line with womanist practical theologian Melva Sampson, a digital griot in her own right and founder of the spiritual community Pink Robe Chronicles, gOD-talk 2.0 identifies Black women as those within "the digital trenches . . . exercising spiritual technologies . . . at the forefront of this particular work."[55] To be clear, Black millennial clergywomen are not the first nor the only religious creatives online, but they are leading digital Black faith in a contemporary era.[56] Black feminist writer Candice Benbow pushes it further in *Essence*: "While Black pastors may have been forced to embrace technology due to the Covid-19 crisis, Black women have always understood its value. . . . Though the presence of traditional Black churches in digital space may be temporary, the ministries of Black women aren't going anywhere."[57] Black millennial women are creating Black religious digital content and claiming digital space as a new spiritual home.

The phenomenon of Black millennials pushing the Black Church into the digital age is more complex than young adults encouraging new trends for old institutions. That this digital awakening erupted during a pandemic reflects a seismic shift in any future understanding of the identity, nature, structure, form, and presence of the Black Church. COVID-19 has opened new possibilities for the Black Church to revive its presence and social witness in the digital sphere. As Jesus taught in the Gospels, whoever seeks to save their life will lose it and those who lose their life will find life. The issue at stake is not whether millennials are leaving religion, but that millennials are leading religion. Note to Black Church: Follow the leaders!

NOTES

1 See Reniqua Allen, "The Missing Black Millennial," *New Republic*, February 20, 2019, https://newrepublic.com.

2 The Pew Research Center conducted the 2014 Religious Landscape Study through telephone interviews of more than thirty-five thousand Americans in all fifty states. The 2014 report is the second study to survey the religious landscape conducted by the Pew Research Center. See Pew Research Center, Religion and Public Life Project, August 14, 2019, www.pewforum.org.

3 Initially housed at the Center for the Study of Race, Politics, and Culture at the University of Chicago, "The Black Youth Project (BYP) is a platform that highlights the voices and ideas of Black millennials. Through knowledge, voice, and action, we work to empower and uplift the lived experiences of young Black Americans today." See Black Youth Project, accessed December 13, 2020, http://blackyouthproject.com. BYP is closely associated with the activist group BYP100, initially convened in 2013 by Black political scientist Cathy Cohen in Chicago. Today, BYP100 claims space as a leading national collective of young Black activists creating justice and freedom for all Black people.

4 COVID-1619 addresses the compounding assaults against Black life since Africans were evicted from their homelands and enslaved on American soil. COVID-45 names the forty-fifth president of the United States, Donald J. Trump, for his tyrannical leadership and failed response to the coronavirus outbreak that resulted in the United States leading in confirmed cases and fatalities.

5 Audra Burch et al, "How Black Lives Matter Reached Every Corner of America," *New York Times*, June 13, 2020, www.nytimes.com.

6   There is much debate around the beginning and ending years of generational cohorts. Pew Research frames the generational cohorts within these categories: Silents (born 1928–1945), Boomers (born 1946–1964), Generation X (born 1965–1980), Millennials (born 1981–1996), Generation Z (born 1996–2010), and Generation Alpha (born 2011–present). I prefer the twenty-year span 1980–2000 that takes account of pre-millennials or xennials, who are born on the borderlines between Gen X'ers and younger millennials, and post-millennials or zennials, who are born on the borderline between older millennials and GenZ's.

7   Author Joshua Mitchell names this rightly: "Lesson number one: not every young adult is a Millennial, and not every Millennial is a young adult." No matter what ages millennial reach, the millennial generation will continue to be millennials (*Black Millennials and the Church: Meet Me Where I Am* [Valley Forge, PA: Judson Press, 2018], 14).

8   Richard Fry, "Millennials Overtake Baby Boomers as America's Largest Generation," Pew Research Center, August 28, 2020, www.pewresearch.org.

9   William H. Frey, "Now, More than Half of Americans Are Millennials or Younger," Brookings, August 14, 2020, www.brookings.edu.

10 Cathy Cohen and Jon C. Rogowski, "Black Millennials in America," *BYP 100*, 2015, https://blackyouthproject.com.

11 Richard Fry, "5 Facts about Millennial Households," Pew Research Center, September 6, 2017. See also Hillary Hoffower, "Black Millennial Households Earn about 60% of What Their White Counterparts Make, and It Highlights Just How Much Worse the Generational Wealth Gap Is along Racial Lines," *Business Insider*, July 23, 2020, www.businessinsider.com.

12 A 2019 Blue Cross Blue Shield report revealed that millennials are less healthy than GenX'ers at the same age. The downward turn in millennials links to six primary behavioral health conditions: ADHD, tobacco use disorder, major depression, substance use disorder, alcohol use disorder, and psychotic disorders. COVID-19 has exacerbated many of these health conditions when combined with feelings of isolation, missing human connection, and lockdown. See "Millennial Health: Trends in Behavioral Health Conditions," Blue Cross Blue Shield, October 15, 2020, www.bcbs.com.

13 See Marc Prensky, *From Digital Natives to Digital Wisdom: Hopeful Essays for 21st Century Learning* (Thousand Oaks, CA: Corwin, 2012).

14 I am making the connection between Prensky's framing of the digital socialization of his students in the early 2000s and social media as catering to millennial interests.

15 It should be no surprise that the Federal Trade Commission filed a lawsuit on December 9, 2020, in the Washington, DC, courts to break up Facebook because of its monopoly practices to buy out its rivals. Additionally, the 2020 Netflix documentary titled *The Social Dilemma* addresses the "dangerous human impact of social networking" from the perspectives of former employees and consultants of the tech giants (e.g., Google, Facebook). Google's firing of ethics researcher

Timnit Gebru, who uncovered unethical business practices in the company's operations, makes a case for tech giants as more than merely "big business," but also a new empire.

16 Nikki Graf, "Today's Young Workers Are More Likely Than Ever to Have a Bachelor's Degree," Pew Research Center, May 16, 2017.

17 Ibid.

18 Michael Lipka, "Millennials Increasingly Are Driving Growth of 'Nones,'" Pew Research Center, May 12, 2015, www.pewresearch.org.

19 Jeff Diamant and Besheer Mohamed, "Black Millennials Are More Religious than Other Millennials," Pew Research Center, July 20, 2018, www.pewresearch.org.

20 Stacey M. Floyd-Thomas et al., *Black Church Studies: An Introduction* (Nashville: Abingdon, 2007), 99.

21 C. Eric Lincoln and Lawrence H. Mamiya, *The Black Church in the African American Experience* (Durham, NC: Duke University Press, 1990), 8.

22 Ibid.

23 While the civil rights movement may be identified as led by the Black Church, it should be noted that a smaller minority of Black churches were active in the actions and demonstrations. The impact of the Kingian shift can also be traced to the split of the National Baptist Convention, USA, the largest Baptist denomination of the nineteenth and twentieth centuries, and the formation of the Progressive National Baptist Convention.

24 The term "Black Church" also links to the evolution of the Duboisian construction of the Negro Church as familial, the center of social life, a theater of amusement, and a political nucleus. See these works to underscore critical valuations of this terminology: W. E. B. DuBois, *The Negro Church* (Atlanta: Atlanta University Press, 1903); Eddie Glaude Jr., "The Black Church Is Dead," *HuffPost*, April 28, 2010, www.huffpost.com; Juan Marcial Floyd-Thomas, *Liberating Black Church History: Making It Plain* (Nashville: Abingdon, 2014); Evelyn Brooks Higginbotham, *Righteous Discontent: The Women's Movement in the Black Baptist Church, 1880–1920* (Cambridge, MA: Harvard University Press, 1993).

25 Lincoln and Mamiya, *Black Church in the African American Experience*, 11–15.

26 Delores S. Williams, *Sisters in the Wilderness: The Challenge of Womanist God-Talk* (Maryknoll, NY: Orbis, 1993), 206.

27 Glaude, "Black Church Is Dead."

28 Ibid.

29 Ibid.

30 Evelyn Brooks Higginbotham. *Righteous Discontent: The Women's Movement in the Black Baptist Church, 1880–1920* (Cambridge, MA: Harvard University Press, 1993).

31 Glaude, "Black Church Is Dead."

32 Ibid.

33 Ibid.

34 Mitchell, *Black Millennials and the Church*, 3.

35 Ibid., 27.

36 D. Danyelle Thomas, "Exodus: Why Black Millennials Are Leaving the Church," *Unfit Christian*, February 8, 2019, www.unfitchristian.com.

37 Brianna K. Parker, *What Google Can't Give: The Relevancy of the Church for Black Millennials in the Tech Age* (Mansfield, TX: Black Millennial Café, 2018), 54.

38 Thomas, "Exodus," 6.

39 See: Keeanga-Yamahtta Taylor, *From #BlackLivesMatter to Black Liberation* (Chicago: Haymarket, 2016); Barbara Ransby, *Making All Black Lives Matter: Reimagining Freedom in the Twenty-First Century* (Oakland: University of California Press, 2018); Patrisse Khan-Cullors and Asha Bandele, *When They Call You a Terrorist: A Story of Black Lives Matter and the Power to Change the World* (New York: Wednesday, 2020); Alicia Garza, *The Purpose of Power: How We Come Together When We Fall Apart* (New York: One World, 2020).

40 Maya King, "The Black Church Can Engage More Black Millennials by Bringing Politics Back into the Pulpit," *Black Youth Project*, September 29, 2017, http://blackyouthproject.com.

41 Ibid.

42 Rev. Jeremiah Wright, "Confusing God and Government," sermon delivered at Trinity United Church of Christ, Chicago, Illinois, April 13, 2003.

43 "Transcript: Barack Obama's Speech on Race," NPR, March 18, 2008, www.npr.org/.

44 Barack Obama, *A Promised Land* (New York: Crown, 2020), 120.

45 Elonda Clay, "Subtle Impact: Technology Trends and the Black Church," *Journal of the Interdenominational Theological Center* 31, no. 1–2 (2004): 153–78, quote at 173.

46 Ibid., 175.

47 Ibid., 154.

48 Ibid., 162.

49 Christian ethicist H. Richard Niebuhr in his 1951 seminal work *Christ and Culture* takes up the enduring problem between Christianity and culture through typologies: "antagonistic" (Christ against culture), "accommodationist" (Christ of culture), "architectonic" (Christ above culture), "oscillatory" (Christ and culture in paradox), and "conversionist" (Christ transforms culture). Similarly, Christian churches approach digital technology with similar stances ranging from extreme opposition to radical transformation.

50 Erika Gault, "'My People Are Free!': Theorizing the Digital Black Church," Fire!!! 6:1 (Spring, 2020), 11–12.

51 Ibid., 5.

52 Since 2018, gOD-Talk has hosted "a series of conversations to uncover how millennials interact with religion and the transformative nature of community, the Internet, and space. gOD-Talk features leading millennial voices and seeks to amplify their experiences in a curated conversation that will be documented and streamed to online audiences. By using a lower case 'g' for the word 'gOD' the program is highlighting the ways in which it will "transgress" traditional/orthodox

boundaries and figurative/literal designations of that which is considered sacred." See "gOD-Talk: A Black Millennials and Faith Conversation," National Museum of African American History and Culture, accessed December 14, 2020, https:// nmaahc.si.edu/god-talk.

53 gOD-talk 2.0 is a live broadcast from the Reginald F. Lewis Museum in Baltimore, Maryland, produced by the National Museum of African American History and Culture and streamed to Facebook. gOD-talk 2.0 engages multiple generations on Black faith in the digital age. See gOD-Talk 2.0 #BlackFaith, October 27, 2020, www.facebook.com/NMAAHC/videos/1049444798830379.

54 Ibid.

55 Ibid.

56 We may point to Juanita Bynum as an early archetype for Black women's religious media. See Monique Moultrie, *Passionate and Pious: Religious Media and Black Women's Sexuality* (Durham, NC: Duke University Press, 2017).

57 Candice Benbow, "While More Black Churches Come Online Due to Coronavirus, Black Women Faith Leaders Have Always Been Here," *Essence*, March 24, 2020, 7, www.essence.com.

3

Live and Let Die

Spirits of White Christian Male Defiance in the Age of COVID-19

CHRISTOPHER M. DRISCOLL

On May 5, 2020, President Donald Trump toured a manufacturing plant in Phoenix, Arizona—Honeywell—that was producing N-95 face masks in response to the COVID-19 crisis. The trip was part of the administration's efforts to champion the working class, alongside a work ethic that would confront fear and uncertainty with American courage. Trump's trip was fashioned in the light of past generals visiting the front lines of the Western Front—only the front lines of the COVID-19 pandemic would be found on manufacturing plant floors.

The trip was carried in the press as yet another instance of Trump's refusal to wear a mask. Even in the actual plant where they were being produced, Trump remained noncommittal on his (own) relationship with masks, which was not so much ineptitude as a dog whistle to those watching who would dare question his white masculine identity. The obviously reckless behavior was an intentional showing of (ostensibly) a particular kind of white masculine courage in the face of adversity. As videos of the tour made their rounds across the internet, folks soon realized that the Guns N' Roses cover of "Live and Let Die" played on a loudspeaker during Trump's tour of the factory. Like so many moments of Trump's presidency, the tour meeting with that soundtrack was yet another moment of Samuel Beckett or Franz Kafka material come to life. The absurdity of the abrasively hackneyed political optics tells a particular truth about the white masculine relationship to death, dying, and one another vis-à-vis those existential circumstances surrounding death. In the face of fear and death, we deny its power while also denying the reality it imposes on us. Such denial, framed in this chapter as defiance, is at the heart of much of white Christian America.

To paraphrase the lyrics of "Live and Let Die," when a crisis or extreme set of adverse circumstances arise, and changing them isn't on the table, it is not our task to question the circumstances, only to confront them. Often, however, such a confrontation doesn't seem to play out in terms of a collective, united response to the threat; rather, other animosities often arise from the confrontation that are then imposed against one another. Trump's momentary anthem reminds us that when standing on the front lines of a pandemic, many of us do not end up directing our energies toward it. Rather, our fears and inadequacies in the face of the large-scale threat are mapped on to our neighbors, civic leaders, and fellow citizens. In what follows, I use this frame of "live and let die" as an entry point for analysis of white masculine American Christian defiance. I first work to contextualize and historicize the white masculine and Christian tendency to act or operate as if defiance is a natural posture toward the world. I then look to two specific contemporary instances of such defiance during the COVID-19 pandemic, with the cases of Georgia governor Brian Kemp's dispute with Atlanta's mayor Kecia Bottoms over mask mandates, and then Christian evangelist Sean Feucht's crusade against COVID-19 policies that he feels threaten expressions of the freedom of religion and his defiant hosting of mass Christian worship services despite stay-at-home orders from state officials. My hope is that readers make use of these cases for further exploration of the variegated and often concealed instances of white masculine Christian defiance that continue to adversely impact the life circumstances of Black and Brown people, as well as of white people.

Before beginning, it bears remembering that Axl Rose, the lead singer of Guns N' Roses, did not write "Live and Let Die." Neither did the equally famous "badass rocker" Slash, the longtime guitarist for the band. They merely covered it. The author of the song that so deeply describes the defiant posture under scrutiny here is none other than a musical icon for Americans, Paul McCartney. In terms of reputation, generation, and listening constituency, McCartney could not be further from Guns N' Roses in our collective consciousness. But in terms of white masculine defiance, both McCartney and Rose represent the same song. The problem of white masculine defiance is not a partisan issue. Neither is it a Trumpian issue, even as the factory scene exemplifies the cavalier hubris of this defiance. The defiance discussed in this chapter is not limited to the bad guys of culture, but also includes our most collectively cherished and revered. McCartney need not now be thought of as a bad guy. Rather, the whole social scene of Trump's promenade through the factory while the McCartney song played created an image of what white masculine defiance is, who is involved in that defiance, and how such defiance is performed. Fortunately for all of us, in our current moment, the certainty and efficacy of this performance is now increasingly contested in productive ways. In service to that contestation, in this chapter I invite readers to see something of themselves—ourselves—in the sights and sounds of Trump, Kemp, Feucht, and so many others who have preceded us. But first I discuss aspects of the history of white Christian defiance.

A History of White Defiance

Historically, white Christians in the Americas have exploited pandemics as opportunities for social advance and shown little regard for people of color who may also be impacted by them. Several demographic studies posit that at the turn of the sixteenth century the world population was approximately four hundred million, of whom eighty million inhabited the Americas. By the middle of the century, out of these eighty million, only ten million remained, with most deaths coming from pandemic, and others from outright war and related forms of human cruelty, such as theft of land, razing of crops, and so on.[1] Sheer contact with whites became death for Black and Brown people; cultural apocalypse ensued. In later centuries, white Americans like Jeffrey Amherst did, in fact, call for distributing smallpox blankets to Native Americans, and others would at times go on to use transmission of disease as a form of biological warfare.[2] More recently, during the Spanish flu pandemic of 1918–1919, violence against Black folks by white folks intensified as Black people were widely blamed for the spread of the virus, even though white folks were the hardest-hit demographic.[3] Historian of religions James W. Perkinson, writing of the forceful insertion of the world's Indigenous peoples into a "Western" cosmology, elaborates on the long-term psychic effects of these historical circumstances, when noting that for Black and Brown folks, "'Death' intruded so precipitously, pandemically, and irresistibly in colonial forms of violence that its cultural 'grammar' was entirely obliterated. It became an ever-present possibility, ready to fall with unpredictable swiftness, uncontrollable randomness, and indecipherable consequence."[4] The white Christian American denial of death has meant certain death for others.

In certain respects, the contemporary moment of dual biological and social pandemics, in addition to our responses to these dangers, follows similar patterns. In 2020, the veritable failure of the US federal government and many state governments to enact adequate policies and protocols for responding to COVID-19 was disparately felt by different communities. It is little wonder that those same communities have risen up in response to yet other expressions of disparate treatment and life circumstances expressed by police brutality, violence, and an ongoing barrage of dead Black men and women. The United States is still a predominantly white nation that would rather ask, "What did the dead do to deserve their death?" than more critical questions of its collective relationship to race and violent disciplining of bodies. Historically, the line distinguishing a biological from a social pandemic is thin and white. A 2020 *Scientific American* article frames some of these consequences in parallel with the demonstrations against white supremacy and police brutality that occurred in the wake of George Floyd's murder:

> American citizens who share George Floyd's skin color are perishing from COVID-19 at shockingly inordinate numbers. Data show that Black Americans face excess COVID-19 death as a result of disparate access to testing, high levels of underlying health conditions, greater occupational exposure, and lower rates of medical insurance coverage. Black bodies have been wounded and strained by decades of discriminatory housing policies, mass incarceration, malnutrition, and trauma. These are the injustices that make them unable to breathe.[5]

Another study, from the Public Religion Research Institute (PRRI), not only confirms the disparate impact of COVID-19 on Black and Brown folks but does so while paying specific attention to religious affiliation. "Directly measuring how religious communities have been impacted by the pandemic is virtually impossible," the study reads, "as there is no source of COVID-19 data by religious affiliation."[6] Accounting not for rates of infection but for geographic proximity to accounted COVID-19 cases per county, the study found that Hispanic Catholics, Jews, Hispanic Protestants, Black Protestants, other nonwhite Catholics, and Muslims were the six most at-risk communities.[7] Buddhism is the category ostensibly dividing Black and Brown traditions from white traditions, with Mormons rounding out the study as the least likely to live in counties hardest hit by COVID-19.

How are we to account for these disparities? In one sense, there is the history already mentioned and its consequences. Historical circumstance has so shaped the practical life options and everyday lives of racialized people that de facto segregation is still often at work in determining where we live, and what resources for health care and wellness are available in a given community. The PRRI's turn to geography is an effort to account for the disparities in terms of this history. But these disparities can also be accounted for in terms of theological ideas referring to God's will and providence, which is to say, God's plan revealed as history. Perkinson emphasizes the range in which whiteness works in the making and being of defiance, suggesting that whiteness

> abreacts "away from" the formless fact of mortality, the beginning of life in dark intimacy, the reproduction of life in a merging that muddles boundaries between bodies. It promises control; it organizes sight as "reflection," as light bouncing off of surface. It resists opacity, interiority, the density of contacting surfaces, the proximity of perishability, the permeability of the body to all other bodies, the wetness of exchange, the "surrounding-ness" of the ground of incubation and end.[8]

Salvation as defiance—defying fact, science, and the ontological conditions of human finitude. Whiteness presupposes itself a life that does not correspond to objective realities or empirical circumstances. Whiteness is framed as a mystical theological quality (in the Durkheimian functional sense), tricking many into thinking its effects are magic, rather than the result of hundreds of years of decisions and distinctions that build up in such a way as to effectively create multiple worlds out of the same raw materials. This defiance offers one way of organizing an analytic approach helpful for revealing whiteness in practice. I turn next to a brief sketch of such an approach.

To Live and Let Die in Defiance

To defy is to resist or refuse to obey something or someone powerful, a transitive verb meant to convey the notion that this resistance or refusal will be met with the full force of power at something or someone's disposal. In such terms, defiance is about eluding these powers, but not overcoming them. Whiteness breaks into modern history as moments of defiance. Here I turn to several disparate—albeit phenomenologically connected—thinkers, including Georgio Agamben, Michel Foucault, Achille Mbembe, Søren Kierkegaard, Martin Heidegger, and James Perkinson, who each contribute to a brief sketch of whiteness's relationship to defiance. In short, whiteness is itself an ontological defiance—a defiance of our shared, mutually interdependent reality, as such.

We might think here of Georgio Agamben's notion of bare life, as a life that carries an element of defiance in its very being.[9] But this seemingly innate, ontological quality of white Christian defiance does not emerge ex nihilo. As the so-called Age of Discovery was to commence, the preeminent European colonial powers of the fifteenth to seventeenth centuries had been controlled by Muslims for nearly seven hundred years. In 1491, Spain defeated the last Muslim stronghold of Grenada, effectively Christianizing western Europe along with racializing western Europe. The following year, 1492, we remember as the year "Columbus sailed the ocean blue," but it was also the year that these European countries effectively began policing on the grounds of whiteness, expelling any remaining Muslims and Jews from the countries. Henceforth, until its gradual diminishment around the period of the Enlightenment, any nonwhite person would need to be Christianized if in Europe. Exploration and colonialism would then impose this social arrangement onto the rest of the world. In short, racialization and Christian exceptionalism are inextricably linked to white defiance, and this defiance simply cannot be explored without ongoing attention to racial and religious difference.

This spark or spirit of defiance, one could argue, indwelt in the movement of Europeans to and on New World shores. Historically, the defiance of European religious authorities on one side of the Atlantic is remembered as heroic and valorous. Religious freedom is a cornerstone of the United States' cultural history as well as its de jure foundation in the country's constitution. On the western side of the Atlantic, the natural world and its earthly powers (Indigenous peoples) are rendered as obstacles within a never-ending quest to overcome the harsh circumstances of a life lived on one's own terms; put another way, defiance in the face of the other, for white Christians, becomes defiance in the face of adversity. In these ways, white defiance is baked into the substance, in the theological sense of this word, of white Christian American identity.

Another way of thinking about defiance is Michel Foucault's notion of governmentality, the interplay "between technologies of domination of others and those of the self."[10] We are, all of us, in an existential dance with the state, impacting our choices of self-expression and movement. For Foucault, defiance includes the confrontation with these state powers, but it also includes the relative space a person makes for self-expression inside of those boundaries imposed by the state. The state power structure designs the parameters of the game we all experience as social life, and our defiance—should such an act be our inclination—happens in the panache, the style, and tactics deployed while playing the game. Sovereignty, in this arrangement, shifts from its expression in the right to take a life or let that life live, and becomes "the right to make live and to let die."[11] Yet missing from Agamben's and Foucault's analyses are sustained critiques of race or of how whiteness impacts understandings or tendencies toward defiance. Agamben and Foucault help to analyze certain aspects of our shared situation together even as they also reinforce the structures of race and whiteness specifically.

The biopolitical "truth game"[12] white Europeans have played has included race for nearly five hundred years, despite some of our best and varied efforts to deny it. To think and act in terms of race became, for these Europeans, a means of directly defying princes and principalities while it also served as a biopolitical tactic for distinguishing oneself in the wake of more fundamental limits imposed by the natural world and the state. So fundamental was racial thinking—and anti-Black racism, specifically—in the making of New World Europeans that "whiteness today functions as a kind of silent *prophylaxis*, policing the borders between (its) more privileged lifeworlds and the social conditions it identifies as 'black' and 'dangerous.' To the degree those social conditions (concentrated impoverishment, exposure to violent drug trades, proximity to toxic waste sites, etc.) in fact result in higher mortality rates and indeed constitute a 'living form of social death,' whiteness emerges as a structure of both avoidance and denial."[13] In this way, whiteness would not be functioning as designed were Agamben or Foucault to center it in analyses. Nevertheless, structural realities such as whiteness shape our existential circumstances such that some of us experience whiteness as "disbelief in death" and others of us, those of us counted as history's others, experience whiteness "as death."[14]

To wit, the necropolitics of Achille Mbembe organizes an ontology of the Black and Brown relationship to death under these conditions.[15] Necropolitics, as an analytic, helps to chart whiteness's imposition of death upon the other, and the other's subsequent circumstances in wake of that imposition of death. Agamben and Foucault, as we might note, take for granted that death is the appropriate frame for analysis (e.g., from the right to kill or not). Mbembe casts light on the taken-for-grantedness of death and death-making to white political arrangements, including analyses thereof.

In an effort to shift the gaze *onto* whiteness, however, I follow Perkinson insofar as he offers a robust historical ontology of whiteness working within (and as) these conditions. Specifically, for Perkinson,

Whiteness . . . is increasingly a category of distance and deception, a veritable incarnation of denial, consciousness without a body, eating the body of its chosen witch, while "witching" its own eating "out of mind." It is a mindless eating, understanding itself as a bodiless mind. In the political economy of the modern slave trade and its continuation as the globalizing system of white supremacist capital, its body, its body is the "blackness" it metabolizes as its own white flesh.[16]

Perhaps most perniciously, insofar as the effort is to overcome death, this "game" of race-making and the instrumentalizing of Blackness is a losing game for all involved. Obviously enough, none of this has enabled white Christian Americans to overcome physical death. Totalizing logics that come at the expense of whole communities never achieve their ends, not even for the beneficiaries. Perhaps some tacit knowledge of this game being a lost cause also shapes white Christian American defiance?

In addition to Agamben and Foucault, Mbembe and Perkinson, just as useful for understanding this defiance is the Danish philosopher

Søren Kierkegaard. In *The Sickness unto Death* (1849), Kierkegaard draws a causal connection between defiance and despair, suggesting that despair is rooted in human weakness, and it often expresses itself as defiance.[17] He notes,

> First comes despair over the earthly or something earthly, then despair over oneself about the eternal. Then comes defiance, which really is despair by the aid of the eternal, the despairing abuse of the eternal in the self to the point of being despairingly determined to be oneself.[18]

For white people, defiance is "despair by the aid of the eternal," insofar as it often expresses itself in and through religious, theological, or otherwise metaphysical registers. This association with religion grants the defiance a legitimacy it might not otherwise have. However, it also complicates the existential circumstances in such a way that the defiant ones perceive themselves as on the winning side of the game of history, as it were. As many readers are likely aware, Kierkegaard ultimately suggests that despair offers an avenue for arriving at authentic faith, but here he cautions readers to distinguish between the despair that leads to faith and the despair borne of defiance:

> The despair which is the passageway to faith is also by the aid of the eternal: by the aid of the eternal the self has courage to lose itself in order to gain itself. Here on the contrary it is not willing to begin by losing itself but wills to be itself.[19]

Kierkegaard's point seems akin to what Foucault eventually characterizes as a difference between modern Western concerns to "know thyself" rather than to "take care of oneself."[20] The German phenomenologist, existentialist, and National Socialist Martin Heidegger helps to exemplify the philosophical parameters of this defiant "will to be itself." As exemplified in his explicit support of National Socialism, Heidegger's notion of being-toward-death demonstrates the lengths some will go to deceive themselves into thinking they've won the game via whiteness, masculinity, and other totalizing notions of normativity. Heidegger is, in this case, an ethnographic example of whom Kierkegaard is talking about. Heidegger writes,

Death does not reveal itself as a loss, but rather as a loss experienced by the survivors. The suffering of this loss, however, does not furnish an approach to the loss of Being as such that is "suffered" by the person who died. We do not experience in a genuine sense the dying of the others but are at most always only "present." . . . In this way the One brings about a *continual putting at ease about death.*[21]

For many white Christian Americans, death is not a "loss" insofar as it is treated as an experience of suffering for the living—the other's suffering becomes my hardship. "Your" death becomes a solution for responding to my death, a bastardization of the tragic hero motif. For many white Christian Americans, the dead do not experience suffering by way of death, and the living "do not experience in a genuine sense the dying of the others." This suggests that an isomorphic relationship exists between mortality rates (for COVID-19 or police shootings—it is all the same for whiteness; it's the death that matters) and narcissistic expressions of defiance. Counterintuitively, the higher the number of deaths, the greater the defiance. For white American Christians, an immense absence of genuine faith (a la Kierkegaard) is expressed as a confession of faith, and feigned responsibility toward one another becomes a method of dismissing the suffering of the dying. Referencing Heidegger's quotation above: "In this way," white Christian Americans "bring about a *continual putting at ease about death.*" We live; they die. We worship; they die.

What of this dynamic remains operative, and what might happen when this tried-and-true mode of relating to the other is questioned or undermined? In what follows, I want to shift from the existential and historical and focus on the contemporary and the concrete, giving attention to two specific instances where this live-and-let-die sensibility was on display during the time of COVID-19.

The Defiant Spirit of White Christian American Capitalism

The first illustration of this defiance was the dispute between Georgia governor Brian Kemp and Atlanta mayor Keisha Lance Bottoms that took place across much of the 2020 COVID-19 quarantine. For a bit of context, white Georgian Brian Kemp has a history of leadership and playing politics that many regard as racist. He narrowly achieved victory in the Georgia gubernatorial race of 2018 against Black candidate and rising star in the Democratic Party Stacey Abrams. Approximately fifty thousand votes separated the two candidates, after a campaign where many accused Kemp of voter suppression. Studies give credence to the accusations. According to Zak Cheney-Rice of *nymag.com*,

> Brian Kemp is Georgia's governor due to one of the most controversial elections in recent memory. As secretary of state since 2010, he had eight years to winnow the electorate to his liking before November 2018, and did so by purging 1.4 million voters from the rolls, placing thousands of registrations on hold, and overseeing the closure or relocation of nearly half of the state's precincts and polling sites. The unstated goal—though it was clear to anyone watching similar efforts by Republicans across the South—was to reduce the voting power of unfavorable constituencies: black people, poor people, students, and others.[22]

Such was the legacy and reputation that followed Kemp into the COVID-19 pandemic. Knowing full well the disparate impact of COVID-19, on July 6, 2020, Kemp declared a "State of Emergency across Georgia" and authorized "the activation of as many as 1,000 Georgia National Guard troops."[23] This was in response to what Kemp's office framed as "weeks of dramatically increased violent crime and property destruction in the City of Atlanta." In fact, the previous weeks had seen the rise of #BlackLivesMatter protesters in the wake of the murders of Ahmaud Arbery and Rayshard Brooks. On February 23, 2020, Arbery had been pursued and murdered by three white vigilantes in Brunswick, Georgia. During spring 2020, public demonstrations increased as more and more information—including video of the murder—was released to the public. It was seventy-four days after the murder that a grand jury finally indicted the three men on charges. Within weeks of these charges being filed, and in the same week that George Floyd was murdered by police in Minneapolis, another black man, Rayshard Brooks, was murdered by Atlanta police officer Garrett Rolfe. Rolfe shot Brooks twice in the back. Brooks died after surgery. The escalation of political action in the wake of Arbery's murder and the eventual indictment, along with the murder of Brooks, meant that Georgia was a particular hotbed of political activity. While

George Floyd became the name most symbolically associated with this moment in US history, his was not an isolated case. These were the circumstances precipitating Kemp's declaration of a state of emergency across Georgia.

Kemp's press release associates Executive Order 07.06.20.01 with gun violence from the previous Fourth of July weekend, which left "over thirty Georgians wounded" and five dead. The effort to address gun violence is, at first glance, admirable even if heavy-handed and austere. But upon closer inspection of the press release, the real motivation for Kemp's activation of the Guardsmen becomes apparent: "Peaceful protests were hijacked by criminals with a dangerous, destructive agenda. Now, innocent Georgians are being targeted, shot, and left for dead," the presser's second paragraph begins. The document continues,

> This lawlessness must be stopped and order restored in our capital city. I have declared a State of Emergency and called up the Georgia Guard because the safety of our citizens comes first. This measure will allow troops to protect state property and dispatch state law enforcement officers to patrol our streets. Enough with the tough talk. We must protect the lives and livelihoods of all Georgians.[24]

Kemp's rhetorical attention to the acute gun violence experienced the previous weekend was mere political cover for his more authoritarian intervention into the weeks-long #BlackLivesMatter protests that had engulfed many US cities in May and June 2020. Kemp seemed to be instrumentalizing the suffering of those who actually had experienced the pain of gun violence. The July 6 press statement had the effect of reminding Georgians where Kemp stood on these twin concerns. It concludes by promising that "the Georgia Guard will provide support at state buildings, including the Georgia State Capital, Georgia Department of Public Safety Headquarters, and the Governor's Mansion."[25] Kemp's first priority was "state property"; second came "the lives and livelihoods of all Georgians." This catchphrase "lives and livelihoods" came to be something of a rallying cry for Kemp and his supporters across the COVID-19 catastrophe. On the surface, these words appear to work to balance the need to keep people safe with keeping the economy thriving. Whether such sentiments were made in earnest or not, the slogan became a euphemism justifying his opening the Georgia economy at a time when health officials were encouraging increased social distancing, mask wearing, and staying inside homes. By the end of the brief, it becomes evident what motivated Kemp the most—the protection of property—especially property related to his own circumstances, even including the Governor's Mansion.

CBS News reported on July 10 that following "a new single-day record for new coronavirus cases . . . Atlanta mayor Keisha Lance Bottoms" ordered "the city to reverse its reopening plan and return to Phase 1."[26] In her press release on the reversal, Mayor Bottoms's guidelines included staying home except for essential travel, and the order made wearing masks in public obligatory.[27] In an interview with Gayle King on *CBS This Morning*, the mayor emphasized that a failure of COVID testing facilities and options in the state, even impacting her own family, "is the reason the virus is continuing to spread." The interview then moved quickly to discuss the Atlanta mask mandate, with King proffering word to viewers that Governor Kemp had already declared the Atlanta mandate "unenforceable" and that, more broadly, "he doesn't seem to be supporting you on this." After noting that several other mayors in the state had also mandated masks for their cities, Mayor Bottoms noted that "the governor seems to be the only elected official, one of the few in the state, that does not think mandating masks is a good idea."[28]

The country would turn its sights more squarely onto the tension between Bottoms and Kemp a few days later, when Governor Kemp's office made a statement via press release undermining Mayor Bottoms, calling the Atlanta mayor's guidance "confusing" and "both non-binding and legally unenforceable."[29] The governor's statement further claimed that the state guidelines were legally binding and effective, and accused Bottoms of failing to enforce "state restrictions." Like his July 6 press release, this one from July 13 also ended by noting that Kemp's motivations were to "help protect the lives and livelihoods of all Georgians."[30] Kemp officially suspended local municipality mask mandates on July 15, when he renewed earlier state regulations and guidelines concerning COVID-19 response. In this iteration, he made clear,

> Any state, county, or municipal law, order, ordinance, rule, or regulation that requires persons to wear face coverings, masks, or shields, or any

other Personal Protective Equipment while in places of public accommodation or public property are suspended to the extent that they are more restrictive than this Executive Order.[31]

The next day, Kemp made his displeasure with Bottoms a matter of legal record when he announced he was suing Bottoms and the city of Atlanta "over the city's mask mandate, claiming the measure violates his emergency orders."[32] Mayor Bottoms responded to the lawsuit publicly by reminding people of the number of Georgians who had died from COVID-19 (to that date), and emphasizing that rather than pay court costs, attorney fees, and other costs associated with the suit, "A better use of taxpayer money would be to expand testing and contact tracing."[33] Bottoms and other mayors were clearly frustrated by Kemp's seeming defiance of medical and health logic. Van Johnson, the mayor of Savannah, said poignantly of the lawsuit, "It is officially official. Governor Kemp does not give a damn about us. Every man and woman for himself/herself. Ignore the science and survive the best you can."[34]

On July 17, 2020, Kemp held a press conference. In his prepared remarks, he seemed most frustrated that Bottoms and other local officials would defy his earlier guidelines. Where the law was concerned, he suggested that wearing masks would never be illegal in his state but defying his authority would be. One journalist asked him what the lawsuit suggested about his own priorities during such a difficult time. He claimed his priorities were clear, before finding three different ways to blame the rising COVID-19 numbers on #BlackLivesMatter mass demonstrations—going so far as to sardonically claim that "his priorities during that time were to keep our city from being burned down."[35] Kemp emphasized his concern to protect "livelihoods," noting that business leaders have had a significant part to play on his COVID-19 task force. He did not hide his economic motivation. In fact, he tacitly shamed those whom he positioned as not being interested in the economic consequences of social distancing. When asked specifically about Bottoms's comment about the lawsuit showing skewed priorities, Kemp suggested that the business owners the suit sought to support were the taxpayers (in this case), and that he was also using COVID-19 CARES Act money to sue the city of Atlanta. Specifically, Kemp said,

Well, the mask mandates are unenforceable. And what people should be thinking about is the livelihoods, those businesses, those hard-working Georgians that are in those businesses—they are paying the taxes that we are using to respond to this, as well as CARES act funding that we've gotten from the federal government.[36]

Kemp followed up many of the subsequent questions by framing mask mandates as examples of governmental overreach. "Government is not going to be the answer to all people's problems,"[37] he stated with derision. Kemp seemed to not capture the evil irony at work in his denouncement of government alongside his admittance that he would gladly take government money.

How are we to understand the logic that guided Kemp's seemingly illogical decision to not mandate masks yet mandate National Guard troops? How could anyone be willing to deploy a military force, the state National Guard, to the heart of its biggest city yet reject the possibility of mandating a face mask while in public? Surely, it isn't as simple as brazen hypocrisy—after all, authenticity tends to matter for white men. Perhaps Kemp's posture is indicative of a common response by white Christian American men to the fact of our own embodiment? When confronted in such a way, Perkinson suggests we oscillate "'plastically' between fantasy and fear. "Where white experience of everyday life takes shape as a form of fascination, moving unimpeded through the consumer spaces of the culture, the reflex in the white body is simply naivete, presumption."[38] Moreover, there is something of masculinity at work in this relationship to bodies. White bodies are, theoretically at least, on the line as well, which leads largely to the rationalization of this mode of governmentality. But they aren't on the line in the same way. And when Kemp was confronted with that disparate reality, he considered the situation of being at odds with an-other as an effort to overcome adversity (in the form of a perceived threat to his autonomy). We might imagine that for many white Christian American men such as Kemp, the live-and-let-die defiant sensibility is both social ontology and policy axiom: govern all for the sake of a few. The goal of such an ontology seems to be little more than the preservation of acute political power and an effort to undergird the structural power of whiteness—in other words, to remain in defiant denial of our varied responsibilities to one another.

Eventually, a judge ruled that Kemp's effort to suspend local jurisdiction regulations would likely prove unconstitutional. Kemp then dropped the suit. In the fall of 2020, Kemp went on what some might call a public relations campaign seeking to mend interracial offenses from the past summer. This even included a sit-down and photo-op meeting with Atlanta rapper Michael "Killer Mike" Render, presumably for the sake of Render's social capital. Many were shocked and angered by Render's associating with Kemp. The anger is understandable, even if misguided (according to both Render and Kemp). Kemp's actions during the COVID-19 pandemic are an expression of the live-and-let-die sensibility that would mortgage Black and Brown well-being for white prosperity and do so under cries of liberty. No amount of face time with wealthy rappers changes that fact.

A Spirit of White Pentecost

On March 14, 2020, US president Donald J. Trump proclaimed the following day a "National Day of Prayer for All Americans Affected by the Coronavirus Pandemic and for our National Response Efforts."[39] March 15 would be a day for "Americans of all faiths and religious traditions and backgrounds to offer prayers for all those affected, including people who have suffered harm or lost loved ones."[40] The proclamation referenced two New Testament verses and one from the Hebrew Bible, ostensibly on brand for an administration determined to propagate the notion of the United States as a Judeo-Christian nation. But more troubling, and fascinating, to be honest, is that the prayer proclamation was filed on the administration's website under "Healthcare." That prayer would be considered "health care" is both a tragic failure of religious literacy and an expression of magical thinking, both of which colored the Trump administration.

Rather than discuss the relatively easy target of Trump, in this section I look to the work and ministry of a blonde-haired, blue-eyed musician and Christian missionary, Sean Feucht, a volunteer worship leader of Bethel Church in Redding, California.[41] As early as the initial COVID-19 state and local lockdown orders in March, communities of faithful Christians began to think about the impact of the pandemic on worship services. One early news story involved Feucht, who had begun hosting "faith 'rallies' on his Instagram page"[42] in the wake of the coronavirus quarantine. His guests on this occasion were pastors of Bethel Church Bill Johnson and Shawn Bolz. Johnson encouraged Christians to use common sense and take general precautions like hand washing, but "warned that believers should not operate in fear."[43] Collectively the three of them painted a portrait of the faithful as defiant in the face of fear. "Being fearful indicates a weak faith" seems to sum up the general theological message. Feucht would amplify this point in the coming months.

At face value, the theology espoused by Feucht and Johnson looks like an otherworldly focused American evangelical call "to be not afraid of the world for you are not of the world." But in fact, Feucht and Bethel Church espouse a theology that has come to be called "Seven Mountains Dominionism,"[44] with the mountains understood as seven "areas of life: family, religion, education, media, entertainment, business, and government."[45] These seven mountains constitute different aspects of social life that the church seeks to occlude. Feucht's brand of Christianity, in this effort, is decidedly this-worldly. As many commentators and scholars note, Christian Dominionism is a threat to the traditional US separation of church and state, wanting to create a Christian American theocracy as a stepping-stone to a "worldwide theocracy," notes Steve Barry for *Patheos.com*.[46] Given these ambitions, Feucht is quite politically active, running a failed 2020 bid for California's Third US Congressional District before creating a political organization called Hold the Line, an effort his website refers to as an "engagement with the church and with millennials to give them courage to stand up and speak truth to our government leaders."[47] In an interview about Hold the Line, Feucht all but makes his Dominionism explicit in that his political interests are an outgrowth of missionizing theology that calls him "to go and change culture and bring the kingdom of God into those spheres of society."[48] In the same interview, his and Dominionism's Christian Nationalism was on full display, when he noted,

America is essentially who the world looks to still as a model of freedom, as a model of a nation that is founded on Judeo-Christian biblical values. So, I think that the more that I travel, the more that I realize the importance of maintaining and building upon the foundation in our nation that the forefathers pioneered . . . ensuring that the America that I grew up in, which was an incredible place, still is an incredible place, full of opportunity. . . . It's just the greatest country in the history of the world.[49]

On the weekend of June 13, 2020, Feucht hosted the "Hope Rally" in Minneapolis, Minnesota, at the exact location where George Floyd had been killed by Minneapolis police. In the previous weeks, the site had become something of a shrine to Floyd and other victims of police violence, and a meeting place for #BlackLivesMatter protesters. Beth Stoneburner, writing for the Friendly Atheist Blog Channel at Patheos. com, cataloged some of the online blowback from Feucht's Hope Rally. One voice on Twitter, Jo Luehmann, noted the irony that "Bethel and Sean don't even support BLM!," before quite succinctly describing how white Evangelicalism works: "This is how little they respect boundaries and consent. They are the center of the universe and we all must bow."[50] Other comments noted the perniciousness of Christian worship music drowning out the voices of protesters and other invited speakers. Many additional comments emphasized that Feucht was neither invited to the city nor encouraged to stick around. The occasion even included an altar call, the moment of a Christian worship service when participants are invited to receive salvation in Jesus Christ, as well as actual Christian baptisms. Feucht turned a political tragedy into an expression of God's grace, occluding the cultural specificities at work for an appeal to homogeneity in Christ. Essentially, he was there to wash Black folks white in Christ. Feucht may as well have been taking direction from sixteenth-century Franciscan monks in their conversion efforts with the Aztec. When the rally ended, Feucht tweeted simply that he had "no words for what god is doing tonight in Minneapolis."[51] For what it's worth, video footage of the occasion shows no sign of God being in attendance.

Originally the rally was to take place at nearby North Central University. However, by the summer of 2020 Feucht had made such a name for himself as a critic of #BlackLivesMatter that the university rescinded his invitation. It was this cancellation that led Feucht to set up his stage at the corner of Thirty-Eighth and Chicago in Minneapolis.[52] As the social unrest continued through June 2020,

Feucht was confronted with rising tides of white Christians speaking up against his Dominionism (not usually calling it this by name). In response, Feucht made it very clear that while "the statement 'black lives matter' is true, the movement is a fraud."[53] Feucht had drawn a proverbial line in the sand of white American Christian faith: "CANCEL CULTURE IS NOT KINGDOM CULTURE," Feucht tweeted, while others of his tweets harkened to spiritual warfare.[54] By the end of the month, Feucht was peddling what he called "Our Pledge: A Biblical Statement on Human Value, Race, and Unity." The statement offered a series of biblical platitudes ultimately emphasizing that God celebrates diversity, but unites all Christians in one person of Jesus Christ. Classic Christian egalitarianism covers what we might call the ontological dimensions of the pledge. The ethical aspect of the pledge, as if tone-deaf to the cries heard among protesters for (literally) centuries, appeals to reconciliation and claims God's priority is a relationship with God calling us to love one another.[55] Feucht brings to mind a statement Lillian Smith made long ago in her memoir of growing up white in the repressive South: "Their religion was too narcissistic to be concerned with anything but a man's body and a man's soul. Like the child in love with his own image and the invalid in love with his own disease, these men of God were in love with Sin which had come from such depths within that they believed they had created it themselves."[56] "What an awesome gift these revivalists possessed," Smith would continue, "for palpating the source of our anxiety!"[57]

In a sense, all of the trouble over black lives mattering was but a prelude for Feucht, who by July 1, 2020, was in the news again as the "victim" of "'Big Tech censorship,' for allegedly preventing his street ministry videos (filmed at peaceful prayer gatherings at protest sites) from being shared and viewed among his followers."[58] While up to the time of this writing, Facebook, the parent company of Instagram, denied any censorship took place, the effect of the publicity was to center Feucht as a poster boy defending religious freedom:

> I did not pick this fight, but I'm here. . . . I feel it is time we push back and stand up against those working to silence the church. . . . God is moving across America and there's a story of reconciliation and hope many are trying to hide![59]

As if to coincide perfectly with Feucht's media martyrdom, a loud faction of white evangelical Christians voiced their anger in early July, in response to California state guidelines issued on July 1 and that included directives to

> Discontinue singing (in rehearsals, services, etc.), chanting, and other practices and performances where there is increased likelihood for transmission from contaminated exhaled droplets.[60]

Feucht found himself the leader of these white Christians offended at California governor Gavin Newsome's mandate against choirs congregating. Newsome's practical guidance to keep all Californians safe elicited a kind of narcissistic injury to Feucht and, clearly, many more. In response, Feucht created an online video and petition called "Let Us Worship," where he states,

> How insane is it that, for the last several weeks, tens of thousands of people have been gathering outdoors, in cities all across California, and they have been screaming and chanting and protesting. And, all the while the state officials are encouraging that as they do this. And then now, the church wants to gather—just like we've been doing for thousands of years to simply worship God, they bring the hammer down against us.[61]

CBN's Starnes ran with a story framed in terms of a big state government impinging on the rights of Christians. Smack dab in the center of the story is a tweet from Feucht, sarcastically welcoming folks to California: "We encourage you to shout with thousands during protests but have banned you from singing in church to God."[62] The sarcasm is telling of a deep historical trend in the United States, wherein pushes for racial equality or equity often give way to white Christians upset that their churches are under attack or that their way of life will be severely truncated.

The rhetorical and political pivot Feucht enacted across the spring and summer of 2020 was a bait-and-switch meant to co-opt the emotional effervescence of the #BlackLivesMatter movement and channel it into white cries and concerns couched as Christian concerns. The move had the effect of positing Black life and concerns as profaning the sacred

Christian commitment, making it increasingly difficult for nonwhites to participate fully in that emotional energy without divesting themselves of concerns born of the Black experience. Concluding the "Let Us Worship" promotional video with a direct comment to the California governor, Feucht equated Newsom to Pharaoh from the Hebrew Bible, reminding that "This is what the Lord says, 'Let my people go, so they may worship.'"[63]

And worship they have done. Accounts from July and August 2020 indicate that under the leadership of Feucht (as well as other prominent evangelical leaders), churches throughout California and the Pacific Northwest hosted massive gatherings in public spaces. Thousands at a beach revival.[64] Between four thousand and seven thousand in Portland on August 8.[65] As COVID-19 raged into 2021, and as unjust police killings continued to set cities on fire with rage from exhausted Black and Brown communities, Feucht was "calling on Christians to rise up in defiance against 'double standard' coronavirus restrictions."[66] This resistance was not without yet other resistance. At the *No Longer Quivering* nonreligious blog at *Patheos.com*, Suzanne Titkemeyer distills the problem with Feucht's defiance quite elegantly:

> This is about the need for Christians to feel that righteous self-justified martyrbating they all love so much. Their need to push their views and wants down everyone else's throats and flip the proverbial bird at anyone trying to make them behave for the common good of everyone. The church might have left the building, but so did love, caring for others and all common sense, just leaving ego, hubris and a persecution complex.[67]

In Feucht's actions across the summer of 2020, we have a distillation of the making of American Christianity *as white*. The statistically verifiable situation of Black and Brown Americans facing police brutality, public executions, and disparate pandemic consequences is transmuted into a feeling of persecution among white Christians, and Feucht's "Let Us Worship" is packaged as a restoration of white religious freedom. The language of unity in Christ, and the rhetoric of religious freedom, serve as the twin means of denying and defying a shared responsibility toward one another. In the work and world of Feucht, "Let us worship" is synonymous with "Live and Let Die."

Conclusion

In this chapter, I have tried to give short historical context to the white American Christian relationship to death and pandemic. I have avoided drawing any conclusions about outright instrumental rationales shaping the actions of Brian Kemp and Sean Feucht, but based on historical circumstance, it would be understandable if readers did just that. In other words, I have reserved judgment as to whether Kemp and Feucht were *purposefully and intentionally* using the circumstances of the pandemic for their own social advance and instead framed their actions in terms of the historical precedent of "defiance." I have sought to sketch out a model for understanding the theological underpinnings of white Christian American defiance, framing that defiance in ultimate terms of a despair borne of weakness. The pandemics of 2020 foreground this weakness in as clear relief as possible. To this extent, I hope this all-too-brief attention to white Christian American defiance might prove useful for readers interested in joining in the fight to stave off rising white tides of American fascism. Should we lose this fight, perhaps this work might contribute to our postmortem.

NOTES

1 Tzvetan Todorov, *The Conquest of America: The Question of the Other* (New York: Harper and Row, 1982), 133. See also Jared Diamond, *Guns, Germs and Steel* (New York: W. W. Norton and Company, 1999).

2 Amherst College, "Frequently Asked Questions," accessed October 30, 2020, www.amherst.edu.

3 "How Racism Shaped the Public Health Response to the 1918 Spanish Flu Pandemic," Medill National Security Zone, accessed October 30, 2020, https://nationalsecurityzone.medill.northwestern.edu; see also John M. Barry, *The Great Influenza, Revised Edition* (Penguin, 2005).

4 James W. Perkinson, *Shamanism, Racism, and Hip Hop Culture: Essays on White Supremacy and Black Subversion* (London: Palgrave Macmillan, 2005), 58.

5 Jennifer Tsai, "COVID-19's Disparate Impacts Are Not a Story about Race," *Scientific American*, September 8, 2020, www.scientificamerican.com.

6 "Estimating COVID-19 Exposure for Religious Subgroups in the United States," *PRRI* (blog), August 5, 2020, www.prri.org.

7 Ibid.

8 Perkinson, *Shamanism*, 124.

9 Georgio Agamben, *Homo Sacer: Sovereign Power and Bare Life* (Stanford, CA: Stanford University Press, 1998).

10 Michel Foucault, *Technologies of the Self* (London: Tavistock, 1988), 19.

11 Michel Foucault, *The Birth of Biopolitics* (London: Picador, 2010).

12 Foucault, *Technologies of the Self*, 18, 39.

13 James W. Perkinson, *White Theology: Outing Supremacy in Modernity* (New York: Palgrave Macmillan, 2004), 166.

14 Ibid.

15 Achille Mbembe, *Necropolitics* (Durham, NC: Duke University Press, 2019).

16 Perkinson, *Shamanism*, 37.

17 Søren Kierkegaard, *The Sickness unto Death* (Princeton, NJ: Princeton University Press, 1941), 76.

18 Ibid.

19 Ibid., 76–77.

20 Foucault, *Technologies of the Self*, 13.

21 Martin Heidegger, in Walter Kaufmann, *The Faith of a Heretic* (Princeton, NJ: Princeton University Press, 1959), 356.

22 Zak Cheney-Rice, "Georgia Is Really Good at Making It Hard for Black People to Vote, Study Finds," *NYMAG*, December 13, 2019, https://nymag.com.

23 "Kemp Declares State of Emergency, Authorizes 1,000 Troops to Protect Georgians," Governor Brian P. Kemp Office of the Governor, July 6, 2020, https://gov.georgia.gov.

24 Ibid.

25 Ibid.

26 Sophie Lewis, "Atlanta Mayor Orders City to Return to Phase 1 as Georgia Breaks Record for New Daily Coronavirus Cases," CBS News, July 10, 2020, www.cbsnews.com.

27 "Mayor Keisha Lance Bottoms Orders City's Phased Reopening Plan to Be Moved Back to Phase I," City of Atlanta press release, July 10, 2020, www.atlantaga.gov.

28 Lewis, "Atlanta Mayor Orders City."

29 "Statement on Atlanta Reverting to 'Phase One,'" Governor Brian P. Kemp Office of the Governor, July 13, 2020, https://gov.georgia.gov.

30 Ibid.

31 "Governor Kemp Suspends Local Mask Mandates," CBS 46 News, July 15, 2020, www.cbs46.com.

32 Veronica Stracqualursi and Paul LeBlanc, "Georgia Governor Sues Atlanta Mayor over City's Mask Mandate," CNN, July 16, 2020, www.cnn.com.

33 Ibid.

34 Ibid.

35 "Gov. Kemp Addresses Georgia after Suing Atlanta over Masks, Restrictions," July 17, 2020, www.youtube.com/watch?v=d7np-8IZg4I&feature=youtu.be.

36 Ibid.

37 Ibid.

38 Perkinson, *Shamanism*, 194–95.

39 "Proclamation on the National Day of Prayer for All Americans Affected by the Coronavirus Pandemic and for Our National Response Efforts," March 14, 2020, https://web.archive.org/web/20210120202043/https://trumpwhitehouse.archives .gov/presidential-actions/proclamation-national-day-prayer-americans-affected -coronavirus-pandemic-national-response-efforts/.

40 Ibid.

41 Mike Mangas and Ashley Gardner, "Bethel Church Not Involved in Worship Gathering Condemned by Public Health," KRCR, July 23, 2020, https://krcrtv.com.

42 Talia Wise, "'Silence Voices of Fear': Bill Johnson, Shawn Bolz, Sean Feucht Hold Faith Rally against Coronavirus," CBN News, March 13, 2020, www1.cbn.com.

43 Ibid.

44 Peter Montgomery, "Sean Feucht Launches Political Group to Mobilize Conservative Christian Millennials," Right Wing Watch, May 14, 2020, www.right wingwatch.org.

45 David R. Brockman, "The Fringe Theology That Could End Religious Freedom," Texas Observer, June 2, 2016, www.texasobserver.org.

46 Jack Matirko, "Dominionism in America Part 5: The Seven Mountains Mandate," For Infernal Use Only (blog), February 20, 2019, www.patheos.com.

47 "Hold the Line," Hold the Line, accessed August 10, 2020, www.holdtheline.live.

48 Virginia Allen, "Christian Missionary's 'Hold the Line' Aims to Engage the Flock Politically," Daily Signal, May 11, 2020, www.dailysignal.com.

49 Ibid.

50 Beth Stoneburner, "A Christian Band Co-Opted the Site of George Floyd's Murder to Win Converts," Friendly Atheist (blog), June 15, 2020, accessed August 10, 2020, https://friendlyatheist.patheos.com/2020/06/15/a-christian-band-co-opted-the -site-of-george-floyds-murder-to-win-converts/.

51 Melissa Turtinen, "Some Aren't Happy Californian Musician Was Performing at George Floyd Memorial," Bring Me the News, June 15, 2020, https://bringmethe news.com.

52 Peter Montgomery, "Sean Feucht Calls Black Lives Matter Movement a 'Fraud,' Seeks to Turn 'Riots' into 'Revival,'" Right Wing Watch, June 18, 2020, www.right wingwatch.org.

53 Sean Feucht and Ryan Bomberger, "White, Woke but Spiritually Broke," 2020, www.youtube.com/watch?v=u7_448bTHL0&feature=youtu.be&t=747.

54 Montgomery, "Sean Feucht Calls."

55 Sean Feucht, "Our Pledge," accessed August 10, 2020, www.seanfeucht.com.

56 Lillian Smith, Killers of the Dream (New York: W. W. Norton & Company, 1949), 105.

57 Ibid., 106.

58 "Christian Worship Leader Leads National Outcry against Instagram for Censorship," LifeSiteNews, July 1, 2020, www.lifesitenews.com.

59 Ibid.

60 Todd Starnes, "California's Governor Forbids Christians from Singing in Church Houses," CBN News, July 3, 2020, www1.cbn.com.

61 "Let Us Worship," 2020, www.youtube.com/watch?time_continue=184&v=ds274k1 HD9U&feature=emb_title.

62 Starnes, "California's Governor Forbids."

63 "Let Us Worship."

64 Caleb Parke, "California Beach Revival Attended by 1,000: 'The Church Has Left the Building,'" Fox News, July 14, 2020, www.foxnews.com.

65 Danielle Wallace, "Portland Sees Thousands Worship amid Coronavirus Restrictions Hours before Riots, Fire at Police Union," Fox News, August 9, 2020, www.foxnews.com.

66 Caleb Parke, "'Let Us Worship' Founder Calls out California Leaders' Coronavirus Lockdown Hypocrisy," Fox News, July 30, 2020, www.foxnews.com.

67 Suzanne Titkemeyer, "Bethel Redding Urging People to Not Socially Distance? Open Thread COVID 19," *No Longer Quivering* (blog), July 20, 2020, www .patheos.com.

4

Where There Are No Answers

Reflecting on Theological Claims in the Age of COVID-19

ANTHONY B. PINN

What does one make of democratic possibility, with all its promises, as Black bodies pile up? Based on my interest in the study of religion, that question generates for me another. Christianity is so intimately connected—through doctrine and performance—to the workings of this nation; can it (should it) survive the demise of the United States' delusion currently under way due to the plague of COVID-19 and continued anti-Black racism?[1]

This isn't the first invisible threat, but for many it's the first experienced as more than a cautionary story recounted by others and from a safe distance. In at least that way, COVID-19 is different. The challenge with COVID-19 is uncertainty—the lack of control over circumstances, and the inability to identify clearly the threat or determine duration. In addition, the virus highlights the human body. Yet Christianity has traditionally had a difficult time with the human body. Drawing on scripture and corresponding doctrine, the body has been understood as the source of problematic desires, the trap holding the soul in place. The body—the physical body—is made hypervisible—suspect and dangerous.[2] Even more liberal views are challenged by the limitations of the larger tradition of which they are a part—and this is a source of schisms, theological debate, and religious frustration. Right now, the body demands attention and the threat it poses isn't summed up through the old moral grammar of puritanical existence. And while this is the case for all bodies, the dilemma is amplified for bodies socially regarded as already marginal due, for example, to race. Praying (i.e., sacred rituals) and preying (i.e., a secular form of sacrifice) are connected as religious rationales that easily justify disregard and antilife activities played out graphically in responses to COVID-19 and #BlackLivesMatter.

The isolation—the confinement of bodies—demands introspection within what is called the "religious." It urges deeper recognition of and accounting for how bodies occupy time and space, and the ways in which that occupation matters beyond the individual. It points out the nature of our connectedness—in terms of the benefits and challenges of that connectedness. The entanglement that is human life is exposed at times like this, and we are forced to negotiate what to make of that connectedness—what about it renders us vulnerable and what of it promotes opportunity.

Thinking Religion during a Plague

With circumstances such as those we faced beginning in early 2020, religious communities typically turn to theology as a way to name, circumscribe, and wrestle with life conditions, because "theology is contextual language—that is, defined by the human situation that gives birth to it."[3] More to the point, within contexts of misery, one might think of theology as "passionate language, the language of commitment, because it is language which seeks to vindicate the afflicted and condemn the enforcers of evil."[4] Yet part of the theological challenge involves deciphering who is afflicted and who should be condemned. Tackling the nature of evil—as this process of deciphering and reconciling entails—often takes the form of theodicy, for example, what can be said about divine justice in light of profound suffering? However, theodicy, as scholars like Terrence Tilley and William R. Jones have argued, never satisfies in the long term, and its failure is even more graphic as the coronavirus devours life.[5] The effort to vindicate God often comes at the expense of humans, whose misery and pain lose some of their significance—the safeguarding of ideals at the expense of the vulnerable.[6]

In fact, theodicy is a dangerous consideration as it disrupts reason and threatens to render faith dysfunctional. What does it mean to vindicate the Divine and sanction suffering in ongoing death-dealing circumstances? What is to be thought and made of suffering that is ongoing and disproportionate? It can't be subdued, yet the theodical question arises anew for the Christian theist with each challenge to the "normal"—to patterns of thinking that serve to reinforce religious-theological assumption. Social distancing and failure to observe this strategy, for example, point to a more earthy challenge and moral failure: anthropodicy, which concerns itself with the human role in suffering—the effort to interrogate and justify human action over against its consequences.[7] Within the context of religion in general and theology in particular, it amplifies the grammar of good and evil. COVID-19 ties together the natural religious impulse to think about God (theodicy) and the demand to be mindful of the human (anthropodicy): what is this virus, and what of our encounter with it, in terms of scope and scale?

There are limits to what theological insights offer embodied challenges. Theology operates based on the assumption of insiders and outsiders, of a rationale that cuts against reason—both challenging and embracing logic. In this instance, theology offers a language of life undercut by the uncertainty of the moment—and what this moment means for the nature of life moving forward. The theodicy question has no answer—the challenge is earthier than theodicy can manage, but anthropodicy doesn't satisfy either. Theodicy positions anxiety in terms of vertical relationships—the human condition explained through a relationship to a cosmic logic beyond our ability to comprehend. Anthropodicy concerns itself with attempting to explain human experience from within the confines of human history—what we do as embodied beings and what we might say about that arrangement in light of human reason. At best, it requires human accountability and responsibility in a manner not demanded through theodicy; but in the long run, it is a way of thinking that doesn't demand much other than a source of blame already known to us. Neither, however, can fully satisfy a situation that seems to point out the best and worst elements of human behavior—marking out human thinking, but doing that both affirms and degrades human life. Each of these two approaches leaves us flat—still facing circumstances that theological language is ill-equipped to describe and resolve.

Christian communities have not been without a response to these challenging times—attempting to make religious sense of circumstances that target some fundamental assumptions regarding collective life. And they do this using theology as a language meant to offer stability and comfort by pointing out the basic problem at work and the resolution available. While this is a general effort within Christian circles, it is most graphically present in the rhetoric and actions of religious leaders. Ministers like Rodney Howard-Browne of Tampa push to maintain pre-virus patterns of activity despite the escalating threat to health and well-being locally, nationally, and even globally.[8] Challenges to this particular theologized response—of Christian business as usual—are viewed as an attack on Christians, for whom this virus is something of a test of faith: to alter practice is to weaken faith.[9] Others see the virus as pointing to an existing moral failure not simply of Christian communities but of the nation as a whole that resulted in God's wrath. In a word, it is a consequence of moral failure.[10] In either case, a rigid commitment to religious business as usual expressed as an act of religious commitment ignores threats to physical life.

Antimaskers, for example, provide at least two examples of problematic theologizing. First, there is the overdetermination of faith that saturated perspective on collective life marked by the assumption that belief in God is a safeguard against infection—a troubling belief that proper spiritual positioning over and against the world protects one from the world. In addition, there's something akin to a distorted theological anthropology by means of which the *imago dei* argument is played out through visibility of this likeness. As one politician in Ohio noted, "one of those [Judeo-Christian] principles is that we are all created in the image and likeness of God. That image is seen the most by our face. I will not wear a mask."[11] This, I would add, is tied to a dwarfed sense of empathy and a radical individualism, which equates divine creation with radical independence. However, as should be obvious, there is a political dimension to this theological argument whereby true "free will" is equated with a type of individualized political anarchic mood, whereby citizenship is equated with an antiregulation stance. To wear a mask, some argue, is to be dehumanized or distorted—to lose what is distinctively human about themselves. As the slogan goes, "I will not be muzzled like a mad dog!"[12]

The impact of this virus is far-reaching in that it challenges physical well-being, political ideology, and socioeconomic infrastructure in the present moment moving forward, but it also disrupts historical narratives. In a word, it dismantles the assumed special status of the United States and hampers the ability to market the nation as having a unique global position. This grand legend is shaken on a variety of fronts as this unseen virus destroys without regard for the United States' understanding of itself as beyond the reach of most troubles that afflict the rest of the world. After all, isn't this the land of "*life*, liberty, and the pursuit of happiness"? Anxiety reigns as the ability to bracket and control death is shattered. The dominant ideology is weakened as the body count rises. We hunker down and try to think and act in a way that befits a new normal.

The functions of the body are highlighted by the viral threat and expressed through the strange practice of gathering—hoarding toilet paper is just one ritualized response to traumatic uncertainty. Life is stripped down to basic parameters and activities, and we are forced to explore what we need over against what we want—and this is difficult within a social world that blurs the line between the two. Ritual practices meant to distract, to point toward something beyond the materiality of the body, are suspended, and we are forced to spend time alone, and in those private spaces create ways to be connected and comforted.

Christianity's entanglement in the sociopolitical efforts of the United States has come to define much of this religion's nature—with its grammar of meaning equated to political inclinations. To be clear, this statement is not to lament the loss of some type of essence, the assumption that Christianity can or has ever been more than a particular coding of mundane interests and concerns. Both the right and the left find comfort and confirmation in the use of Christianity's infrastructure, rendering it of no moral or ethical distinctiveness. Affirm life or take life—each can be justified using the same religious-theological language. That is to say, the "magic" of faith shrouding religious-theological performance fails to constitute a difference. Defined by this ritual-theological infrastructure, Christianity offers nothing unique to service the demands of this particular racial justice–seeking moment. As liberation theologians including James Cone have noted, in such circumstances it is a tool of white supremacy, a device used to buttress modalities of white nationalist desire.

I imagine some will object to this characterization. Still, when applied to the deadly circumstances that despised populations face in the United States, through its primary and most widely noted tools, Christianity affords no sustainable (moral or ethical) articulated distinction between murderer and murdered. The grammar of rightness is applied to those who might be said to safeguard the arrangements of death by not opposing white privilege (e.g., "All Lives Matter") and those who seek to demolish the tools of death (e.g., "Black Lives Matter"). This safeguarding of certain arrangements of death is, at times, also performed through the rejection of the face covering as a strike against their "God-given" rights and liberties as the preferred population safeguarded by divine intervention against disease.

Mind the "Gap"

Back to my initial question: Is there anything of Christianity that can or should be preserved during this time of lucid challenge to the deadly arrangement of collective life? More to the point, what of it is left in the aftermath of the pull on its rituals and the push of its perceptions—its theological grammar of faith in and against the world—from both the right and the left? I suggest that if anything remains of value in Christianity, it has to do with its grammar of the "gap"—that is, what remains after the push and pull on its thinking and performance, when all else has been stripped away.

My concern here isn't a question of God's existence or location—an issue of knowledge limitations and the meaning of God—but rather my aim to is name the place of radical trauma and uncertainty. If one turns to the existential thought of Søren Kierkegaard, for instance, the gap might be represented in the affective space when, in his first telling of the story (Genesis 22), Abraham takes Isaac to sacrifice him in accordance with the will of God, and Sarah watches as her husband and son leave. It is the space between familiarity and the uncertainty of disappearance, when "Sarah looked out of the window after them until they had passed down the valley and she could see them no more."[13] It is the space of the radical turn—the "instant" between Abraham's "turned away" from Isaac and Isaac's seeing him again when "Abraham's face . . . was changed, his glance was wild, his form was horror."[14] Thinking of Abraham and Isaac, the gap is the place of "contradiction."[15] The gap is that which faith—Kierkegaard would have us believe—covers; but faith easily bends to the mundane needs and explanations of collective life. From Kierkegaard's world to ours, there is considerable cultural distance to cover. So while Kierkegaard speaks of Abraham and Sarah, there are also Hagar and her son—at a time before Isaac.

Hagar and Abraham's son, Ishmael, is destined to be in relationship to a community, but he is denied status as being of divine and salvific promise. So powerfully described by Delores Williams, the gap is the location of anguish experienced by Hagar between the promise associated with Abraham and acceptance of exclusion through her return to Abraham's camp—that is, the "wilderness experience."[16] It is wilderness as a space of collapse (what Williams calls "women's alienation and isolation, economic deprivation"[17]), before an effort to reconstitute relationships. Even before the wilderness, the graphic encounter with the gap—Hagar's marginalization and sociocultural vulnerability—is present and forceful. She is a servant to Abraham's wife, Sarah, which—as readers of the story come to learn—involves loss of determination of activity and being. She is to fulfill Sarah's desires—even when this means surrendering her body to Abraham. Williams makes clear that this isn't simply a mundane social arrangement—as traumatic and destructive as that in itself would be—but rather it is the structuring of a divine preference. "God," writes Williams, "is clearly partial to Sarah,"[18] and this preference for Sarah exposes Hagar and her body to the needs and wants of others. Hagar seeks resolve by leaving her arrangements—rejecting her existential plight and entering instead a space of uncertainty, a place of negation: no community, no family, no social arrangements, and no recognizable markers of connection. She enters the wilderness. Herein is another manifestation of the gap—a place marked by a void of certainty, structure, and coherence. It is the space between the past and prospects of a future—a location named by the terror of the present. Think of the gap as the moment at which Hagar recognizes the death of her misery and the closeness of demise— the space before she is sent back, and before the question of being is resolved. According to the story,

> She wandered off into the desert of Beersheba. When the skin of water was finished she abandoned the child under a bush. Then she went and sat down at a distance, about bowshot away, thinking "I cannot bear to see the child die." Sitting at a distance, she began to sob.[19]

"Sitting at a distance"—the gap is the space between fleeing Sarah and being "found" by the angel. It is not primarily a problem of language, but rather has an affective quality constituted as a moment oversaturated with instability. Instead, it is the geography of affectively arranged obtuseness just before Kelly Brown Douglas's question, "What are we to hope for?"[20] Pushing forward from Douglas and using the language of demise defining the current moment, the gap is the dissonance between white lies and Black life mattering.

Furthermore, the gap can be understood as the space of paradox between the cross and the lynching tree, as narrated by James Cone.[21] In *The Cross and the Lynching Tree*, Cone writes, "Can the cross redeem the lynching tree? Can the lynching tree liberate the cross and make it real in American history?"[22] This marker of demise lends historicity to the real suffering of the oppressed, and the cross points out a larger meaning for that real suffering; in so doing it isolates the gap for consideration. In his last theological text—*Said I Wasn't Gonna Tell Nobody*, Cone frames this gap—this location of instability and radical uncertainty—in terms of theodicy: "Throughout the twentieth century," he writes, "African Americans continued to struggle to reconcile their faith in God's justice and love with the persistence of black suffering. Writer James Baldwin spoke for many when asking, 'If [God's] love was so great, and if He loved all His children, why were we, the blacks, cast down so far?'"—and here's the key, the theological shift that I believe his engagement with moralism makes theological and ethically feasible: "No one knows the answer to that question."[23] What Cone seems to come to find with theodicy is absurdity, or the gap in terms of the limitation on language's ability to capture the full content of the space. It is the prime theological question asked and met with a silence that names the gap or what Williams calls the wilderness. This silence does not end inquiry but rather fuels attention to new questions, a redefining of ethics away from theoretical consideration to the substance, the uncomfortable conditions of life. It, the silence, is a starting point.[24] Cone's theological project involves a rejection of a certain mode of the divine to the degree his thinking offers no firm resolution to the theodicy dilemma. His is an appeal to living, as Richard Wright reflects when thinking about life in the Jim Crow South, by means of an embodied response to the world in which "our songs and dances are our banner of hope flung desperately up in the face of a world that has pushed us to the wall."[25]

Figures like Wright provide a language—improvise a grammar—of life without certainties. They speak of the present—its pain and misery—without surrender. These artists offer imaginative frameworks that signify teleological projections. One might think of this moment of recognition as a moment of lucidity exemplified, I would argue, by artist. It has everything to do with the artist's depth of engagement with absurdity, with misery and the silence of the world. Take note, for example, of Michel Fabre's description of Richard Wright. Fabre writes that Wright "had suffered the traumatic experience of oppression and his intuition was subtle enough, his historical culture rich enough to enable him to feel all of this perhaps more vividly than anyone else. The wound of racial oppression and the negative aspects of his education actually endowed him with a special insight, the double vision of belonging to two cultures (American and Afro American) which he was then able to convey in forceful and understandable language, even if rapid historical and social change sometimes prevent him from creating the most adequate symbols of it."[26] The key here is special insight—a mode of observation and naming that might elsewhere be called awareness that, to borrow from Wright, keeps one from being "driven out of life."[27] Perhaps, as Cone's frequent turn to African American literature might be said to reflect, there is something about the gap that makes art necessary. This story of death could speak to the world as only the artist can—like the Black artist who recognizes the world is the briar patch and African Americans are Br'er Rabbit, finding the ability to exist over against the inhospitable nature of the context. Art—in this case, literature—is a poetic acknowledgment of the gap.

Mindful of Cone and art, I want to offer an answer to the original question. What religion, in this case Christianity, might offer at this moment is a call to acknowledge the gap as poetic negation of our assumed grammar and vocabulary for describing life. Yet what religion can't provide at this moment is a viable way to fill that gap. The gap isn't adequately captured or filled through theological and doctrinal pronouncements of care and comfort. (I think something of this realization is to be found in early critiques of recognized religious leaders and their efforts to "lead" the struggle offered by #BlackLivesMatter advocates.) Recognition of the gap before an effort to fill it with anything doesn't promise transformation, no more than protests against injustice necessarily translate into new modalities of living together. But such recognition does honor the awful nature of the problem we face. In other words, perhaps what religion offers—all it can offer—at this point is a highlighting of vulnerability and uncertainty as the place from which we work.

Camus and the Plague

Cone wrestles with the significance of the gap early through a turn to figures such as Albert Camus. Mindful of this, I want to give consideration, as Cone did, to Camus's *The Plague*.[28]

I imagine many look to *The Plague* for what it might offer in terms of familiarity—that is to say, circumstances like our own that suggest we aren't the first to encounter death from a source we can't properly name or control. Others might find helpful the story's rehearsal of science as they work to critique the ridiculous response of some conservative evangelicals who assume divine purpose in this moment of death, which in turn props up their theologized attack on difference—for example, gays and lesbians. Others might find of interest the effort of church representatives to find a theological narrative that tames death. Still others might find most appealing the novel's turn to human effort to address material circumstances in the face of failed religious claims.

Cone makes use of Camus from his earlier writings, in that Camus and other Black moralists, like Richard Wright, get at the nature of what I'm calling the gap; yet we can gather more than description from Camus. As Cone reflects, attention to thinkers such as Albert Camus motivated him "to do in theology what they did in literature."[29] *The Plague*, Cone notes in his final book, offered a way to wrestle with fundamental questions unanswerable from a theological perspective—questions, as I would name them—of the gap.[30] For Cone, Camus and *The Plague* appeal because they shed light on what Cone (and Williams) understands as a type of misery unto death—that is, Black (and gendered) suffering—but in a more general sense *The Plague* can be said to speak to the gap because the gap is marked by an affective confrontation with uncertainty that can be constitutive of death—physical or ontologi-cal. The gap is that place—as Kierkegaard, Williams, and Cone might be said to describe it—of a void, where the past and present are emptied and what remains is a particular type of anxiety—of a vulnerability that is almost too much.

Traditional responses to the gap attempt resolution by denying one el-ement of the dilemma addresses human need for salvation by destroying the integrity of suffering, rendering it purposeful and redemptive. This effort to dismantle, to deny the silence of the world, by forcing an answer and pretending it is this larger response is what Cone seeks to avoid. He maintains the tension—acknowledges the silence of the world with respect to Black suffering. This sense of recognition—to use Camus's word, aspiration[31]—is akin to awareness in that it is an intense focus on the world. Such is a different approach to uncertainty.

With Camus, Cone is reminded of the human confronted by the gap—to the existential consequences of the gap, and to theologically linger over the gap. For Cone, doing so involves attention to the real and persistent nature of Black suffering—without effort to sanction the suffering, or in other words, to render the gap (i.e., the distance between suffering and liberation) salvific. Turning to *The Plague*, Cone remem-bers Rieux's response to Father Paneloux regarding the death of an in-nocent child—with Rieux refusing to "love a scheme of things in which children are put to torture"[32]—and Cone says, "It is not permissible to appeal to the idea that God's will is inscrutable or that the righteous sufferer will be rewarded in heaven."[33] In making such a claim, Cone refuses to collapse the gap.

In part, the ongoing value of *The Plague* during this tense moment on the world stage confronting COVID-19 as a new disease—as well as a reason it could help Cone theologize—is the fluidity of trauma it allows: the source of trauma addressed, the nature of demise, the form of uncer-tainty that shifts to fit the circumstances of the reader.[34] Cone by turning to *The Plague* could thus speak of the gap as the space of unaccounted-for Black suffering. With the blues there is the narration of the tragic that finds in that recognition of the tragic—or one might say the absurd—determination to linger at the gap. Cone calls this "transcendence" while still swimming in the stuff of existential conditions, or "transcendence as persistent struggle,"[35] and Camus names it "happiness"—as in one "must imagine Sisyphus happy," although still bound to his labor. This isn't the articulation of a goal over against circumstances, but rather persistence of struggle within the present. Cone, one might say, turns to Camus to reconstitute moral and ethical purpose in conversation with one who appreciates and names the gap. For Cone, it is in the challenge of suffering, and for Camus it is the space of nausea—or the absurd—as a place of silence that resists traditional theologizing efforts.

The fragile and troubled nature of life has been exposed and, naturally, we look for ways to absorb and process this reality—to make sense of our circumstances. The standard, social effort to isolate death (and those likely to bring it into our personal circumstances) and thereby safeguard against it has failed. Examples or models of how to think about the angst of demise help, which is where Camus enters the picture. While an award-winning intellectual favored by many academics, the North African Camus also wrote of existential circumstances of war and want that tapped into life conditions experienced by and of concern to a general public.

Even if Cone did not appeal to Camus's exploration of death and uncertainty, there would be reason to reflect on it here, in light of COVID-19. After all, as Stephen Metcalf and so many others might agree, "Its relevance lashes you across the face."[36] It captures and presents an example of exposure—of uncertainty—of a gap between what we know and what we desire. Philosopher Alain de Botton puts it this way: Camus "was drawn to his theme because he believed that the actual historical incidents we call plagues are merely concentrations of a universal precondition, dramatic instances of a perpetual rule: that all human beings are vulnerable to being randomly exterminated at any time, by a virus, an accident or the actions of our fellow man."[37] One might think of this in terms of humanly enacted disregard that drove Hagar to the brink of death, the cruelty that almost cost Isaac his life, or the Black suffering that Cone struggles to name. In any of these contexts, one might think of *The Plague*'s relevance.[38]

The French Algerian context is the place of Camus's youth. It is where he lived in poverty with his grandmother, mother, and brother, where he played football and attended school. It is also the location for the novel, the place that slowly succumbs to a plague. Over the course of its pages, the novel chronicles the existential, affective, and psychological response to a deadly virus spread from animals to humans—made visible only as it destroys the physical and emotional integrity of its host. Science seeks to tame, if not end, the virus, and religion seeks to understand (perhaps even justify) it in relationship to the nature and meaning of humanity in relationship to a grand unity of life.

Human mechanisms of explanation ultimately fail to satisfy, even if they serve to explain the how of death. We are left with the existential challenge of why this death and the means by which to address that question without, at the same time, degrading the integrity of life. As the novel points out, human connections might provide a bit of comfort within the context of absurdity that is our relationship to the world— but nothing stems the tide of death. All that is altered through our thinking and doing within a context of uncertainty and invisible threat is how one embraces this particular possibility of death. As the novel makes clear, we are powerless—our tools dulled by the persistence of demise. However, the gap—the place of the plague—isn't the "end"; that would make circumstances easier. Rather, the gap is felt as a threat—a potentiality—the possibility of undesired demise.

This is a muffled but sustained perseverance of humanity despite circumstances—the integrity and value of life found in the living. We learn, in this place, to confront ourselves. At the place of the gap the theological tendency is to look for God; but Camus indicates—and Cone recognized this—we must confront ourselves.[39] Camus reminds readers of the interconnected nature of all life—the manner in which human existence is tied to other modes of life, seen and unseen. But then there are the final lines of the book:

> The plague bacillus never dies or disappears for good; that it can lie dormant for years and years in furniture and linen-chests; that it bides its time in bedrooms, cellars, trunks and book-shelves; and perhaps the day would come when, for the bane and the enlightening of men, it roused up its rats again and sent them forth to die in a happy city.[40]

There is nothing particularly optimistic about this ending, but I would argue it offers something of deep and abiding value. Attention to these concluding words urges a sense that agency isn't restricted to humans— and this is a taming of the worst of our anthropocentric tendencies.

Instead, he cautions readers to recognize life is subject to the movement and activity of material forces humans can't control: this virus doesn't care about human wants and desires. The human animal doesn't simply impose its will on the world—such thinking is a terrible distortion of circumstances. Things impact us, inform us, shape us—in a sense determine the nature and meaning of human life. In a word, we are not only part of the world but we are also dependent upon a world that doesn't bend to our will and doesn't prioritize the criteria for our well-being. What this should produce is humility, a bit of perspective, that conditions how we move through the world—that measures our "touch" and tames our intentions through recognition that human life isn't guaranteed. The moral framework for life is modified in this way—highlighting a concern for codes of doing and thinking that commit to a balancing of needs.

We are vulnerable, forced to recognize the connected nature of life and death. And what's more, we lack the ability to clearly identify and gear up against an enemy that can't be seen—that uses humans as hosts, many of who willingly infect. What we also see is the manner in which difference breeds a type of disregard. In other words, the virus also serves to amplify the vulnerability of particular populations who are already at risk in the United States. Vulnerability is layered on vulnerability.

Yet this vulnerability isn't experienced the same. Camus's story takes place within French Algeria—a location of colonial context that marks difference as problematic. While not identical, the geography of the United States and the threat of COVID-19 also entail trauma amplified by racialization that can weaponize the virus: think of white nationalists wanting to use the virus to attack despised populations. Also worth noting is the way in which social marginalization—of African Americans, for instance—amplifies rates of infection and death.[41] The deadly combination of racism and classism intensifies already troubling practices of injustice. To be Black in the United States is to face the ever present potential of death—think of Sandra Bland or Michael Brown—through visible forces of social control, and now the invisible latches onto these bodies and marks them for death intensified by racialized access to testing and medical assistance. The virus exposes and makes more graphic the toxic dimensions of our social world: we encounter the gap. Viral circumstances will change, but will the deadly connotations of marginalization in its various forms do so also?

What to Do?

Perhaps most difficult, however, is the way in which the end of *The Plague* challenges a basic assumption: proper strategies for collective life are outcome-driven, with a clear goal achieved. But according to Camus, we don't win. The plague ends, but it can come again—emerge out of hiding to hamper life. Citizens of Oran in the novel celebrate a victory of sorts, but the end of the plague isn't a win over death—rather a break in the action. In our world changed by COVID-19, we do well to heed Camus's warning: there are threats that we can't conquer. That is to say, this virus and its impact should remind us that outcome-driven strategies aren't useful. The idea that we act in the world with the intent of safeguarding life because our goals will be fulfilled is a poor approach, particularly for humanists who make no claims to cosmic aid.

More appropriate in a context where the plague may once again reach out to kill is a sense of perpetual rebellion—a steadfastness in our confrontation with the gap—an effort to name the unnamable: an understanding that we struggle to improve circumstances for all of life because we can, not because we will be successful. The gap remains—highlighted and announced through one form of plague or another. There is a tragicomic quality of life that should remind us of the interrelated nature of life and death, as well as the manner in which our best efforts often betray us.

So why struggle to make improvements? Why work against the spread of this virus? Why attempt to safeguard life in such uncertain times? Why not just surrender and assume this is the end of things as we've known them? Why? Simply *because we can* and not because we are sure or even likely to find victory and the fulfillment of our efforts.

Think about this in relationship to Camus's depiction of Sisyphus and his stone. Punished by the gods, Sisyphus is tasked with moving his stone up a hill, only to have it come back down, and the process starts again . . . forever. According to Camus, one might think this would defeat him—this is surely what the gods anticipated—because there is no final outcome, no victory. But he continues his task, with full awareness of his circumstances. The short story that names the larger collection—*The Myth of Sisyphus and Other Essays*—ends with these words:

I leave Sisyphus at the foot of the mountain! One always finds one's burden again. But Sisyphus teaches the higher fidelity that negates the gods and raises rocks. He too concludes that all is well. This universe henceforth without a master seems to him neither sterile nor futile. Each atom of that stone, each mineral flake of that night-filled mountain, in itself forms a world. The struggle itself toward the heights is enough to fill a man's heart. One must imagine Sisyphus happy.

We struggle with our own task, work against the threat of this virus, but as Sisyphus we should do this—continue our efforts—simply because we can. COVID-19 may withdraw—allowing us to leave our homes again, and gather with family and friends—but the virus won't be gone; the threat is ever present. Things are "well" not because the threat has been tamed but because we persist. We encounter the gap and aren't buckled by the uncertainty. We should work facing the gap, and in the doing we imagine ourselves, like Sisyphus, more aware—and through that lucidity able to confront the gap.

This viral challenge can't be contained or managed theologically— what is left to us is ethics comfortable with vulnerability and proposes no final resolution. It is a mode of perpetual struggle—a commitment to recognition of ongoing threats to collective well-being, threats that are both external and internal. Theological proclamations aren't answers that can withstand this threat. The answer is ethics—behavior that enhances life, a time to rethink the markers of healthy personhood and how this obligates us with respect to each other. This isn't so simple as doing the right thing because we see ourselves in others—that's too easy and too self-assured. Rather, we need ways of behaving in the world that entail a deep and abiding appreciation for intersections— fragile connections to others, whether they are like us or not. And that are mindful of humans as only one dimension of a larger framework of living things.

This is an ethics committed to relationship—to an embodied regard for the "other" that doesn't promote a final resolution but rather that understands the need for perpetual effort toward an expanded sense of well-being. It is an ethical posture committed to struggling with uncertainty, recognizing the layered nature of this problem, and sensitive to the impact on the most vulnerable (with this category not limited to human beings). This is an ethical posture that is comfortable with vulnerability and that seeks to promote health and well-being to the degree either is possible within the context of a world that doesn't bend to our desires and wants.

NOTES

1 This chapter brings together and expands upon three pieces: "Mind the Gap: Humanist Thoughts on Christianity in the Age of Black Lives Matter," Berkley Forum, Berkley Center, Georgetown University, June 16, 2020; "Humanism's Vulnerable Human," *The Humanist* (May/June 2020): 19–20; "You Can't Theologize a Virus," *Sacred Matters*, April 13, 2020.

2 See, for example, M. Shawn Copeland, *Enfleshing Freedom: Body, Race, and Being* (Minneapolis: Fortress, 2009); CERCL Collective, *Embodiment and Black Religion: Rethinking the Body in African American Religious Experience* (London: Equinox, 2017); Mark D. Jordan, *Convulsing Bodies: Religion and Resistance in Foucault* (Stanford, CA: Stanford University Press, 2014); Kelly Brown Douglas, *What's Faith Got to Do with It? Black Bodies / Christian Souls* (Maryknoll, NY: Orbis, 2005).

3 James Cone, *A Black Theology of Liberation*, 20th ann. ed. (Maryknoll, NY: Orbis, 1993), xi.

4 Ibid., 17.

5 See Terrence Tilley, *The Evils of Theodicy* (Eugene, OR: Wipf and Stock, 2000); William R. Jones, *Is God a White Racist? A Preamble to Black Theology* (Boston: Beacon, 1996).

6 For more attention to my thinking on theodicy than provided here, see Pinn, *Why, Lord? Suffering and Evil in Black Theology* (New York: Continuum, 1995). For a more general discussion of theodicy, see, for example, John Hick, *Evil and the God of Love* (New York: Springer, 2010); Stephen T. Davis, *Encountering Evil: Live Options in Theodicy*, new ed. (Louisville, KY: Westminster John Knox, 2001); Wendy Farley, *Tragic Vision and Divine Compassion: A Contemporary Theodicy* (Louisville, KY: Westminster/John Knox, 1990); Emilie Townes, ed., *A Troubling in My Soul: Womanist Perspectives on Evil and Suffering* (Maryknoll, NY: Orbis, 1993).

7 I take up anthropodicy in "Is One Person's Theodicy Another's Anthropodicy? Preliminary Considerations," *Free Inquiry* 36, no. 2 (February/March 2016), https://secularhumanism.org.

8 Daniel Burke, "Police Arrest Florida Pastor for Holding Church Services Despite Stay-at-Home Order," CNN, March 30, 2020, www.cnn.com.

9 Candice Marie Benbow, "Coronavirus Is Forcing Black Churches to Make Tough Choices," *Zora,* March 18, 2020, https://zora.medium.com.

10 Will Peischel, "One of Trump's Favorite Pastors Says, 'All Natural Disasters Can Ultimately Be Traced to Sin,'" *Mother Jones*, March 14, 2020, www.motherjones .com.

11 Jackie Salo, "Ohio Lawmaker Refuses to Wear Mask Because Faces Are the 'Likeness of God,'" *New York Post*, May 5, 2020, https://nypost.com.

12 Will Bunch, "America Is Drunk on a Warped Idea of Freedom, and Now It's Killing People," *Philadelphia Inquirer*, June 28, 2020, www.inquirer.com.

13 Søren Kierkegaard, *Fear and Trembling* (Dublin: Merchant, 2012), 11–12.

14 Ibid., 12.

15 Ibid., 25.

16 Delores Williams, *Sisters in the Wilderness: The Challenge of Womanist God-Talk*, anniversary ed. (Maryknoll, NY: Orbis, 2013).

17 Ibid., 26.

18 Ibid., 145.

19 Genesis 21:15–16, as rendered in Williams, *Sisters in the Wilderness*, 30.

20 Kelly Brown Douglas, *Stand Your Ground: Black Bodies and the Justice of God* (Maryknoll, NY: Orbis, 2015).

21 James H. Cone, *The Cross and the Lynching Tree* (Maryknoll, NY: Orbis, 2011), 74.

22 Ibid., 161. Also see Cone, *God of the Oppressed* (New York: Harper, 1975). Much of what Cone and other Black theologians argue regarding God and redemption is undercut by William R. Jones, *Is God a White Racist? A Preamble to Black Theology* (Boston: Beacon, 1997).

23 Cone, *Cross and the Lynching Tree*, 28.

24 Robert Zaretsky, *A Life Worth Living* (Cambridge, MA: Harvard University Press, 2013), 23.

25 Richard Wright, *12 Million Black Voices* (New York: Basic, 2008), 130.

26 Michel Fabre, *The Unfinished Quest of Richard Wright*, 2nd ed. (Urbana: University of Illinois Press, 1993), xxxii.

27 Richard Wright, *White Man, Listen!* (New York: HarperPerennial, 1995), 95.

28 Albert Camus, *The Plague* (New York: Vintage International, 1991).

29 James Cone, *I Said I Wasn't Gonna Tell Nobody* (Maryknoll, NY: Orbis, 2018), 13.

30 Ibid., 124.

31 Albert Camus, *Myth of Sisyphus and Other Essays* (New York: Vintage International, 1991), 54.

32 Quoted in Cone, *Black Theology and Black Power* (Maryknoll, NY: Orbis, 1989), 124.

33 Ibid., 124.

34 In saying this, I am playing off the openness to multiple reads noted by Stephen Eric Bronner. See Bronner, *Camus: Portrait of a Moralist* (Chicago: University of Chicago Press, 1999), 70.

35 Cone, *God of the Oppressed*, 27, 29.

36 Stephen Metcalf, "Albert Camus' 'The Plague' and Our Own Great Reset," *Los Angeles Times*, March 23, 2020, www.latimes.com.

37 Alain de Botton, "Camus on the Coronavirus," *New York Times*, March 19, 2020, www.nytimes.com.

38 In fact, the publisher reports that the end of February 2020 showed an increase in sales of about 150 percent over the previous year. "Why You Should Read The Plague: The Albert Camus Novel the Coronavirus Has Made a Bestseller Again," *Literature*, March 13, 2020, www.openculture.com.

39 James Cone, *A Black Theology of Liberation*, 84.

40 Camus, *The Plague*, 308.

41 Sociologist Tony Brown argues for a direct relationship between anti-Black racism and health issues for African Americans. See, for example, R. Jay Turner, Tony N. Brown, and William B. Hale, "Race, Socioeconomic Position, and Physical Health: A Descriptive Analysis." *Journal of Health and Social Behavior* 58, no. 1: 23–36; Whitney N. Pirtle and Tony N. Brown, "Inconsistency within Expressed and Observed Racial Identifications: Implications for Mental Health Status," *Sociological Perspectives* 59, no. 3 (2016): 582–603.

5

The Corons and American Indian Genocide

Weaponizing Infectious Disease as the Continuation of a eurochristian Religious Project[1]

TINK TINKER (WAZHAZHE / OSAGE NATION)

Our young daughter started middle school as a sixth grader at the American Indian Academy of Denver, working in an unfamiliar online classroom structure from home because of the pandemic. Early on, we had a Zoom meeting (aren't all meetings now Zoom?) with a couple of her teachers. One Native teacher noted that many folk across the continent at that time saw the pandemic as "the apocalypse." Yet, she allowed, we Natives have survived so many apocalypses during the eurochristian conquest of Turtle Island;[2] this was just another one. Among other memories of genocide, American Indians carry the persistent memory that infectious disease was always a tool of eurochristian conquest and domination. We've done this before.[3]

Apocalypse

We do not have the space here to catalog all the dates and locations of the human and viral colonial invasions that have fractured Indigenous Nations and cultures during the past five hundred years. The words of these invaders stand as their own testimony to the tightly interwoven theology and practice that allowed them to see and use disease as a means to implement their god's plan for christian conquest and domination. Whether it was biblical notions of a "miraculous pestilence" come to the new world, or Daniel Denton's celebration of a "Divine Hand" making way for english settlement through deadly disease among the Natives, or Cotton Mather's joy over the clearing of "pernicious creatures" to make room for "better growth," or John Winthrop's zero-sum game of the Natives' death by sickness or submission to eurochristian domination—these earliest stories of eurochristian invasion of the continent reveal how the christian invaders saw disease as divine aid toward achieving the eurochristian goal of Native removal: that is, of Native genocide.

These earliest theological exhortations calling this calamity among Native Peoples a good and godly thing for eurochristian domination carried through all of the settling of the americas. In north america, we hear it repeatedly in the multiple Trails of Tears that reduced numerous Native Nations to the most threadbare hope of continued existence. It was a natural progression, it seems, that allowed the u.s., as a protestant nation, to adopt roman catholic civil law, called the "Doctrine-of-christian-Discovery," in order to justify their invasion and killing of the Native Peoples of Turtle Island as a less-than, non-christian People. From the beginning of the eurochristian invasion of Turtle Island until today, theology, religion, disease, and civil law are thoroughly intertwined.[4] For u.s. supreme court justice John Marshall, faith in Jesus Christ made the murder of Indian Peoples both righteous and legal.[5]

Let me take you back to one of the early english "Doctrine-of-christian-Discovery" claims to the domination of the north american continent—to an english king by the name of James Stuart, the same James who sponsored the groundbreaking english translation of the eurochristian bible, the so-called king James version (kjv) still in use today. The first genocidal eurochristian disease pandemic swept through northeast Turtle Island (the part they called new england) only a couple of years before the english moved north to invade those Native Lands to claim them. A very high percentage of coastal Native residents died from this (novel) foreign disease. The earliest english eurochristian response to Native dying was to rejoice—politically, theologically (i.e., religiously), and legally when their diseases unleashed genocidal pandemics among Native Peoples, so that by 1620 this king was able to credit his god with clearing the land for eurochristian invasion. Note his wording in this legal edict giving American Indian Lands to the colonialist corporation called "plymouth company": "There hath by God's Visitation reigned a wonderfull Plague, together with many horrible Slaugthers, and Murthers, committed amoungst the Sauages and brutish People there." Here is James Stuart's full sentence:

And also for that We have been further given certainly to knowe, that within these late Yeares there hath by God's Visitation reigned a wonderfull Plague, together with many horrible Slaugthers, and Murthers, committed amoungst the Sauages and brutish People there, heertofore inhabiting, in a Manner to the utter Destruction, Deuastacion, and Depopulacion of that whole Territorye, so that there is not left for many Leagues together in a Manner, any that doe claime or challenge any Kind of Interests therein, nor any other Superiour Lord or Souveraigne to make Claime "hereunto, whereby We in our Judgment are persuaded and satisfied that the appointed Time is come in which Almighty God in his great Goodness and Bountie towards Us and our People, hath thought fitt and determined, that those large and goodly Territoryes, deserted as it were by their naturall Inhabitants, should be possessed and enjoyed by such of our Subjects and People as heertofore have and hereafter shall by his Mercie and Favour, and by his Powerfull Arme, be directed and conducted thither.[6]

Indeed, it is a wonderful and powerful god who can clear whole populations of human beings to make way for "his" own favorite armed invaders.

Long before they had the science to identify a germ theory, however, eurochristians already knew about disease contagion, going back even to their own bible and certainly through the eurochristian middle ages.[7] Strict laws controlling the behavior of lepers in public were in force throughout the medieval european period.[8] There was even a formal church liturgy to initiate such exclusion in the high middle ages, something called a mass of separation that was performed by a priest at a leper's hut.[9] Just as eurochristians understood social distancing to contain disease transmission, however, they also understood how to weaponize physical proximity with an aim to create massive infection. Hence, they had already long used contagion as a method of warfare. Some historians have argued that the european/mediterranean pandemic called the Black Plague was initiated with the catapulting of infected dead bodies over the walls at the end of a three-year siege of Caffa (1344–1346),[10] and they knew how to capitalize on incidences of contagious disease. When the other colonialist group associated with the plymouth name (the heavily armed mayflower crowd) first arrived, the eurochristian pandemic mentioned in their king's document had paved the way. It had killed some 90-plus percent of the coastal population of what had been already renamed "new England" by the colonialist invaders.[11] The mayflower pilgrims expressed equal gratitude to their god for what they considered his expeditious slaughter of Native Peoples to prepare this new england for occupancy by a "new israel," a "new chosen people."

As Freeland and I argue, one common rationale eurochristians advance for Indian genocide is that most Indian deaths occurred by disease. While there is a numerical truth to the claim,[12] the raw data fails to take into account the exhaustion of Indian folk either enslaved or on the run from the brutality of invasion, leaving them especially vulnerable to the ravages of novel diseases among their populations. As Freeland and I continue to insist, everywhere eurochristian peoples went,

> they actively participated in the violent destruction of the Indigenous peoples by both direct killing as well as in that more enduring subjugation characterized as "conversion" to "civilization," a process that ensured cultural, political, and economic destruction. By destroying the culture, the colonizers actively destroyed native lives by denying them their usual access to food, traditional medicines, and cultural/religious ceremonies. The three active agents of disease, war, and cultural destruction, then, all worked simultaneously to generate a most efficient killing machine.[13]

On the other hand, we now know that many of the diseases were actually intentional infections caused by agents of the eurochristian invasion. Barbara Mann has written most powerfully about this proclivity of eurochristian warfare in Indian Country in a book titled *The Tainted Gift: The Disease Method of Frontier Expansion.*[14]

This historical trauma is the unshakeable memory that reared up in the minds of all Native folk as we confronted the reality of the 2020 global coronavirus pandemic. American Indian Peoples have a long and vicious history through the whole of this hemisphere with infectious diseases being used as a modality of conquest, and the religion of the eurochristian colonizer always was a part of the equation. Religion provides the easy rationale and actually drives domination. One close

Native colleague insisted that I should make this chapter very brief, allowing for only my title and this query: Are there any questions? But the problem is that eurochristians have such a short memory and are so deeply rooted in a habitual flurry of denial mechanisms and the deeply romantic imaginary narrative of their own conquest of the continent as an unmitigated good that they will often be left baffled by any real evidence to the contrary. So, as always, we are forced to explain. To explain ourselves, to fill in details, historical details that our eurochristian relatives have conveniently forgotten, erased from their memories even as they created monuments to mark the romance of their own presence and conquest of this continent called Turtle Island.[15]

The Corons

This current pandemic has wreaked its own havoc among People of Color, poor folk in the u.s., and particularly Native Peoples in hugely disproportionate magnitudes compared to its effect on White eurochristian society. It has amplified vulnerabilities that are already present in American Indian communities as a result of 528 years of invasion, conquest, and colonization, with the repeated introduction of infectious diseases. From an Indian perspective, it seems as if this pandemic actually allowed the sociopolitical whole to function in ways that work—have always worked—toward the earliest goal of the eurochristian invaders to erase any lingering Native presence or identity on the continent other than the colonizers' romantic and overtly racist mascot-ization. Today, Native Peoples control only a tiny part of their original homeland territories, but Natives still control considerable access to what natural extractive resources the eurochristian industrialist elites consider precious. They had deemed these lands largely economically unviable a century and a half ago when Indians were forced onto desperate and semiarid reservations. Yet suddenly today, having discovered those subsurface resources, the colonialists want what the Natives have left. And COVID-19 is giving them cover for extending their reach. Somewhere deep in the eurochristian colonial subconsciousness, there remains a narrative of a justifiable abjection of Native Peoples. Hence, Native genocide can be explained as some sort of a natural, if not outright godly, prerequisite of some cosmic eschatological design. Today's alternative is to blame

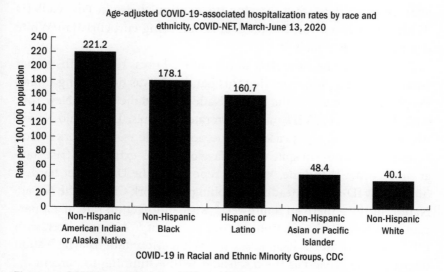

Figure 5.1. COVID-19 in Racial and Ethnic Minority Groups. Source: "Health Equity Considerations and Racial and Ethnic Minority Groups," Centers for Disease Control and Prevention, February 12, 2021.[16]

the Native, their inadequacies and their natural inabilities, for their own demise—even in the face of stark evidence to the contrary.

In early July 2020, the u.s. federal Centers for Disease Control and Prevention (CDC) published a startling comparative chart, tracing the hospitalization rates for different racialized ethnic groups in the u.s. As is immediately apparent, People of Color (PoC) are far more likely than eurochristian folk to contract more lethal pathologies with this virus. And American Indian Peoples, the aboriginal inhabitants of the continent, are the most vulnerable statistically. Indians required hospitalization at a rate nearly six times that of eurochristians / White americans.

Journalists reported in late July that Donald Trump continued publicly to shirk responsibility for and struggled to cover up his own presidential incompetence by blaming People of Color for the spread of this pandemic,[17] even as his top national infectious disease advisor, Anthony Fauci, acknowledged that Black, Indigenous, and Latinx communities have been hit hardest by this pandemic.[18] By August 5, CNN reported an even greater disparity in infection rates among children based on ethnicity, skin color, and socioeconomic status in the u.s.[19] By February

2021, research data were showing the continued rise in PoC COVID deaths, with American Indian deaths outpacing eurochristian/White deaths by nearly double.[20]

It had already become clear in the national press two months earlier (mid-May 2020), however, that this pandemic was devastating Indian Peoples in particular, as the Navajo Nation passed the state of New York with the highest COVID-19 infection rate in the u.s. The Navajo Nation was experiencing 2,304 cases per 100,000 people vs. New York's 1,806 cases per 100,000—in spite of the Navajo Nation's extremely strict stay-at-home order.[21] In June, WebMD reported, "The U.S. center hardest hit by COVID-19 isn't headline-grabbing New York City; it's the Navajo Nation in the American Southwest," with an infection rate of 3.4 percent vs. a New York infection rate of 1.9 percent.[22] A month later, with little notice outside of local press, the White Mountain Apache Nation displaced the Navajo as the u.s. leader with a stunning 10 percent infection rate.[23] Indeed, five Indian National reservation communities were far outdistancing any u.s. state in mid-June: after White Mountain came the Zia, San Felipe, Navajo, and Kewa Nations.[24] A month later the Mississippi Band of Choctaw Nation doubled the infection rate of the White Mountain Apache, and eight Indian Nations were outdistancing any state, again, largely unnoticed by any non-Native press.[25] Nations like the Cheyenne River Lakota and Pine Ridge, both in south Dakota, avoided such ignominy only because their leadership flat-out defied that state's governor, who presumed to have authority over another sovereign Nation. They put up roadblock checkpoints to reduce traffic through their reservation boundaries—on so-called federal highways.[26]

The COVID-19 pandemic put Native Peoples throughout the hemisphere on high alert. Historical memories of disease as a eurochristian weapon of invasion are intermingled with alarm at the deadliness of this current virus. Yet few non-Natives remember that infectious disease was always a favorite way for the eurochristians to clear the land they so coveted of its rightful Native inhabitants[27]—because it allowed for plausible deniability and the claim of christian innocence. Yet today, those eurochristian folk still covet those Native lands that are left, mostly to further their extractive industries—from mines, tar sands, and shale oil deposits to the pipelines used to transfer that Native wealth (Native capital?) to eurochristian processing factories. COVID-19 made that process much easier as eurochristian governments worked to limit large gatherings (read, e.g., pipeline protests) while pipeline equipment delivery services and construction (threatening Indigenous territories) were summarily labeled as essential work. So, full speed ahead, and thanks be to god for COVID-19. It has become second nature to use disease, especially pandemic disease, as a legitimate excuse for grabbing Indigenous Lands and natural resources.

Today the main colonialist concern is not the mere *taking* of Indian Lands, although the Trump administration certainly tried to do that in the case of Mashpee Land on Cape Cod.[28] Rather, today the issue is ensuring that eurochristian captains of industry can continue to rape Indian natural resources without legal or moral accountability, and COVID-19 made that much easier as it rendered protest and resistance much more difficult. Reports persist of pipeline companies using the COVID quarantine time to covertly move in equipment for their next pipeline expansion opportunity. The provincial energy minister in Alberta, Canada, went so far as to say explicitly that companies should use the pandemic as a cover to subvert Native protests, given the restrictions on the size of any gathering.[29]

At the same time, the u.s. federal government continues to invent ways to circumvent its Treaty responsibilities toward Indian Peoples. A prime example is the Trump administration's long delay in the delivery of CARES Act funding to Indian Nations to help their containment of the viral spread.[30] Whether one calls this delay aggression or microaggression, it demonstrates the willful negligence of the u.s. federal government toward Indian Peoples—particularly, we might note, with regard to Treaty Obligations rooted in article vi of the u.s. constitution. My argument here is that even the procedural negligence practiced by the u.s. federal government has its roots in the subliminal depths of the eurochristian religious psyche. I mean here to call up both the extent to which Indian Peoples can be ignored and neglected in spite of Treaties because the dominant thinking is so rooted in the righteousness of the eurochristian conquest and domination of Native Peoples, and the extent to which the democratic capitalist system has become equally rooted in the deep consciousness of eurochristian colonialist folk. And I want to be clear that this sort of framing of reality is in my mind the substance of religious thinking at a structural level.[31]

Make no mistake about it: the reigning political economy of the u.s. is thoroughly steeped in that religious psyche, even without using the language of jesus or god, and that is even more apparent in this time of broad social crisis around the pandemic. Democratic capitalism is much more than an economic theory. It is founded in and framed by the soft substance of religious thinking that caused the lieutenant governor of the state of Texas, Dan Patrick, to claim that elderly americans, including himself, should be willing to die from COVID-19 in order to save the american economy.[32] That is religious language, traditional eurochristian religious language, the language of sacrifice and salvation, language that is inherently anthropocentric. It is rooted in that White Supremacist religious notion that frames american Exceptionalism as such a politically pious and devout faith.[33] Using more secularized synonyms, we might say patriotic and dutiful, but piety and devotion are just under the surface. This is so deeply rooted in that habitual structure of White Supremacist thinking that democratic capitalism, as it has morphed in north America, is the only possibility imaginable for humans to govern themselves. It is preternaturally correct, both politically and economically undergirded by a patriotic spirituality, something that must be evangelically imposed on other countries—for their own betterment in the image of god or the image of the u.s. On the other hand, American Indians remember too vividly that our ancestors died of infectious diseases precisely to build the u.s. economy and national wealth.[34] And, contra Dan Patrick, too many of those Natives who died in past pandemics or have died of today's coronavirus have been those elders who are carriers of the cultural traditions and remaining fluent speakers of Native languages.

As Indian Peoples became increasingly infected and began dying in Indian communities across Turtle Island in early 2020, Indian memories of that history of Indian genocide leapt back to life. Indians, unfortunately, know how to do this. It seems that the eurochristian colonial power structure also remembers. One Indian community asked for face masks and testing supplies to help combat the COVID-19 pandemic; they received a shipment of body bags. "My team turned ghost white," said Esther Lucero, chief executive officer of the Seattle Indian Health Board. "We asked for tests, and they sent us a box of body bags." The package, filled with zippered white bags, came with beige tags instructing, "Attach to toe."[35] A one-off mistake? Or is it every ten years? To wit, in 2009 during another pandemic: "The Canadian government sent body bags to some remote Indian reserves (in Manitoba) . . . , sending a jarring message at odds with its promise that [it was] ready for the H1N1 flu."[36]

Survival: Enemies or Relatives?

I began this chapter with an insight from a teacher at my daughter's school, the American Indian Academy of Denver. This teacher named what we Indian people know so well—that we have endured centuries of eurochristian conquest and domination, and yet our worldview and cultures and customs are still vibrant and very much a part of our everyday lives as Indigenous Peoples. This is true even in the time of the novel coronavirus. For the eurochristian world, the response to the virus falls into their usual framed dichotomy of good versus evil. Any internet search on the keywords "COVID" and "evil" returns a multitude of results that all contain "evil" in the title. And as we have seen in the history of the eurochristian invasion and colonization of Turtle Island, anything deemed evil must be viewed through the lens of a righteous battle, a godly enterprise, where the enemy must be vanquished through force. In the COVID era, we are seeing the militarization of the discourse about the virus.

Is the real enemy the virus itself? Or is it a political system that has, through generations, ensured Native demise through strategic use of disease and dispossession of our Lands? More generally, from an Indian perspective, the total inadequacy of the government, particularly the u.s. federal government, has helped make this pandemic so catastrophic for people on this continent.

This brings us to one last deeply religious eurochristian aspect of the COVID crisis, and one that affects Indian Peoples as much as it does others in this broadly colonized society. Namely, I am concerned about this metaphorical militarization of COVID and the COVID response—a framing of the pandemic that goes hand in hand with the eurochristian "angry and punitive god" fantasy that I mentioned earlier. Why must any exceptional action be cast through a militarized filter? Suddenly, every nurse, every grocery clerk, every "essential" employee is working on the "front line" of some militarized conflict. They are envisioned as frontline workers in the struggle to defeat the enemy coronavirus. In no way do I intend to demean or minimize their courage or the importance of what they do for the greater social whole. Rather, in moments of reflection during home quarantine, I have come to recognize a deeper worldview difference in the eurochristian response to this pandemic.

Something deeply embedded in the eurochristian religious psyche generates war imagery as the default response to any natural-world moment of imbalance that threatens humans, including this global pandemic. From an Indian perspective, however, the coronavirus is not an enemy. Rather, the global conditions that humans have created, with their state governments and wealth-generating industries, have given rise to the spread of this novel virus; the organism is a natural response to the imbalances resulting from human greed and overextension. For the eurochristian, however, the natural world is too often a threat to be vanquished and controlled by noble human warriors. This was starkly illustrated by a Chicago news editorial published in the wake of Hurricane Katrina, proclaiming, "human nature is stronger than mother nature." Those words eventually became a fundraising slogan for hurricane relief.[37]

We can easily see that the historic eurochristian religion has always been framed by military metaphors. This can be traced in more modern times in hymns like "onward christian soldiers" or "Stand up, stand up for Jesus, ye soldiers of the cross" to the older hymnody cast regularly in terms of christian triumph, triumph in a cosmic struggle between good and evil in which the christ event secures victory over death and the devil, the personification of evil. The military metaphorizing of christian faith can be tracked in medieval european thought through the actual military crusades to conquer Palestinians' Lands, which are held to be inherently christian, as well as the proliferation of religious orders of knights like the knights templar, the hospitallers of st. john, or the teutonic knights, who served their god by arming up and fighting and killing the enemies / infidels of their god. That framing does not simply go away over time; rather it morphs today into a variety of secular mutations. For instance, political campaigns, marketing campaigns, or funding campaigns for colleges or churches frame their everyday activities as military actions, campaigns, or movements of an army through the countryside. And of course, the cosmic struggle between good and evil characterizes nearly every aspect of u.s. foreign policy, or it morphs into the militarized, heavily armed christian identity / white nationalist movement. And indeed that is what we have in the response to COVID-19. The current high priests of eurochristian religion, the physicians and the scientists, are then deployed to slay the dragon and defeat the COVID-19 enemy.

In this way, then, the sociopolitical whole has militarized COVID as some wicked enemy of the people. Disease and death are enemies for which the christian religion is the answer, since their jesus won the victory over death. All of this underscores the particularity of the salvific eurochristian worldview at its deepest. Of course coronavirus is the enemy since humans are the apex of their god's anthropocentric creation and of utmost importance. Anthropocentrism is the foundation of the whole of militarized religion and culture in the euro-west.

For American Indian Peoples, living a traditional culture, the pandemic is framed in a completely different way. This novel coronavirus is simply another life form. It is simply doing its best to make sure that it propagates and stays alive. Human beings just happen to be the best and most readily available hosts at the time. As I have reminded my students on many occasions, an Indigenous worldview or cosmology is thoroughly rational. There is a reciprocal balance to all elements of the universe—a natural algorithm, we might say. In a typical healing ceremony, the *ieska*, or interpreter, would eventually ask the disease (the cancer, the virus, or whatever ails the supplicant) to leave the person and go away to another part of the universe where it might no longer be a danger to any other living being. The disease or unsettling spirit presence is never "destroyed," but rather it is dealt with respectfully in a way that sends it off somewhere else to continue its own life apart from us. There is no evil; there is only balance and imbalance, harmony and disharmony. Oren Lyons reminded us all back in 1987: "From where we come from, the natural law is simple in this case: We will suffer in exact ratio to our transgressions, and the damage done may be permanent to life as we know it today."[38]

From an American Indian perspective, it is just another relative, not nearly as much to be feared as is the u.s. federal government and its extractive industries in their relationships with Indian Peoples. But this virus, like every virus, has only one goal. That goal is to stay alive and to do what it must to replicate and reproduce itself. It is doing what viruses do naturally. Humans have just proven to be very amenable hosts for COVID-19, so they readily attach to us in order to thrive and populate. Respecting the virus as a relative does not mean that I will not also do my utmost to stay alive and to keep my family alive. That is my responsibility, but we cannot do that successfully by naming another life form as an enemy. Indeed, if there is an enemy, it seems that the real enemy is the stupidity of human beings who no longer remember how to live in a balanced relationship with the world around us, whose activity in the world has pressured the novel coronavirus away from its usual habitat.

American Indians hold a vastly different worldview from eurochristians, even of our more liberal allies and especially those New Age religionists who spuriously claim to have adopted our worldview—as if it were that easy. Most importantly for this chapter on the coronavirus, our worldview sees all of life as interrelated and connected through relationship. My daughter is buffalo clan and has a particularly close relationship with the Buffalo Nation, but at age eleven she is self-conscious of being in relationship these days with butterflies, moths, grasshoppers, and spiders. She fearlessly tracks down spiders in our home to collect them and place them carefully outside the home so that they do not get stepped on or damaged. That is relationship.

Some years ago, we rebuilt our *iⁿ uⁿgliⁿ tse* (our sitting-with-the-stones house, what eurochristians call a sweat lodge) on a new site to allow the Earth to renew itself at the old site. By the second time we used the lodge, some red ants had also moved in and begun building a new nest right in the back of the lodge, something that we did not notice at first. Then, in the midst of ceremony, several persons in the lodge got bit by these ants, which were now objecting to our invading their home. These lodges take considerable time and energy to build, involving collecting enough willows to make the half-dome structure, a particularly difficult task for urban Indians who have to travel out of the city to gather willows, especially to gather them legally. Later that week a couple of us went back out to the lodge and without covering it sat down for ceremony in the lodge. We began by making an offering of apology to those ants, but then we spoke with those relatives to ask them in a good way, a heartfelt way, if they might move their home over some ways to allow us to continue to meet in the site we had built our lodge. A few days later, when we went back out for our usual ceremony, the ants had indeed moved to another location, requiring us to respond with a thank-you in that day's ceremony. And there were two new anthills just a short way away on either side of our lodge.

We can add one thing here. Those ants already knew that we had a deep respect for them as relatives. About fifty yards from the lodge site itself, in a break in the scrub oaks covering the Land, was a place where we were able to park two or three cars. One of our elders noticed one day that some red ants had built a home right in the middle of that *parking* space. So, out of respect for their home, the old man dragged three large tree stumps from our firewood pile and placed them on top of the ant lodge to prevent anyone from parking on top of the ants. He reduced our parking space, obviously, but we were able to maintain a good relationship with the Ant Nation. Twenty-five years later, the remnants of those logs are still sitting on top of that ant home, protecting them from an inadvertent human invasion and destruction. You see, this novel coronavirus, like those red ants, have their own life and ways and certainly deserve to live and do what they do. We humans need to respect that even as we try to protect ourselves from their harmful effects on our human bodies. As his uncle explains to Tayo in Silko's novel *Ceremony*, nothing in the world is all good or all bad. In our Indian understanding of the world, every living thing, including rocks, have their own life and place in the cosmic whole. And each has its own role in maintaining the balance of the whole. And all of them are our relatives: like those red ants, even this virus.[39]

Declaring COVID-19 to be an enemy to be wiped out would be too anthropocentric and ultimately too self-destructive. Perhaps we need to rethink how we humans have overrun the planet and made usual places of habitation no longer habitable. We have violated our relationships and agreements with all the other nonhuman nations who live on this planet. So instead of declaring them enemies, the real questions are how we might find a way to live in the world together and how we can take care of ourselves without merely blaming the viral other. In order to survive and thrive, we must think in terms of relationship rather than domination and eradication. How do we live in balance—as Indian Peoples always have with the world around them—with these threatening new viruses? Is getting a vaccine a way to sustain a relationship with this virus? Yes: we can ask this virus to find a home that is not deadly to two-leggeds, so that the relationship can continue as a more balanced one. I certainly embrace the vaccine—but not at the cost of making enemies of the corons or any new novel virus that might appear over the horizon. The problem with making enemies is that the list of possible new enemies that we must confront never ends. We need a better metaphor for framing our lives and our existence on this earth and a better way of maintaining our health and balance.

In an important sense, of course, we humans created this pandemic around COVID-19. That is, we created the expanded natural habitat that made the spread of this virus inevitable by crowding those natural host animals with our ever-spreading human populations, industries, technologies, and so on. Viruses that were once living in remote corners of the earth are finding that those corners are not so remote anymore. Bat caves are increasingly being encroached on by expanding urban metropolises, meaning that humans are increasingly invading those corners to extract natural resources even from the bats themselves. Humans simply cannot forever expand into new territories without experiencing consequences—as we have so dramatically discovered in this pandemic moment and will rediscover with the next. The novel coronavirus COVID-19 is certainly not the last.

In the meantime, we need to call on our eurochristian relatives and others around the globe to learn how to live with their nonhuman relatives in harmony and balance, to see these others as relatives rather than resources to be used up or enemies to be destroyed. As a beginning, we call upon our eurochristian relatives to learn how to live in a healthy, healing relationship with the Natives of this Land, with American Indian Nations.

NOTES

1 My idiosyncratic convention for capitalizing or not-capitalizing initial letters of certain words is very intentional. Using the lower case "christian" or "puritan" or even "u.s." allows readers to avoid unnecessary automatic normativizing or universalizing of the principal institutional religious, political, or social quotients of the christian euro-west. At the same time I insist on capitalizing American Indian, Native, and White (both as nouns and as adjectives). "White" intends to indicate a clear cultural pattern invested in Whiteness that is all too often overlooked

or even denied by american Whites. At the same time, I leave my synonym for White, "eurochristian," uncapitalized to avoid any unnecessary centering of the european or christian Self in the mind of the reader.

2   The eurochristian invaders renamed everything. Turtle Island they now call north america.

3   For my sociological usage of the category signifier *eurochristian* see my essay, "What Are We Going to Do with White People?," *The New Polis*, December 17, 2019, https://thenewpolis.com.

4   Steve Newcomb, *Pagans in the Promised Land: Decoding the Doctrine of Chrisitan Discovery* (Golden, CO: Fulcrum, 2008).

5   Johnson v. M'Intosh (1823). To wit, the unanimous decision for the court by justice John Marshall. Marshall is crystal clear that religion, the christian religion of the invader, makes the conquest, killing, and Land theft both moral and especially legal:

> On the **discovery** of this immense continent, the great nations of Europe were eager to appropriate to themselves so much of it as they could respectively acquire. Its vast extent offered an ample field to the ambition and enterprise of all; and the character and religion of its inhabitants afforded an apology for considering them as a people over whom the superior genius of Europe might claim an ascendency. The potentates of the old world found no difficulty in convincing themselves that they made ample compensation to the inhabitants of the new, by bestowing on them civilization and Christianity, in exchange for unlimited independence. But, as they were all in pursuit of nearly the same object, it was necessary, in order to avoid conflicting settlements, and consequent war with each other, to establish a principle, which all should acknowledge as the law by which the right of acquisition, which they all asserted, should be regulated as between themselves. This principle was, that discovery gave title to the government by whose subjects, or by whose authority, it was made, **against all other European governments**, which title might be consummated by possession. (Emphases added)

6   "The Charter of New England: 1620," *The Federal and State Constitutions Colonial Charters, and Other Organic Laws of the States, Territories, and Colonies Now or Heretofore Forming the United States of America*, compiled and edited under the Act of Congress of June 30, 1906 by Francis Newton Thorpe (Washington, DC: Government Printing Office, 1909), Yale Law School Avalon Project, accessed May 17, 2020, https://avalon.law.yale.edu.

7   Kenrad E. Nelson and Carolyn F. Williams, "Early History of Infections Disease," in Kenrad E. Nelson and Carolyn F. Williams, eds., *Infectious Disease Epidemiology: Theory and Practice*, 3rd ed. (Burlington, MA: Jones and Bartlett Learning, 2014), 3–18. For eurochristian biblical injunctions, see Leviticus 13:44–46 which states, "Now whosoever shall be defiled with the leprosy, and is separated by the judgment of the priest, shall have his clothes hanging loose, his

head bare, his mouth covered with a cloth, and he shall cry out that he is defiled and unclean. All the time that he is infected and unclean, he shall dwell alone without the camp."

8 Church councils and royal courts both established laws segregating lepers and forcing them to persistently self-identify in public. See Herbert C. Covey, "People with Leprosy (Hansen's Disease) during the Middle Ages," *Social Science Journal* 38, no. 2 (2001): www.tandfonline.com.

9 One example is recorded by liturgical scholar Edmond Martene, *De Antiquis Ecclesiae Ritibus* (1783), Ordo I. For another, see Alficia Sehgal, *Leprosy* (New York: Infobase, 2006), 15.

10 Jeanne Guillemin, *Biological Weapons: From the Invention of State-Sponsored Programs to Contemporary Bioterrorism* (New York: Columbia University Press, 2005), 3; Mark Wheelis, "Biological Warfare at the 1346 Siege of Caffa," *Emerging Infectious Diseases* 8, no. 9 (2002): 971–75, https://wwwnc.cdc.gov. One of Wheelis's annotations suggests, "Medieval society lacked a coherent theory of disease causation. Three notions coexisted in a somewhat contradictory mixture: 1) disease was a divine punishment for individual or collective transgression; 2) disease was the result of 'miasma,' or the stench of decay; and 3) disease was the result of person-to-person contagion."

11 John Smith, former leader of Jamestown, sailed the coast exploring invasion sites in 1614 and formally named new england as colonial property in a map published in 1616.

12 Tink Tinker and Mark Freeland, "Thief, Slave-Trader, Murderer: Christopher Columbus and Caribbean Population Decline," *Wicazo Sa Review* (Spring 2008): 36.

13 Ibid.

14 Barbara Alice Mann, *The Tainted Gift: The Disease Method of Frontier Expansion* (Santa Barbara: Praeger, 2009). Using primary-source evidence, Mann closely analyzes four historical occurrences between 1760 and 1850 when infectious disease was deliberately spread among Indian communities.

15 Throughout June and July 2020, of course, many of those icons of eurochristian civil worship have come tumbling down in the eruption of the Black Lives Matter protests. Besides the statues of confederate defenders of chattel slavery that came down in that period, we saw the downfall of Columbus statues across the continent, even in Columbus, Ohio; statues of "saint" Junípero Serra in California—to the consternation of ignorant catholic archbishops; and statues of romantic christian heroes like Kit Carson, the Indian murderer.

16 For a later report, see Pinar Karaca-Mandic, Archelle Georgiou, and Sourmya Sen, "Assessment of COVID-19 Hospitalizations by Race/Ethnicity in 12 States," *JAMA Internal Medicine*, August 17, 2020, doi:10.1001/jamainternmed.2020.3857, https://jamanetwork.com. CDC updates of its COVID-related racial-ethnic statistics indicated little substantial change. American Latinos and American Indians continued to lead all hospitalizations for COVID, followed closely by

African Americans, and all three categories ranked hospitalizations at three to four times the rate for White COVID sufferers (CDC, "COVID-19 Racial and Ethnic Health Disparities," updated December 10, 2020). Also note the very similar mid-November report: Aris Folley, "Black, Latino and Native American People Being Hospitalized with COVID-19 at Roughly Four Times Rate of White Counterparts: CDC," *The Hill*, November 17, 2020. The overrepresentation of Indians, Blacks, and Latinos was consistent and persistent over the first ten months of the pandemic.

17 Lindsey Ellefson, "MSNBC's Scarborough: Trump Is 'Blaming Black and Brown People' for Coronavirus Rise," The Wrap, July 23, 2020, www.msn.com.

18 "Dr. Fauci on Why Coronavirus Is Wreaking Havoc on Black Communities," CBS News, July 30, 2020, www.msn.com.

19 Madeline Holcomb, "Schools Find There's No One-Size-Fits-All Approach to Returning to Campus during Coronavirus Outbreak," CNN, August 5, 2020. Also see "Children from Minority and Lower Socioeconomic Backgrounds at Greater Risk," August 5, 2020, www.cnn.com.

20 Nina Lakhani, "Exclusive: Indigenous Americans Dying from Covid at Twice the Rate of White Americans: One in Every 475 Native Americans Has Died since the Pandemic Began," *The Guardian*, February 4, 2021, www.theguardian.com.

21 Hollie Silverman, Konstantin Toropin, Sara Sidner, and Leslie Perrot, "Navajo Nation Surpasses New York State for the Highest Covid-19 Infection Rate in the US," CNN, May 18, 2020, www.cnn.com.

22 Alan Mozes, "Covid-19 Ravages the Navajo Nation," *WebMD: HealthDay Reporter*, June 9, 2020, www.webmd.com.

23 Chelsea Curtis, "10% of Arizona Reservation Has Covid-19, and Many Have No Drinking Water," *Arizona Republic*, July 17, 2020, www.azcentral.com.

24 Yaodong Gu, "Native American Communities Hit Harder Than Some States, Research Finds," *Cronkite News*, June 15, 2020, www.indianz.com. Also, according to the report,

> The disproportionate impact COVID-19 has had on minorities underscores the longstanding failure of federal officials to respond to the needs of Native Americans, Rep. Betty McCollum said Thursday in a subcommittee meeting on the Indian Health Service. "Five tribes are experiencing more instances of coronavirus per 100,000 citizens than any states, including New York," the Minnesota Democrat said, citing data from the American Indian Studies Center at UCLA and Indian Country Today. According to a data visualization posted by UCLA researchers, if COVID-19 infection rates were scaled per 100,000 people and if tribes were states, the top five infection rates nationwide would be tribes [sic] (UCLA American Indian Studies Center, "Coronavirus in Indian Country: Latest Case Counts," last update June 16, 2020, www.aisc.ucla.edu).
> In late July, UCLA listed seven Native Nations exceeding the infection rate of New York and all other states (updated for mid-July: UCLA American

Indian Studies Center, "Coronavirus in Indian Country: Latest Case Counts," data last updated on July 20, 2020, for data through July 14, 2020, www.aisc .ucla.edu.

25 "Coronavirus in Indian Country: Latest Case Counts," last updated July 20, 2020.

26 David K. Li, "South Dakota Tribes Defy Governor and Maintain Checkpoints in Coronavirus Fight," NBC News, May 10, 2020, www.nbcnews.com. "We have every legal right to do what we're doing," said Cheyenne River Sioux tribe chairman Harold Frazier. "We're just doing preventative action."

27 The best analysis of the later period in the eurochristian-induced disease method of conquest is Mann, *Tainted Gift*. The desire for American Indian Lands is clearly articulated in american eurochristian legal theory by supreme court justice John Marshall in his unanimous decision in Johnson v. M'Intosh (1823). See note 4 in this chapter.

28 "Secretary of the Interior Has Ordered Mashpee Wompanoag Tribe 'Disestablished,' Tribe Says," CBS Boston, March 28, 2020, https://boston.cbslo cal.com. After a court ruling blocked the DOI move, the Mashpee got strong congressional support in the house of representatives (Mashpee-Wampanoag Nation, "Mashpee Wampanoag Tribe Applauds Legislation Passed by U.S. House to Protect Land," https://mashpeewampanoagtribe-nsn.gov).

29 Melanie Woods, "Alberta Energy Minister Says Pandemic Gathering Ban a "Great Time' for Pipelines: Energy Minister Sonya Savage Said Bans on Gatherings Like Protests Makes Pipeline Construction Easier," *Huffington Post*, May 2, 2020, www .huffingtonpost.ca.

30 Acee Agoyo, "'We Got These Monies Late': Trump Administration Makes Tribes Wait More Than 80 Days for Full COVID-19 Relief," *indianz.com*, June 17, 2020, www.indianz.com; Jennifer Bendery, "Republicans Spin Trump's Awful Record on Tribal Issues to Make It Sound Amazing," *Politics: Huffington Post*, August 25, 2020, www.huffpost.com. The CARES Act did include a historic $8 billion for tribes, but that's only because Senate Democrats fought to include it. The White House wanted to give tribes $0. And once the bill became law, the Trump administration failed to distribute that money for weeks—leaving tribes with no federal help as Native American communities were ravaged by the coronavirus. See "Tribal Nations More Vulnerable to COVID-19 Impacts, Need Additional Fiscal Aid," Center on Budget and Policy Priorities, www.cbpp.org.

31 I should note here that I treat religion as largely a modern invented category. It is a broad eurochristian category of cognition that, in my mind, became inclusive of deeply held social and political normatives in the eurochristian and globalized social whole. Insofar as it is usually imposed on the colonized Other, it is always an invented term used to extend colonialist control over the Other. As such, American Indians had (and have had) no religion until the advent of eurochristian missionaries and their modalities of conversion therapy. It is a category, then, that simply cannot function as a useful descriptor of any reality in a precolonial, traditional, or decolonized American Indian world. See my

own work for the argument that "religion" has nothing to do with any reality in the traditional American Indian world: Tinker, "Religious Studies: The Final Colonization of American Indians," *Religious Theory*, e-supplement to *Journal of Cultural and Religious Theory*, June 1, 2020, http://jcrt.org. For the invention of religion, see also David Chidester, *Empire of Religion: Imperialism and Comparative Religion* (Chicago: University of Chicago Press, 2013). Chidester had previously demonstrated that whether colonial interpreters identified Natives in southern Africa as having a religion or not depended largely on the political needs of the eurochristian colonizer at any given moment. See his *Savage Systems: Colonialism and Comparative Religion in Southern Africa* (Charlottesville: University of Virginia Press, 1996).

32 Jamie Knodel, "Texas Lt. Gov. Dan Patrick Suggests He and Other Seniors Willing to Die to Get Economy Going again," NBC News, March 24, 2020, www.nbcnews.com.

33 One is reminded, at least obliquely, of Bellah's notion of american civil religion in this regard. See Robert N. Bellah, "Civil Religion in America," *Daedalus* 96, no. 1 (Winter 1967): 1–21, www.robertbellah.com.

34 Again, see Mann, *Tainted Gift*.

35 Eric Ortiz, "Native American Health Center Asked for COVID-19 Supplies. It Got Body Bags Instead," NBC News, May 6, 2020, www.nbcnews.com.

36 "Body Bags Disrupt Canada's Flu-Readiness Message," Reuters, September 16, 2009, https://ca.reuters.com.

37 David Hiller, "To Our Readers," *Chicago Tribune*, September 4, 2005, www.chicagotribune.com.

38 Oren Lyons, "Traditional Native Perspectives," *Orion Nature Quarterly* 9, no. 3 (Summer 1990): 33–34. From a talk given at the Fourth World Wilderness Congress in Denver, in 1987.

39 See "The Irrelevance of Euro-christian Dichotomies for Indigenous Peoples: Beyond Non-violence to a Vision of Cosmic Balance," in Irfan A. Omar and Joshua Burns, eds., *Peacemaking and the Challenge of Violence in World Religions* (Hoboken, NJ: Wiley-Blackwell, 2015), 206–29.

6

Love Crafts Countries

Loving beyond the White Divide—A Story of Blackness, Korea, and Transformative Power on the Damascus Road

BLANCHE BONG COOK

Onshore, holding everything together, but willing to risk and go far out to sea, courage, domesticity. This is what Black people mean to me and still mean to each other, but for me, the history of the place of Black people in his country is so varied, complex, and beautiful, and impactful—made a big impact. Nobody could have loved as much as we did, went on with life as much as we did—carried on—and considering the efforts to make sure we never did—Considering that—it is amazing.
—Toni Morrison, *The Pieces That I Am*

Nobody is free until everybody is free.
—Fannie Lou Hamer

The visionary television series *Lovecraft Country* illuminates the absurdity of being Black in America. Through the use of Afrofuturism, *Lovecraft Country* exposes the perilous nature, unfathomable nightmare, and unspeakable horror of white supremacist terrorism and the perennial precarity of being Black—a knowledge that, at any moment, the state can end your life and you will be blamed for your own death (Trayvon Martin, Michael Brown, Sandra Bland, and Breonna Taylor all starred in their own nightmare made real).[1] By collapsing space and time and enlisting the stuff of nightmares, *Lovecraft* maps the ravages of white supremacy and Black terror. The drama starts with the lead Black protagonists taking a road trip through the American South, only to be chased by life-size COVID-like viruses—giant man-eating gelatinous amphibians that emerge from the earth's core. These bumpy, bulbous monsters, however, pale in comparison to the white police officers (and other white terrorists) who dispense random and relentless legally sanctioned violence with the relish and euphoria of a grinning lynch mob. Pouring battery acid into gaping wounds and drawing an even tighter fit between horror and Black reality, the white antagonists gaslight the Black protagonists—subjecting them to supernatural illusions, making them doubt the reality of the attacks against them, or making them think the terrorism is imagined.[2] Compare Trayvon Martin, a seventeen-year-old Black teenager walking to a candy store only to find himself attacked by a monster, and blamed for his own murder in a court of law and public opinion. Like rape victims, casualties of police violence cannot expose the violation, because upsetting the power structure makes it upset—the violator never wants his savagery revealed and laid bare for all the world to see. Similar to the plight of so-called Korean comfort women—the hundreds of thousands of women and girls the Japanese imperial soldiers enslaved sexually in military brothels from Seoul to Singapore—when these women sought redress, the Japanese became upset and experienced "apology fatigue." These are *Lovecraft* spaces.

Despite its ghoulishness, *Lovecraft* also addresses Afro-pessimism, specifically the transformative power to step outside one's material conditions in order to find love, solidarity, and purpose. Lovecraft Country occupants can see beyond the material evil of power as it is a raced, classed, and gendered white heteropatriarchy (the "WHP"), and find value and love in their fellow Lovecraftian dwellers, which sustains them beyond death and brings them joy in this often hellish world. "Weeping may endure through the night, but joy comes with the morning" (Psalm 30:5). As Toni Morrison observes, despite all that Black people have been through, who has ever loved more?

Despite gestures toward formal equality, the existence of Black people remains in a perennial COVID crisis. By every measure, Black people have languished on the front lines of neoliberalism, dying at disparate rates in a two-tiered health care system of life for the wealthy and death for the poor. COVID merely exposed what was always there—systemic and institutional inequality. Systemic inequality brings police violence into stark relief because state-sanctioned violence is a dramatic representation of the absurdity of being Black in America day to day, minute by minute. The videos of white police officers killing Black people make what should never have been comfortable uncomfortable. The videos make it difficult, though not impossible, to avert the eyes and pretend as if you don't know or just don't care. Set against this backdrop are the 2016 and 2020 presidential elections, where the majority of white people voted for Donald Trump, a man who symbolizes a culture of contempt for women, people of color, and immigrants. Decades of dog-whistle politics have arguably conjured up the devil. The perceived loss of exclusive white control over jobs, education, and intimate spaces has enlarged a chasm between working people across races while the wealthy steadily enact upwardly mobile distributions of wealth—a clever political maneuver as old as the Tilden-Hayes Compromise of 1877 and the destruction of the New Deal constituency—using race to pit poor and working-class whites against people of color while the rich get richer—a most effective political shiny bauble (distract by dangling an attractive toy on a string and steal the wallet).

During another state of crisis, the Korean War, my parents, an African American GI and a Korean woman, met, married, and remained inseparable beyond death. In their union, they offered an alternative vision of community in stark contrast to the seventy-two million Trump followers. In the face of disaster and impending doom, they retreated together in solidarity, like the Korean merchant and Black protesters against police violence in Spike Lee's *Do the Right Thing*. In the middle of an uprising, the Korean merchant and Black protesters acknowledged each other as "Same. Same." They reached over the divide of honorary whiteness and dishonorable Blackness to find solidarity in the face of calamity. Like Saul, after God knocks him off his horse, while he is in hot pursuit of Christians to kill, Paul emerges in solidarity with his fellow citizens of the Lovecraft Countries—the places of endless precarity. God shows up in crisis. God shows up in Lovecraft Countries—in a manger, on the cross, and in tears. Rather than doubling down on his hegemonic supremacy as a Pharisaic hunter and lyncher of Christians, Paul finds solidarity with those he once despised. As Martin Luther King observes, in moments of hegemonic crisis, God shows up and transforms consciousness, making the body ready for communion and solidarity with the world, an intersectionally transcendent gift.

This chapter explores intersectional consciousness and redemptive love as a prototype for solidarity among subaltern occupants of the Lovecraft Countries, places of absurdly relentless precarity. It is also a love story set in the Korean War and Black working-class South Side of Chicago with two protagonists that love beyond the white heteropatriarchal divide. My mother did not hypersexualize my father with Mandingo fantasies. My father did not use my mother as a yellow proxy to get closer to white women and whiteness. My mother did not call my father "Geomdungi," the Korean "N" word for Black people. She called him "Yobo," the Korean word for "my darling." My parents stepped outside the fantastic hegemonic imagination and white heteropatriarchal systems of valuation from the slave block to the lynching tree and mass incarceration. Instead, they found transcendental value in one another and solidarity that lasted beyond death.

This chapter proceeds in three parts: (1) Love (2) crafts (3) countries. Desire creates territorial boundaries (or countries), not glacial fissures on the cartography of a map or a god that doles out land. The geopolitics of space governs bodies. Desire negotiates power, politics, and policy as it problematizes people and creates peril. In these yet-to-be United States, the WHP usurps all of the space and situates vulnerable bodies in places of precarity for the specific purpose of exploitation, both for labor and for sex (slavery, ghettoes, and brothels, all Lovecraft Country). This power of spacing and placing is as much about love as it is about hate. The WHP loves itself as much as it hates the other. Lynchings, for example, celebrate the death of Black people and the love of white people.

Part one addresses two competing ideas of love: contempt-based love, on the one hand, and solidarity and mutuality, on the other. Contempt-based love is the love language of the WHP—WHP appeal; it is predicated on contempt for Blacks, persons of color, women, and immigrants. Contempt-based love highlights the unique nature of my parents' union and the need for a transformational consciousness rooted in intersectionality as an antidote to white heteronormativity, particularly in a time of crisis. Part one describes a highly unlikely love story between a Black man and a Korean woman, during the Korean War, that spans from Korea to Chicago's South Side; Lovecraft places central to a match that could only be made in heaven. Part Two (crafts) analyzes agency, briefly describing my tenure as a federal prosecutor with the United States Department of Justice (DOJ) and active participation in mass incarceration--locking up drug dealers and gun toters as a prelude to Saul's conversion through inversion on that Damascus road. Paul's conversion is a theoretical model and analytical framework for examining the transformation of the fantastic hegemonic imagination into a liberatory intersectional consciousness that stands in solidarity with fellow subaltern dwellers of the Lovecraft Countries. Part Three (countries) discusses Paul's newfound world in a larger scheme of social justice as conceived in the writings of Dr. Martin Luther King and capsulated in Kimberlé Williams Crenshaw's intersectionality. In sum, we can emerge from COVID and live together, or we can continue our treachery in silos and die.

Contempt-Based Love

America is at war with itself, rotting on a battlefield of fading identities lost in contempt, cruelty, and exclusion. Decades of Richard Nixon dog whistling and the GOP's Southern Strategy have resurrected a faded imperialist identity, predicated on the intersecting valences of the WHP. Daily, our senses are assaulted with images of state-sanctioned violence against Black bodies, #MeToo cruelty toward women, and unprecedented numbers of the poor languishing on the front lines of COVID-19 and neoliberalism, dying in a two-tiered health care system—private health care and life for the wealthy, no health care or public health care and death for the poor. On the environmental front, the same cruelty resonates in the UN secretary-general Antonio Guterres's admonition, "Humanity has declared war on nature."[3]

Although COVID unleashed biblical proportions of suffering and despair—killing millions worldwide and destroying economies—it does not explain Trump's refusal to launch federally coordinated initiatives to mitigate COVID-caused devastation or his supporters' refusal to wear masks. Protection from outside invasion is the federal government's raison d'être. Instead, as Anthony Farley argues, the constant drumbeat of Pied Piper dog whistling has conjured a demonic suicide mission for millions with a domestic abuser who vows, "If I cannot have America, nobody can."

Pitting poor and working-class whites against people and beings of color (Mexican rapists, Muslim terrorists, Black suburban invaders, and Chinese viruses), while the elite enact upwardly distributive tax relief for the wealthy, is a centuries-old "shiny bauble." It is an effective conflation of race, class, and gender that convinces poor and working-class whites to turn their ire outward on the vulnerable and to anchor their identities in moral righteousness and God-given supremacy. As President Lyndon B. Johnson famously quipped, "If you can convince the lowest white man he's better than the best colored man, he won't notice you're picking his pocket. Hell, give him somebody to look down on, and he'll empty his pockets for you."[4]

For many Trump supporters, the diminishing value of whiteness, and, more generally, the WHP, occasioned a mental breakdown. The contrasting images of Trump, on the one hand, and President Barack Obama and Vice President Kamala Harris, on the other, reflect a dialectical tension in the American psyche. On the one hand, many believe that the civil rights and feminist movements have yet to be realized, necessitating the #BlackLivesMatter and #MeToo movements. On the other hand, a rabid base feels utterly victimized, ravaged, and humiliated by the gains of the civil rights and feminist movements. On the one hand are those who experience police violence, sexual harassment, and poverty as routine—a constant state of COVID-like crisis. On the other hand are those who believe that the routine is perfectly deserved. For many, eight years of Black bodies inhabiting the White House during the Obama administration indicated that America had turned the corner and emerged out of its white supremacist clutches. For others, eight years of Black bodies inhabiting the White House occasioned an absolute psychotic break and nightmare, a final evil in a long-ebbing and gnawing away at formerly exclusive white monopolies on housing; education; employment, with bountiful factory jobs and robust pensions; safe, monochromatic suburbs; power. The loss of White House exclusivity was a final nail in the coffin signaling that white America had been left behind for darkness and evil. The battle cry and rage behind "Make America Great Again" burned like fentanyl in the veins of those who harkened back to legacy, heritage, and a bygone nostalgia for unquestioned white supremacy, exclusivity, and moral superiority. Make no mistake: A utopia for some is a nightmare or dystopia for others.

Within this particular historical empire of white turmoil, angst, and suffering, Trump emerged as the great white hope, a messianic figure with WHP appeal sent to restore the prince and the principalities of white supremacy to their honorable throne. Trump arrived on the wings of fine-tuned, dog whistling rhetoric designed to re-elevate whiteness to its temple of supremacy and pedestal of moral righteousness. For his targeted demographic, white supremacy has always been god, and integration and diversity have defiled, marred, cheapened, and sullied god, crying out for vindication and revenge.

The dystopian nightmare occasioned by the gains of the civil rights and feminist movements can be neither oversimplified nor discounted. Without hyperbole, we are witnessing a global rise in nationalism unseen since World War II. Disenfranchised French, Brexiteers, Trump-supporting Hungarians, and rainforest-demolishing Brazilians are gaining momentum daily—airing their aggrieved white status together at real-time internet speeds, with ever-increasing frequency, efficiency, and political organizing. Nationalists have reached across the ocean to find each other and have found euphoria in their shared contempt for the "other."

The perceived loosening of the grip of white supremacy is not only an international cause célèbre, but it is materialized in real terms—"a decline of the white working-class."[5] Trump's base supporters are dying at rates unseen since the AIDS epidemic.[6] According to the Deaton-Case report, these mortality rates are caused by drugs, alcohol, and suicide, concentrated among less educated, late-middle-age whites.[7] Trump's base is America's most righteous and aggrieved, yearning for a bygone era of once-exclusive claims to lily-white power.[8] Far from hyperbole, this loss of whiteness occasions real angst and death.[9]

It is worth deconstructing and decoding the nuance and sophistication of Trumpian hegemonic political messaging and maneuvering—"Make America Great Again." Like a sex trafficker whispering into the ears of a victim, the messaging provides opium and succor and satisfies something for which the soul is longing; at the same time, the pimp has every intention of sending the lost and longing listener out on the stroll only to scoff at her demise from disease. Like dog whistles, the latest well-heeled and refined hegemonic messaging of the WHP, paradigmatically exemplified in Trump, operates at many levels: The references are readily recognizable by his followers (Muslim terrorist, Mexican rapists, and safe, monochromatic suburbs), but simultaneously, they leave room for deniability. Most importantly, however, the messages provide a platform for moral righteousness and the restoration of white heteropatriarchal moral superiority. At the same time, denial is embedded in the ideological façade of the state.

Cruelty, exclusion, and savagery are bonding agents between Trump and his seventy-two million supporters, providing what Lili Loofbourow calls "a vehicle of intimacy through shared contempt."[10] In aptly describing the way Trumpism becomes a cultural identity, religion, worship service, and code of ethics, writer Adam Serwer places his finger squarely on the Trumpian zeitgeist as follows:

> Trump's only true skill is the con; his only fundamental belief is that the United States is the birthright of straight, white, Christian men, and his only real, authentic pleasure is in cruelty. It is that cruelty, and the delight it brings them, that binds his most ardent supporters to him, in shared scorn for those they hate and fear: immigrants, black voters, feminists, and treasonous white men who empathize with any of those who would steal their birthright. The president's ability to execute that cruelty through word and deed makes them euphoric. It makes them feel good, it makes them feel proud, it makes them feel happy, it makes them feel united. And as long as he makes them feel that way, they will let him get away with anything, no matter what it costs them.[11]

Trump and his followers understand that the WHP is a love-driven politic, sowing love and euphoria for itself and contempt for others. The WHP, like lynchings or gang rape, is desire, requiring action for satisfaction. The WHP is as much about love as about hate. Lynchings are contempt for Black people and love for white people. There is contempt for the object of derision or scorn, but there is ecstasy in the mob—a thickness in the solidarity of thieves. Through the spectacle (lynching and rape), the violators find their way to each other in orgiastic revelry—a real hootenanny, all whipped up. The WHP explains why challenges to its completeness and total existence are critiqued as "outside agitators"—those challenging what we love and how we love. As the WHP is love, it explains the limitless devotion of seventy-two million who know absolutely no limits, because love has no limits. There is no bottom.

Trump traffics in WHP appeal—a contempt-based love language with geopolitical scope, whispered in the seductive tone of a domestic abuser, triggering ecstasy and longing in his listeners. "MAGA" is a deep-seated yearning, craving, and lament for love and loss, as well as the hope and promise of restoration, like German national pride after suffering humiliation in World War I. The WHP has all of the trappings of love, including a willingness to nurture, protect, and guard unto death. The machinations of the WHP are difficult to detect, diagnose, and dislodge. Although Blacks experience the WHP as contempt, it is a love language for whites. Who wants to get rid of love, let alone quickly? Lynchings, gang rapes, and police violence are simultaneously spectacle and a love language. Lynchings not only celebrate the death of the object, but the euphoric reunion of the audience—the enthralled and rapturous white audience is celebrating its love of whiteness. Trump rallies were filled with cries of rage, joy, adoring love, and ecstasy, a much-needed release from the humiliation of the civil rights and feminist movements. Tapping his WHP, Trump and his globally collected social media network perfected an identity-based geopolitics of love and grievance. WHP appeal is seduction through limitless savagery; it is fundamentally exquisite because it is so near perfection and is complete. As Robin D'Angelo says of white privilege, to give up 2 percent is too much.

Ian Haney Lopez confined dog-whistling to the territorial borders of America. Trump, however, expanded what Juan Floyd Thomas calls a "dog-whistling love-driven geopolitics" beyond the US territorial borders to the world stage, where the coin of the realm has a basic duality—those we love and those we hate—love on one side for all who find ecstasy in nationalism and, on the other side, hatred for those identified as the objects of nationalists' contempt. "Kung Flu" and the "Chinese virus" identify love for anyone who desires to make the Pacific Rim the source and site of disease and contagion—a yellow peril—a perennial disgust harkening back to the early 1900s and the stuff of nightmares that besieged and tormented H. P. Lovecraft and preoccupied his writing.

The demonization of Black people and the simultaneous overvalorization of whiteness, however, are not restricted to whites. The urge to dissociate oneself from the powerless—namely Blacks—and to associate oneself with the powerful—namely whites—lies at the heart of the immigrant experience and the American assimilation process. American identity is negotiated at the intersection of what Stacey Floyd Thomas calls "honorary whiteness and dishonorable Blackness." In describing this magnetic gravitational pull toward power, and simultaneous contempt for the powerless, comedian Richard Pryor stated that immigrants became American "by learning to how to say 'nigger.'"[12] Similarly, Toni Morrison argued that, in the United States, learning to distinguish oneself from and express contempt for Blacks is part of the ritual through which immigrant groups assimilate. As Morrison explains, "If there were no black people here in this country, it would have been Balkanized. . . . When [immigrants] got off the boat, the second word they learned was 'nigger.'"[13]

Polling data from the 2020 presidential election demonstrates that the gravitational pull toward white supremacy, and Black demonization for all immigrant groups, endures across the racial board. Trump's persistent vitriol directed at the "Chinese virus" did not spare Asians, the otherwise "model minority," from a meteoric rise in hate crimes.[14] Despite his constant use of "the Chinese virus" to deflect from his incompetency and handling of COVID, Trump maintained 30 percent of the Asian vote. In explaining this head-scratching love of the model minorities for Trump, Viet Thanh Nguyen explains, "There is a significant minority of Asian Americans who are deeply invested in white supremacy, white privilege, white allies, and standing with whiteness because they recognize that this is the path to power and profit and inclusion in America."[15] This is not to say that America does not direct its white supremacist ire toward Asians as well. America's championing of Asians as a model minority is hardly a reverence for Asians, but rather it is a vehicle for signifying a deliberate critique of Blacks as lazy, and an excuse to ignore discrimination against Asians[16]—as if to say, "See they can do it and because they did it, we don't need to do anything special for you or them."

In addition to anti-Blackness by Koreans, tensions between Koreans and Black people coexist on the valence of class. Many immigrant groups have played the part of the merchant class in Black communities. From Jewish landlords to Korean hair product sellers, ethnic groups often fill the role of the merchant class and despise their Black clientele.

Spike Lee's *Do the Right Thing* dramatized the tensions between Koreans and Blacks as an exposé on the riots in Koreatown after the Rodney King beating and Latasha Harlins's killing by a Korean merchant, Soon Ja Du. This conflict is played out when Radio Raheem has a confrontation with the Korean owners of the local bodega for his D batteries to power his "ghetto" blaster. Negativity ensues. But when white cops strangle Radio Raheem to death, the ire of a Black uprising turns toward the shop and its Korean owners. To this, the Korean shopkeeper stands in solidarity with the protesters and says, "You, me. Same. Same."

Mutuality, Solidarity, and Faith-Based Love

My parents met in their own Lovecraft Country—in the middle of war, across an ocean of racialized differences. During the Korean War, my father, a Black American GI, and my mother, a Korean woman, forged an alliance and became inseparable beyond death. They retreated from hate in solidarity and melted into one unit, equally yoked. Working tirelessly, four full-time jobs at a time, they built a life together, privately educating all three of their Black children, and living in a home my father's equally hardworking mother (Blanche) prayed into existence. Lovecraft Countries focus the mind on prayer. Both of my parents were made of a mettle similar in stubborn strength to that which possessed Europeans to enslave millions of Africans for centuries—the substance that made fledgling nations, like the United States, world powers in a flash of history[17]—the God-given capacity to endure and survive unspeakable savagery—the epistemological knowledge that when caught between a rock and a hard place, love demands that you become hewers of rock, using your desire to transform earth and stone into art and monuments of justice. My parents exemplified an alternative vision of solidarity, association, and intimacy—one that contrasts sharply with our current historical moment of resurgent white supremacy, nationalism, contempt, and exclusion. Rather than engage each other in supremacists' practices of exclusion and valuation, they stepped outside imperialism and militarism and recognized in each other unending and lasting value.

Instead of playing into the fantastic hegemonic imagination of Blackness and Yellowness, my parents transcended the trappings of white overvalorization and Black demonization. They saw each other outside the white heteropatriarchal gaze. Their story, unlike so much white supremacy or Asian anti-Blackness, was not one of racial animosity but rather racial solidarity and not on white heteropatriarchal terms. My mother did not hypersexualize my father. She was not plagued with Mandingo fantasies—a centuries-long global obsession with hypersexualizing Black people, a constant preoccupation with Black genitalia—for example, the Hottentot Venus, Black men in drag, and Willie Horton-esque Black male rapists. I recall my father telling us how, during the war, the white soldiers would tell the Korean women that the Black soldiers had tails. The WHP has historically placed a value on Black bodies in multitudinous ways, from the slave auction blocks to the $6 million figure Black families receive when white officers kill their loved ones.[18] My mother saw outside these processes of valuation and found devotion.

Far from hypersexualization, my mother loved my father. For eight-and-one-half years, she was his sole caregiver after his first stroke left him infantilized. After nearly fifty years of marriage, she refused to relinquish his care to anyone because she knew that no one would ever care for him the way she would. He was a dark Black man, in a world that despises Black people. She was five feet tall, weighing less than 130 pounds. My father, before the strokes too numerous to count, was five-feet-nine, weighing over 300 pounds—a man more than twice her size. Love can make you do the impossible: Riffing from *Jingle Jangle*, love is the square root of the impossible. She bathed, fed, and changed him faithfully three times a day for eight-and-one-half years, allowing him to live out his life and to die with dignity. Although emotionally and physically fatigued from seeing a once-healthy Titian dwindle slowly away with every stroke, she knew that relinquishing a dark Black man (any Black person) to a care facility would mean neglect, discrimination, and suffering, a result that was intolerable and unfathomable for her. A puny mind cannot understand that kind of love.

Rather than engaging the structural and institutional sexual exploitation of foreign women, which the armed forces facilitated and encouraged through military brothels, my father saw the humanity in my mother. He adored my mother. Saturday mornings were regularly spent at the kitchen table with my dad telling stories about how they met. My parents are from cultures rooted in poverty, perennial suffering, and institutional and structural domination. Within their shared experience of poverty, they found something in the other to value that transcended the exclusionary practices of white supremacy, hypersexualization, and the internalization of dominant discourses of hatred and cruelty. They created a different vision of identity, intimacy, and godliness. They were a match that could only be made in heaven, and for their faithfulness, they found a lifetime of devotion that extended beyond the grave.

My father was not attracted to my mother as a yellow proxy for white women. He would tell any stranger on any public or private street in a nanosecond, "I didn't marry her because I thought I was too good for a Black woman. I married her because I loved her." He was not possessed of the idea that he could only experience manhood through the possession of a white woman or that he could lurch closer to manhood through sexual and intimate proximity to white women. Instead, my parents found something between them that collapsed both time and space.

Korea is a tiny country situated between two world powers, China and Japan, both of which for centuries have persistently fought their border wars over Korea's territorial boundaries. Imperialist expansion left Korea in a perennial state of rape and plunder. During Japan's colonial rule of Korea, between 1931 and 1945, the Japanese Imperial Army systematized its rapes by sexually enslaving hundreds of thousands of girls and women in military brothels, running from Seoul to Singapore.[19] Victims reported girls as young as eight and small groups of girls sexually servicing forty to fifty Japanese soldiers daily.[20]

During the Korean War, Koreans, like Black Americans, lived with the precarity of knowing that, at any moment, state-sanctioned violence could end your life—your time ended—and that racism can not only control your time, but imprison you in particular places for unbridled exploitation by force of law. Moreover, Koreans and Black Americans share a common experience of gaslighting, where the rape victim or victim of other forms of brutality is revictimized and turned into a spectacle while seeking vindication and redress. In classic cases of victim blaming, the victim comes forward seeking redress for unspeakable savagery and thereby becomes "the problem," suffering another round of savagery for having exposed the toxicity of the violators. In the case of the Japanese-branded comfort women—the name the Japanese soldiers gave to the girls they abducted and held as sex captives for decades—the victims of these militarized brothels are met with denial, victim blaming, lying, and an absence of remorse by the Japanese government, in what has been dubbed "apology fatigue."[21]

Similarly, in the case of African American victims of legally sanctioned violence, the criminal justice system is the site of revictimization, obfuscation, and spectacle. Whole epistemological systems intended to redress harm, such as the criminal justice system, instead vilify the victim and valorize the preparator. Take the case of Emmet Till, a fifteen-year-old whom a group of white men tortured, beat, whipped, tied to a metal fan, and drowned for allegedly whistling at a white woman. After six minutes of deliberation, an all-white jury acquitted his killers and allowed them to walk free, laugh, and enjoy cigars with their wives. Or Trayvon Martin, a seventeen-year-old walking to a candy store, who was stalked by a self-appointed neighborhood watchman, killed, and blamed for his own death. The trial of George Zimmerman, the man who shot Martin, vilified Martin and liberated Zimmerman. During the trial, one of Zimmerman's defense attorneys took photographs of himself grinning, smiling, and licking ice cream with his children with a caption reading, "We beat stupidity."[22] In sum, Koreans and Black people both understand, "All wars are fought twice, the first time in the battlefield, the second time in memory."[23]

When Till's mother opened her son's casket so that all the world could see what white people had done to her child, my father, a young man, went to see Till's massacred body. The sight of his tortured body, broken and shattered, flayed with crevices and bloating, left a lasting, lifelong impression on my father. Years later, when my mother arrived at the airport in America to marry him, he hid behind a pillar. Later when she asked him why he was hiding, he said, "White men might kill me for marrying you." My father, mind you, was all man, a man's man, in his prime a body-builder and weightlifter. He could lift a thirty-pound radiator like a box of tissue, but the body of Emmett Till did exactly what it was it intended to do—it sent a searing message that if you crossed the boundary of white supremacy, you did so at your peril.

While serving in Korea, my father required a hernia operation. He had a very strong body—a football player, weightlifter, nonsmoker, and nondrinker. (The fantastic hegemonic imagination does not recognize Black men—pure of heart and body—like that.) Despite his Herculean strength, he was alone. My father told my mother he was going away for surgery and not to worry because he would be back. My father told us about how he pulled duty in large open fields in Korea at night and the loneliness that would kick in. He got through those moments with prayer and knowing he could see my mom when it was all over, longingly stating, "I could go see her." While in the hospital recovering from surgery, he looked up to see my mom and her friend. Her friend knew where the hospital was, and they traveled there together—over thirty miles by foot and makeshift buses. His heart was so full. His heart would fill again and again, every time he told the story, which included many, many Saturday breakfasts with his family. Decades later, after his first stroke, my mom stayed with him in the hospital for thirty days, sleeping on a cot every night by his side. My dad had his first stroke in a hospital. He also died in a hospital. When he recovered from the first stroke, he was completely dazed, confused, and foggy. After the first stroke, he kept looking to my mom to explain what happened. I remember watching him looking directly into her eyes and marveling at how he had someone so solidly in his corner that he could fully trust at his most vulnerable point in life and he knew it. He knew he could trust her in every way, and he could. I wonder if when he saw my mom turn that doorknob in that hospital in Korea, if his mind's eye saw the end, and who would be standing there without fail next to him the whole way.

My parents remained married until my father died nearly fifty-four years later. Over the ocean and many years, when asked how he got such a good wife, he would say, "God did that." My mother and father are Bong and Albert Cook. My mother no longer has to lift a man twice her size. A lesser woman would be relieved. She is lost without him.

Agent of the State

Both my father and I were agents of the state. He, a drafted young African American man, and me, a former federal prosecutor—an assistant United States attorney for the United States Department of Justice, to be precise, the highest form of law enforcement in the country. Although my father was forced to become part of the American imperialism campaign, I volunteered. We were both, in varying degrees, complicit in our own demise, me far more so than he. As Ji-Ah, the Korean love interest of Atticus, a young Black American GI during the Korean War, in the television series *Lovecraft Country*, says to him, "Why do you fight for a country that doesn't care about you?"—indeed a metaethical question at the heart of hegemonic complicity.

As a federal prosecutor of large-scale drug organizations and gun toters, I believed that what I was doing was right. I was ridding vulnerable communities of a cancerous sore. Michelle Alexander's *The New Jim Crow* and the Great Recession transformed my mind. During the Great Recession, I did not see the same thirst to imprison those responsible for unregulated banking practices that led to collapses in world economies like the salivating I saw for incarcerating drug dealers. There was no war on Wall Street remotely comparable to the war on drugs, which some have called the war on Black men. Alexander established an empirical and well-reasoned case for thoroughly disparate incarceration rates by race; a history of the police force controlling Black bodies; and a relentless perception of Black people as dangerous, suspicious, and in need of being controlled. From 1980 to 2008, the number of incarcerated persons quadrupled from five hundred thousand to 2.3 million,[24] with the United States incarcerating 25 percent of the world's prisoners—making America the most carceral nation in history.[25] The stark contrast between the incarceration rates related to the war on drugs and the absence of an outcry for a war on Wall Street made me endlessly question whom we pathologize and what activity we criminalize.

Saul

Like America, Saul is one of the most notorious mass incarcerators in human history. His identity and sense of being are grounded in playing and performing on vulnerable bodies. It is his love language—producing in him a wild-eyed joy and glee.[26] In his conversion on the road to Damascus, Saul is in hot pursuit of Christians—the followers of The Way. As an agent of the state—the Roman imperial power—Saul intends to hunt, shackle, and chain as many Christians as possible. In his mind's eye, he is on a mission to tame and destroy evil. In his fantasies, he will subject his prisoners to his authority and he will render them helpless and defenseless to his power. Saul is seeking his own personal Tulsa. Killing, controlling, and taming Christians—like the taming of Black people—is the business of the state. For Saul, a lawyer and chief law enforcement officer, taming the despised makes him feel good. Cruelty is the point. In subduing evil, he believes he is morally righteous and that he is, therefore, worthy of valorization. Taming, killing, and torturing the despised evil is the love language he shares with other perceived members of the exalted community. It makes his chest swell and his back straighten, and it fixes his gaze—looking like a Confederate statue or founding father mounted on a horse. This same chemistry of feeling empowered Derek Chauvin, lyncher of George Floyd, to stare unflinchingly into the video cameras while kneeling on the neck of soft human tissue, with his hands casually in his pockets, self-assuredly conducting a much-needed public lesson. Chauvin's physicality reflected the mortal righteousness of believing that he was taming evil. By way of another analogy, the deliberate failure to obtain any criminal charges or an indictment against the white police officers who killed Michael Brown, Tamir Rice, and Breonna Taylor, all Black youths, achieved the same task as the killings themselves—the vilification of Black people, the valorization of white police officers, and the reassurance of white heteropatriarchal preeminence, vindication, safety, and security. The lynching of Black people is a love language, reflected in the yard signs extolling solidarity with the police stating: "We love and support the police." The signs valorize the ability to put down evil and the shared cultural identity and sense of moral righteousness that come with it.

Puffed up and bloated with his moral righteousness and the force of law as his obfuscating shield, Saul journeys to Damascus, "breathing threats and murder against the disciples of the Lord."[27] While on his mission, God smacks Saul from his horse and blinds him for three days (in the name of the father, son, and holy ghost). Saul, a renowned persecutor and Pharisee, one of the highest forms of ruling-class law enforcement, is emasculated, made low, and leveled to the ground. He is now an inhabitant of Lovecraft Country. He has been subjected to a random act of violence. He now understands an existence predicated on vulnerability to random acts of violence and the fantastic hegemonic imagination. Saul's fall from the upper-class echelons demonstrates an inverted order (conversion through inversion) where Saul, once a proud, profane agent of the state, is now a blind man—an occupant of the Lovecraft Country or low places—inhabited by the people he once persecuted—the low ground and a place of endless precarity.[28] Saul is now an occupant of the areas in which life can end in a nanosecond through state-sanctioned violence—a place where you can be hunted (Ahmaud Arbery); a place where the state can not only take your life, but blame you for your death; a place where you can walk out of your garage (Andre Maurice Hill); walk inside your home (Casey Goodson Jr.); sit on your couch and eat a bowl of ice cream (Botham Jean); sleep in your bed (Breonna Taylor); or look outside your window (Atatiana Jefferson); and the police can kill you and you are blamed for your murder, while your killer is valorized with yard signs that say, "We respect and support the police."

After Saul is healed, at the hands of a Christian—the people he formerly despised—Saul transforms into Paul, a name derived from the Latin adjective for "small" or "humble." Paul emerges from his helplessness, the scales fall from his eyes, he sees through the eyes of God (not man, particularly not the oppressive man), and he cries throughout the synagogues that Jesus is the son of God. In the rising tide of his helplessness, he recognizes a potential lesson for all of us, during COVID, "You me. Same. Same."

Paul becomes a living, breathing example of the transformative power of crisis to quicken the spirit and change the mind of the oppressor and make him stand in solidarity with the oppressed against the destructive imperial order for the larger good of full human flourishing. Saul is an insider made outsider. His positioning in the margins alongside his fellow colonized subalterns informs his critical disposition and point of view (his positionality). A taste of the misery Saul once inflicted humbles and transforms him. As Zora Neale Hurston states, "You have to go there to know there."[29] Saul, however, is not a mere tourist in these places—ready to smile, pretend, and make gestures toward equality (like diversity initiatives that act as fodder for symbolism, but do nothing to change systemic racism); rather, Paul's soul is saved from his own savagery, active thwarting of justice, and complicity in a cultural identity, heritage, and legacy grounded in treachery. He emerges from his conversion as a former agent of the state turned fervent social justice warrior.

Paul's road to Damascus algorithmically captures conscientization, a conversion through inversion that ignites a transformative consciousness pricked by social crisis. It is this entire process of conscientization that Martin Luther King Jr. brilliantly captures in his "Letter from

Birmingham Jail." In his letter, King wrote to the white clergy who called for an end to the civil rights movement, much like current BLM detractors. The clergy called out "the outside agitators"—those who do not understand our culture, those who will not wait for a more opportune time, those who will not allow things to get better if they would just let time run its course, or those who just are not right for our culture at all—in a word "extremists."[30] In his letter, King likens himself to Paul, refusing to be silenced, rendered invisible, and made to wait; instead, like Paul, King must cry out for every race to hear with the utmost immediacy—right here, right now—with the immediacy that Chauvin knelt on Floyd's neck.

The southern white clergy would rather preach the gospel and ignore racial and economic exploitation. Context, however, renders content. Emptying content of its context allows the inherent ambiguity of language to be co-opted in the service of the WHP. When the WHP is unmoored from its long and treacherous history, it evades detection through ambiguity and becomes an endlessly adaptable virus, morphing from slavery to Jim Crow to mass incarceration to police violence. Stripping doctrine, whether legal or religious, from the material reality of inequality and treachery allows the WHP to perpetuate as normal, natural, and just the way things are. As Kimberlé Crenshaw argues, when white supremacy is unmoored from its historical underpinnings and socioeconomic material realities, "reverse discrimination" becomes just as bad as four hundred years of systemic and institutional racism. Remedial efforts to hire or educate persons of color, for example, become bad for whites. When civil rights discourse and gains are unmoored from the historical treatment of Black Americans, Trump can tap the WHP and use civil rights rhetoric to claim that diversity initiatives, Critical Race Theory, and the 1619 Project are racist and anti-American (unless, of course, racism, hegemony, white supremacy, and white heteronormativity are American), all the while actively undermining democratic processes like voting and the Constitution.

Intersectionality

COVID has placed the world on the road to Damascus. We can continue in our savagery and die, or we can emerge in solidarity and live.

Saul, like my parents, emerged from darkness and found solidarity in the shared experiences of Lovecraft Countries. Like Paul, my parents engaged in a transformative, interconnected, and intersectional consciousness—a redemptive love,[31] which allowed them to see the full humanity and complexity in each other and thereby receive salvation, love, healing, and devotion. Intersectionality is an algorithm for transformative social change and an antidote for a world in crisis. As a planet ravaged by COVID, we can recognize our inextricably intertwined interconnectedness and share our love to survive (wearing a mask and globally collective science), or we can continue in silos of savagery that seduce tyrants to lay up with one another on pillows of evil and whisper the contempt-based love language and sweet nothings of villainy (geopolitical dog whistling with Trump, Putin, Bolsonaro, and Kim Jong-un, all snuggled up)—a guaranteed formula for Holocaust disaster.

Intersectionality recognizes the complex, cumulative ways in which the effects of multiple forms of discrimination (such as racism, sexism, and classism) combine, overlap, and intersect, particularly in the experiences of those who dwell in the margins.[32] Intersectionality cuts through layers of Foucauldian obfuscation: Saul is wrapped in moral righteousness, a false sense of his superiority, and an equally false sense of evil. Like slaveowners, persecutors, and the anti–civil rights movement white clergy, Saul believes that a Black body (in Saul's case, a Christian body) is dangerous, suspicious, and in need of being tamed. Saul believes that playing and performing on vulnerable bodies is right. This false overvalorization and demonization dichotomy obfuscates Saul's savagery and treachery from the world and himself. It is Derek Chauvin's false sense of his own moral righteousness and superiority and his equally false belief in George Floyd's demonization and inferiority that allowed him to sit on Floyd's neck for nearly nine minutes and stare directly into the camera. A failure to acknowledge the inextricable links between racism, sexism, and classism re-creates structural patterns and political strategies that sustain inequality and inequity. These structural patterns make victims of George Floyds, and treacherous savages of Saul and Chauvin.

Although the civil rights, Black power, and feminist movements of the 1960s and 1970s expanded civil rights, none fully embraced the other or an intersectional agenda.[33] Perhaps, as Kimberlé Crenshaw suggests, the current political crisis reflects a failure of the popular political movements and second-wave feminism to embrace intersectionality, and an understanding that racism, sexism, and classism not only overlap but that each also supports and sustains the work of the other.[34] Had the feminist movement, for example, fully embraced intersectionality, might it have acknowledged that the killings of the Emmett Tills and Trayvon Martins could explain the rise of Donald Trump? Or that the demonization of Black men as the prototype for criminality immunizes the treachery of the majority from detection? When we calibrate our minds to see only criminality and treachery in Black bodies, we immunize ourselves from treachery and savagery in white bodies. By way of illustration, when rape is only rape when committed by a Black male against a white female, several things happen. Only Black men are capable of committing rape. White women are only raped when raped by a Black male. Majority men are incapable of committing rape. And Black women are unrapeable.[35]

This architectural framework lodged in the brain is particularly problematic because the vast majority of sexualized violence cases are not interracial, but rather intraracial, that is committed within racial groups. Thus, when we can only train our minds to see sexual violence as that between Black men and white women, the overwhelming majority of sexual violence cases are rendered undetectable and invisible. A failure to adopt intersectionality sustains rape culture and sexual violation. The lasting impact of a failure to embrace intersectionality not only creates and sustains vulnerability for women, but it impacts us all. Savagery is hidden and innocence is lost. When the shiny baubles of Muslim terrorists, Mexican walls, and Chinese viruses are constantly dangled, incompetence is shrouded, and middle-class ambitions and livable wages evaporate. Our fixation on permutations of the Black male rapists and Black bogeyman —and our obsession with building a wall to keep ourselves immunized from outside contaminants that might come and steal our jobs and admissions to colleges and universities, as well as rape our women—distracted our attention from the incompetence that failed to mitigate a pandemic crisis.

Willful blindness, ignorance, or a refusal to recognize the ways in which racism feeds both classism and sexism replicates consistent and unrelenting hegemonic patterns, particularly complicity in self-destruction. The internalization of dominant discourses in the hegemonic process is so thoroughly effective that humanity itself becomes a poster child for its own degradation: Saul was a prisoner to his own self-destruction and an active participant in losing any semblance of humanity. He believed that what he was doing was right. He believed himself to be ridding society of evil. Understanding the inextricably intertwining and interconnectedness of race, class, and gender can heal a festering disease with all of its bulbous ugliness and purulent scales—exposing it to the precious antiseptic light of day—where it can be detected and cured of its infernal vileness. Like a multiheaded Hydra or constantly mutating virus—endlessly adaptable from slavery, to Jim Crow, to mass incarceration—white heteropatriarchy can never be cured, if it remains undetectable. Like Saul, it must emerge from the darkness with all its ugliness and scales in order to receive air and light.

An intersectional agenda and transformational consciousness not only liberate us from the tyrannies of hegemony and evil but can help us recognize humanity and the full possibility of human flourishing. Paul remained in the Lovecraft Country declaring salvation. A recognition of our interconnectedness can restore humanity to those whose suffering goes unrecognizable, undetectable, and invisible. Like Paul, an interconnected consciousness can help us to not only stand in solidarity in Lovecraft Country but to receive salvation from our own treachery, and release from hegemonic complicity in destruction, healing, love, and devotion. In Lovecraft Country, the margin becomes the center informing a new day.[36] As Jacquelyn Grant states, when the bottom gets lifted up, everyone can stand. Through the eyes of the WHP George Floyd was an ant to be stepped on. Through an intersectional consciousness, he was a human being to be loved. An intersectional consciousness enables us to heed the messianic clarion call of Martin Luther King Jr.: "Injustice anywhere is a threat to justice everywhere. We are caught in an inescapable network of mutuality, tied in a single garment of destiny. Whatever affects one directly affects all indirectly."[37]

NOTES

1 In remarking on *Lovecraft*, Misha Green, the story's writer, stated, "In horror, there's a level of anxiety that your life can be taken at any moment. That's the Black experience." Salamishah Tillet, "Living While Black in 'Lovecraft Country,'" *New York Times*, August 7, 2020.

2 Mike Hale, "'Lovecraft Country' Review: Nightmare on Jim Crow Street," *New York Times*, August 13, 2020, www.nytimes.com.

3 Lulu Garcia-Navarro and Steve Inskeep, News Brief, NPR, December 3, 2020.

4 Bill D. Moyers, "What a Real President Was Like," *Washington Post*, November 13, 1988, www.washingtonpost.com.

5 Lenny Bernstein and Joel Achenbach, "A Group of Middle-Aged Whites in the U.S. Is Dying at a Startling Rate," *Washington Post*, November 2, 2015; "The Forces Driving Middle-Aged White People's 'Deaths of Despair,'" NPR, March 23, 2017, www.npr.org.

6 Gina Kolata, "Death Rates Rising for Middle-Aged White Americans, Study Finds," *New York Times*, November 2, 2015, www.nytimes.com.

7 Angus Deaton and Anne Case, "Rising Morbidity and Mortality in Midlife among White Non-Hispanic Americans in the 21st Century," *Proceedings of the National Academy of Sciences* 112, no. 49 (December 8, 2015): 15078–83; see also Bernstein and Achenbach, "Group of Middle-Aged Whites."

8 McKay Coppins, "The Gospel According to Trump," *New York Times*, January 18, 2016, www.nytimes.com.

9 Deaton and Case, "Rising Morbidity and Mortality"; see also Bernstein and Achenbach, "Group of Middle-Aged Whites."

10 Adam Serwer, "The Cruelty Is the Point," *The Atlantic*, October 3, 2018, www.theatlantic.com.

11 Ibid.

12 Richard Pryor, *That Nigger's Crazy* (Reprise MS 2241, 1974).

13 "The Pain of Being Black," *Time*, May 22, 1989.

14 Sabrina Tavernise and Richard A. Oppel Jr., "Spit On, Yelled At, Attacked: Chinese-Americans Fear for Their Safety," *New York Times*, March 23, 2020, www.nytimes.com.

15 Kimberlé Crenshaw, "Where Do We Go From Here: Chaos or Community?," *Intersectionality Matters* (podcast), episode 30.

16 Robert S. Chang, "Toward an Asian American Legal Scholarship: Critical Race Theory, Post-Structuralism, and Narrative Space," *California Law Review* 81 (1993): 1241–323, see 1260.

17 Nikole Hannah-Jones, "The 1619 Project," *New York Times Magazine*, August 18, 2019.

18 Daniel Marans, "$6 Million Is the Going Rate For Killing Unarmed Black People," April 24, 2016, *Huffington Post*, www.huffpost.com.

19 Julie McCarthy, "Philippine Survivor Recounts Her Struggle as a 'Comfort Woman' for Wartime Japan," NPR, November 29, 2020, www.npr.org; Christine Hauser, "'It Is Not Coming Down': San Francisco Defends 'Comfort Women' Statue as Japan Protests," *New York Times*, October 4, 2018, www.nytimes.com.

20 McCarthy, "Philippine Survivor Recounts."

21 Ibid.

22 Ryan Grenoble, "George Zimmerman's Lawyer, Daughter Celebrate with Ice Cream, Share Photo on Instagram," *Huffington Post*, June 28, 2013, www.huffpost.com.

23 Viet Thanh Nguyen, Nothing Ever Dies: Vietnam and the Memory of War (Cambridge: Harvard University Press, 2016), 4.

24 See generally Zach Newman, "'Hands Up, Don't Shoot': Policing, Fatal Force, and Equal Protection in the Age of Colorblindness, *Hastings Constitutional Law Quarterly* 43 (2015): 117–60, see 135.

25 Ibid., 135; see also NAACP, Criminal Justice Fact Sheet, last visited November 22, 2016, www.naacp.org.

26 Saul witnesses the lynching of Stephen, the first martyr of Jesus, and approves of the killing (Acts 8:1).

27 Acts 9:1.

28 Brittany E. Wilson, "The Blinding of Paul and the Power of God: Masculinity, Sight, and Self-Control in Acts," *Journal of Biblical Literature* 133, no. 2 (Summer 2014): 367–87, www.jstor.org.

29 Zora Neale Hurston, *Their Eyes Were Watching God* (New York: Harper Perennial Modern Classics edition, 2006), 192.

30 Lisa M. Bowens, *African American Readings of Paul: Reception, Resistance, and Transformation* (Grand Rapids: Eerdmans, 2020), 256.

31 Stacey Floyd Thomas, ed., *Deeper Shades of Purple* (New York: NYU Press 2006), 142.

32 See generally Kimberlé W. Crenshaw, "Mapping the Margins: Intersectionality, Identity Politics, and Violence against Women of Color," *Stanford Law Review* 43 (1991): 1241–99.

33 Ibid.

34 Ibid.

35 Dorothy E. Roberts, "Rape, Violence, and Women's Autonomy," *Chicago-Kent Law Review* 69 (1993): 359–88, see 365; see generally Crenshaw, "Mapping the Margins."

36 Mari J. Matsuda, "Looking to the Bottom: Critical Legal Studies and Reparations," *Harvard Civil Rights-Civil Liberties Law Review* 22 (1987): 323–99, see 325.

37 Martin Luther King, Jr., "Letter from Birmingham Jail," April 16, 1963, www .csuchico.edu.

7

Insure Domestic Tranquility

The Uncivil, Un-Christian, and Unconstitutional
Crisis in a COVID-19-Era America

MIGUEL A. DE LA TORRE

The first nineteen words enshrined in the Preamble of the US Constitution provide a vision for a republic that has yet to be realized: "We the people of the United States, in order to form a perfect union, establish justice, insure domestic tranquility." The founding fathers (mothers were excluded from envisioning a nation) created a new way of self-governance that entrusted the people ("people" defined as landholding white men)—not some deity—to create a political structure committed to the presupposition of preserving and perpetuating a social order absent of strife and fear of governmental encroachment upon the unalienable rights to life, liberty, and the pursuit of happiness. These first nineteen words provided the formula by which a more perfect union could be formed upon the concept of establishing justice. Only through the establishment of justice can domestic tranquility be ensured. Not to sound trite, but as the protest chant reminds us, "No justice, no peace!"

But these same founding fathers—many of whom engaged in the indefensible practice of owning Black bodies and who spearheaded the invasion of the so-called untamed West by first eradicating the land of Indians—were unable to establish justice for all, lest it threaten their unearned power, privilege, and profit. Justice was reserved exclusively for those who resembled the founding fathers, so ensuring domestic tranquility was limited to white male landholders, at least until 1856 when white males were allowed to vote in all states regardless of property ownership. The establishment of white affirmative action corresponded with the foundation of the republic. The same Constitution, while promising justice and domestic tranquility for whites, also preserved their supremacy over an enslaved Black populace through the Three-Fifths Clause and the Fugitive Slave Clause. In the white male imagination, the injustice of depriving nonwhites of life, liberty, and the pursuit of happiness had to be construed and defined as justice. Interpreting the constitutional Preamble call to establish justice while securing racial and ethnic injustices required verbal contortions that would make any Kama Sutra aficionado envious. But calling injustices "just" required more than simply some governmental pronouncement; it necessitated a sacred blessing.

The founders needed a religion to consecrate the satanic call for oppression and repression. Fredrick Douglass vividly captured the blasphemy of white Christianity when he wrote,

> The slave auctioneer's bell and the church-going bell chime in with each other, and the bitter cries of the heartbroken slave are drowned in the religious shouts of his pious master. Revivals of religion and revivals in the slave-trade go hand in hand together. The slave prison and the church stand near each other. The clanking of fetters and the rattling of chains in the prison, and the pious psalm and solemn prayer in the church, may be heard at the same time. The dealers in the bodies and souls of men erect their stand in the presence of the pulpit, and they mutually help each other. The dealer gives his blood-stained gold to support the pulpit, and the pulpit, in return, covers his infernal business with the garb of Christianity. Here we have religion and robbery the allies of each other— devils dressed in angels' robes, and hell presenting the semblance of paradise.[1]

The gospel preached by the Brown Jewish rabbi two millennia ago is a lifeless spirituality in the hands of Eurocentric Christians because it was designed, since its foundation, to bring death to so many who fall short of the white ideal. Taking Douglass seriously, Christianity had already died in the hands of white Christians centuries before their Faustian bargain was ever struck to elect Donald Trump. The existential threat to communities of color caused by the fusing and confusing of white supremacy with Christian salvation was exacerbated by the COVID-19 pandemic of 2020. For the very well-being and survival of Latinx, it is not simply enough to reject white Christianity; it must be fully opposed.

Latinx have a calling to dig the graves for a white Christianity that spiritualizes our repression.

The knee of white supremacy upon the neck of one defenseless and subdued Black man for eight minutes and forty-six seconds illustrates the physical violence required to maintain and sustain domestic tranquility through the domination of bodies with darker skin pigmentation—bodies regularly defined by the dominant culture as dirty, dangerous, and diseased. The police, with a history to "protect and serve" whites from the menace of color, could always kill with impunity those who fall short of the white ideal. Individualizing violence, putting a face to the existential threat faced by all people of color, regardless of the shade of their hue, the accent in their voice, or the social capital they possess, galvanized a nation—for a moment—to declare that Black lives indeed matter. And while avoiding the white racist retort that "all lives matter," Latinx still must ask: What does it mean to be Brown while Black lives matter? How do individual acts of violence by law enforcement officers against Latinx fit the overall, predominant Black/white dichotomy imposed on the discourse of race and racism in the United States? In the moment of nationwide protest during a national lockdown due to a global pandemic, thousands of Brown children being held in cages at detention camps by US Immigration and Customs Enforcement (ICE) set up in locales like Tornillo, Texas, are absent from this discourse. Ignored is that in areas where there are large Latinx populations, including California, Arizona, and Texas, Brown folk represent almost half of those who die at the hands of police officers.[2]

One is hard pressed to find media coverage concerning the 497 Brown corpses found in 2019 alone littering our nation's southwestern borders—the corpses of those who sought to cross the barriers designed to separate their cheap labor from their Brown bodies.[3] Four Brown bodies (that we know of, for official numbers are grossly underestimated) perish every three days along our southwestern border to "establish justice, insure domestic tranquility." Interviews conducted over two years by the pro-immigrant organization No More Deaths documented over 32,075 incidents of abuse (including death while in detention) imposed upon Brown bodies during short-term Border Patrol incarceration.[4] And if those bodies are feminine, the threat of sexual terror prevails, as women of color held at ICE detention centers face unnecessary and nonconsensual medical procedures, including unwanted gynecological surgeries like hysterectomies.[5]

The political, philosophical, and theological virus undergirding the individual violence imposed on the Black body of George Floyd is the same political, philosophical, and theological infection responsible for the disproportionate number of Brown and Black bodies succumbing to the ravishes of COVID-19. But in this moment of shared decimation during an era where viruses are not discriminators as to which lives are relegated to the underside of white law, embracing some zero-sum mentality would prove fatal. The strategy of divide (communities of color) and conquer (by the dominant culture) requires opposition through solidarity—hence the need to focus on what it means to be Brown at the intersection of the coronavirus pandemic and #BlackLivesMatter national protests.

The COVID Threat to Latinx

Donald Trump is not responsible for causing the coronavirus. Pandemics occur indiscriminative to whomsoever rules. He is, however, responsible for the excessive body count caused by his early denials of the threat and conflicting policies in handling the danger. His incompetency led to an unmitigated failure in ensuring domestic tranquility for all Americans, earning the nation the undesirable and unwanted title of global epicenter. With just 4.25 percent of the world's population, the United States—by 2020 year's end—represented almost 24 percent of the world's recorded infections and almost 19 percent of global deaths due to COVID-19.[6] And while all who live within the US border are at risk, contrary to public outcries of national solidarity, we are not all in this together. Even though no scientific evidence exists indicating that Latinx are inherently more susceptible to contracting the virus, we are discovering that Latinx are bearing a heavier burden of the pandemic. One reason is that, because Latinx disproportionately congregate at the lower rungs of the nation's economic structures, they lack the financial means by which to stay home and remain safe.

For example, when the coronavirus first spread through the fields and processing plants of California's Central Valley, the Latinx workforce was given a choice: work at great personal risk or stay home without pay. Graciela Ramirez, a machine operator at Ruiz Foods—the nation's largest manufacturer of frozen burritos—like so many others, could not survive without her $750-a-week job. Sheltering in place is seldom an option for those living on the margins, paycheck to paycheck. During the March–April lockdown, the low-income Latinx were disproportionately the so-called essential workers who kept the bare-bones economy operating for the rest of us. Soon Ramirez was infected with the virus, contributing to the grim demographics that Latinx far outpace the rest of the nation in infections. Although 18 percent of the population, they represent 34 percent of COVID cases nationwide. In North Carolina, where Latinx constitute 10 percent of the population, they report 46 percent of all infections, and in Wisconsin where Latinx make up 7 percent of the population, they encompass 33 percent of those who contracted the virus.[7] Ramirez and many Latinx like her represent the cannon fodder in the economic battle waged to minimize the consequential market downturns caused by governmental failures to ensure domestic tranquility by containing the spread of COVID-19.

Jose Ayala, age forty-four, a maintenance worker at the Tyson Foods pork plant in Waterloo, Iowa, died on May 25, 2020, of COVID-19 complications. He was one of the workers, many of whom are immigrants, who labored elbow to elbow at conveyor belts without protective gear like masks or shields as hogs carcasses zipped by. When pressured by town officials on April 10 of that same year to temporarily close their largest pork operations, responsible for 4 percent of US pork consumption, Tyson—more concerned with corporate profitability—refused to do so as workers in need of a paycheck showed up infected to work. So many fell ill that by April 22 they were forced to close the plant due to absenteeism. About 1,031 of the plant's 2,800—mostly immigrant—workers were reported to have contracted the coronavirus. Soon it spread to workers elsewhere, making Waterloo the hardest-hit city in Iowa. Tyson's closure was short-lived as pork shortages spread throughout the nation, leading President Trump on April 28 to sign an executive order declaring meat supply as a "critical infrastructure." Mentioning only Tyson, he suggested shielding the company from liabilities for its disregard of basic safety standards for their predominantly immigrant and Latinx workforce. On May 7 the factory reopened. Eating pork chops apparently trumps the welfare of immigrant workers.[8] The importance of ensuring that a gluttonous America is not deprived of the privilege to consume a cheap, plentiful supply of meat as often as it desires requires the cheapening of Brown lives to ensure a steady and continuous flow of consumer goods.

Ramirez and Ayala constitute acceptable collateral damage when ensuring that the engines of savage capitalism continue to hum. But rather than blaming institutional racism for their predicament, victims are instead blamed for their own dilemma. Medical doctor and Ohio state senator Stephen Huffmann asked, "Could it just be that African-Americans or the colored population do not wash their hands as well as other groups or wear a mask or do not socially distance themselves? Could that be the explanation of why the higher incidence?"[9] The reason Latinx, as "the colored population," are dying of coronavirus at higher rates is, the good doctor suggests, they are simply dirty.

In reality, being relegated to live in dirty neighborhoods is one of the major contributors for Latinx's disproportionately higher rates of infection. Environmental racism means Latinx face greater exposure to COVID-19. Elyria Swansea, who lives in Globeville, Colorado—a predominantly poor Latinx Denver neighborhood—experiences, along with her neighbors, higher hospitalization rates for COVID of 2.9 people per 1,000. Those living in the predominantly white Denver neighborhood of Country Club, located six miles due south, report a hospitalization rate for COVID of only 0.3 people per 1,000. Hence Latinx living in Globeville are almost ten times as likely as their white neighbors to the south to be hospitalized for the coronavirus. The culprit is not that Latinx are dirty but rather that the air they breathe is dirty. Air-quality monitoring conducted over the past five years indicates Globeville frequently exceeded EPA's safety limits.[10] Because a correlation exists between air pollution and susceptibility to COVID-19; where they are forced to live due to institutionalized racism and economic deprivation increases their probability of contracting the coronavirus. A Harvard study released in April 2020 demonstrated how a small increase in long-term exposure to air pollution leads to a large increase in COVID-19 death rates.[11]

While Latinx, as essential workers, face higher infection rates for keeping the economic engines running, they are rewarded with governmental policies that scapegoat them as a major cause for the disease's rampant spread. We are already familiar with Trump's racist usage of the terms "China virus," "Wuhan virus," and "kung flu," responsible for violence unleashed upon the Asian community. In California alone, over eight hundred hate incidents against Asian Americans (of which eighty-one involved a physical assault) related to COVID-19 occurred between March and June 2020.[12] But fostering hatred is not limited to Asian Americans. COVID-19 has been used as an excuse to implement more draconian anti-immigration policies, most notably aimed at migrants and refugees from Latin America.

No member of the Trump administration was more responsible for normalizing and legitimizing anti-Latinx hatred than the president's senior adviser Stephen Miller. He has a history of employing obscure laws that were originally designed to protect the nation from overseas diseases to restrict the migration of Brown bodies. In his mind, and in the minds of so many of his compatriots, Latinx possess diseased bodies. When the 2018 Central American caravan was heading for the border, Miller sought nonexistent evidence of disease-carrying Brown bodies. Although about a dozen migrants fell ill while in custody and two under the age of ten died due to the negligence of border authorities, Miller at that time argued in favor for sealing the border from a perceived health threat without any foreknowledge of this pandemic in sight. When a 2019 mumps epidemic broke out at detention facilities throughout six states, and later that year when the flu crippled one facility, Miller once again sought to seal the border with Mexico as a health precaution. Within days of the first confirmed coronavirus case in the United States, the administration finally moved to effectively shut the border to almost all migrants.[13]

As the coronavirus began to spread nationally, Latinx, seen and defined as diseased, were blamed. "We need a wall more than ever," the president tweeted on March 10, 2020, as a remedy to the "China virus." But as a deteriorating economy in Mexico, some five months after sealing the border, pushed migrants north, the anti-Brown rhetoric of diseased Latinx bodies only increased. "Despite the dangers posed by COVID-19, illegal immigration [sic]—it continues," pronounced the acting commissioner of Custom and Border Protection, Mark Morgan. He went on to state, "[Undocumented immigrants are] putting Americans at risk." He argued for finishing Trump's wall to forestall immigration and the spread of coronavirus by infected migrants.[14] Never let the fear of a pandemic go to waste without manipulating that fear to advance anti-Latinx sentiments and xenophobic policies, or failing to profit off said fear, as illustrated by Steve Bannon—former White House chief strategist—who began "We Build the Wall" to collect contributions by diehard xenophobes to construct the wall along the southern border. Five miles of the wall were constructed with funds collected; about $25 million were diverted to personal accounts.[15]

Originally, fear of terrorism led to anti-Muslim violence, peaking in 2016. Shortly afterward, violence toward Latinx was reintroduced as the new norm, shifting the object to be hated by stroking fear of immigrants.[16] During spring 2020, this hatred led the United States to seal its borders. Miller, the architect of the 2017 Muslim travel bans and Latinx family separation strategy, has regularly promoted theories popular with white supremacist groups, forwarding racist material from the white nationalist website VDare, and sending emails to the alt-right news network Breitbart expressing white nationalist racist conspiracies concerns about "white genocide" committed by people of color.[17] Let's be clear: he is fine with immigration, as long as the immigrants are white and do not come from what Trump called "shithole countries."[18] It's Brown immigrants whom he detests. His anti-Latinx rhetoric reinforces an institutional violence responsible for the overabundance of hate crimes that Latinx face—reaching a sixteen-year high by 2018.[19] Subsequent to Trump's inauguration, some 1,020 hate groups—a number that surged after Trump took office[20]—perpetrated thug violence fueled by xenophobic hatred, the new political norm. Since 2016, the nation has moved beyond a society checked by political correctness, with poorly masked racism and ethnic discrimination, to outright resentment and retaliation against Latinx communities.

Once reserved for Latinx immigrant communities, this retaliation is now being exported to their white allies. When Trump, in April 2020, called upon "real Americans" to liberate their state from the health safety guidance enacted by predominantly Democratic governors, white citizens—along with heavily armed white supremacy groups (e.g., the Boogaloo Boys), stormed several state capitals to protest stay-at-home orders. In Lansing, Michigan, armed extremist groups showed up, yelling at and threatening law enforcement. Police simply stood there, refusing to interfere or make arrests. One protester, who subsequently was arrested, threatened to kill Michigan governor Gretchen Whitmer.[21] When protesters are white, police seek to peacefully defuse tensions, but when protesters are of color—for example, marching after the police murders of George Floyd, Breonna Taylor, and other Black victims— then law enforcement response is violent, employing the same strategies and abuses that Brown bodies face daily on the southern border. Take the federal response to the predominately peaceful and unarmed protest in Portland, Oregon, before federal agents were dispatched. Unleashed on the city of Portland, these unmarked and unidentified Trump agents brutalized peaceful protesters, fired pepper spray and rubber bullets into the crowd, and snatched unnamed people off the streets and tossed them into unmarked vans without identifying themselves. Similar ex-tramilitary agents who employ excessive force with little regard for the law are also assigned to the Border Patrol.[22] The violence that white Portlanders faced, which shocked white America, is what has always been the norm for Latinx along our southwestern border, but largely ignored by the press. Permission to abuse Latinx eventually spills over to anyone—including whites—who stand in solidarity with repressed communities of color. White supremacy employs violence to ensure the domestic tranquility of whites, even against other whites who refuse to live into the unearned power, privilege, and profit that said domestic tranquility ensures.

Safeguarding domestic tranquility for whites requires legitimization of lethal government policies for those outside of the protected class and those within who dare to stand in solidarity with them. To maintain and sustain domestic tranquility for white America, people like Graciela Ramirez must risk their lives as essential workers. People like Jose Ayala must die to ensure a food supply for carnivores. People like Elyria Swansea must be defined as dirty and relegated to neighborhoods where environmental racism places her at greater risk. Unnamed and unseen children must be defined as diseased and thrown into cages, becoming dispensable so that a privileged segment of society can enjoy their justice and domestic tranquility.

Though the threat of the coronavirus has dissipated, the emotional scars caused by COVID-19 upon the Latinx ethos may unfortunately continue for generations. The country will lack the ability to bring forth a more perfect union as long as the fear and hatred of Latinx remain unabetted. In a post-coronavirus world, we can move toward curing what has historically ailed this nation or continue ignoring the virus that goes on laying the body politic to waste. We are left wondering if in the aftermath of the pandemic, can we dare to hope for healing? But healing cannot come forth if Latinx refuse to decolonize their own minds, if they continue to be the white voices speaking through Brown faces seeking the justification of white supremacy for either fame or profit. As horrific as what Latinx face to exist at the underside of white peace and security, worse is when so-called Latinx religious leaders become apologists for white supremacy. To hope requires slaying the tenets of white Christianity and rejecting the Brown faces who support the political policies detrimental to the Latinx's existential being.

Brown Faces with White Voices

On January 3, 2020, the self-proclaimed Latinx apostle Guillermo Maldonado held an "Evangelicals for Trump" rally at his seven-thousand-seat sanctuary, Ministerio Internacional El Rey Jesús in Miami, Florida. There, several evangelical leaders gathered to lay hands on the president. "Father," cried out Maldonado, "we give you the praise and honor and we ask you that [Trump] can be the Cyrus to bring reaffirmation, to bring change into this nation, and all the nations of the Earth will say America is the greatest nation of the Earth."[23] There is profit to be gained in anointing Trump as a modern-day King Cyrus. Comparing Trump to the sixth-century BCE pagan Persian monarch provides the means by which biblical principles concerning virtues can be ignored in favor of political expedience. Abandoning all of the prerequisite piety litmus tests by which other presidents and presidential candidates previously were judged allows evangelicals to embrace a procurer of political cruelty, a swindler, an adulterer, and a habitual liar, because God chooses imperfect humans to accomplish God's will. These "supporters of faith," in their red MAGA caps, came to worship *el rey* Donald who, rather than claiming to stand with God, announced, "I really believe we have God on our side."[24] As Maldonado endangers the souls of his congregation, so too does he endanger their health. He informed his parishioners that fear of the coronavirus can be attributed to a "demonic spirit." He encouraged his congregation to attend Sunday services and ignore official pleas to avoid crowded spaces: "Do you believe God would bring his people to his house to be contagious with the virus? Of course not."[25]

All too often, blaming white people for the death-dealing oppression faced by Latinx becomes too easy and too simplistic of a response. And while Euroamericans should certainly be held accountable for their participation in the normalization of racist social structures, communities of color must also wrestle with their own complicity in the repression of their own community—out of ignorance or as a compromising strategy to profit or advance. Although 70 percent of Latinx helped deliver key swing states during the 2020 election and thus deny Trump a second term, it is still troubling that, based on exit polls, Trump did better among Latinx than he did four years earlier—4 percent better among Latinos and 5 percent better among Latinas. This is important when we consider that 2020 marks the first time Latinx overtook African Americans' electoral participation, becoming the largest minoritized voting bloc.[26]

Since childhood, Latinx have been taught to see, define, and interpret society through white eyes—specifically white male cis-gendered eyes. Learning to define one's own body through the eyes of the dominant culture contributes to the colonization of Latinx minds, which either excuses or justifies a white nationalist Christianity that provides validation for the theft, enslavement, genocide, and rape of bodies falling short of the white ideal. Violence toward Latinx in the past and violence experienced by Latinx today in the form of disproportionately higher deaths due to the coronavirus require the legitimization and normalization of a white Christianity that morally and spiritually defends the indefensible. Weak and diseased Latinx bodies ravished by COVID-19 validate the supremacy of whiteness and vindicate neoliberal advances that continue to contribute to their unmerited power, profit, and privilege.

What happens when the colonization of Latinx minds is so successful that they learn to define their own bodies, consciously or unconsciously, through Eurocentric political paradigms like ensuring domestic tranquility. Once Latinx minds are colonized, their bodies can be controlled with little effort. They can be expected to vote against their own self-interest. The search, therefore, is on to find a Brown face with a white voice to be placed on a pedestal to serve as an official spokesperson for the Latinx community. These colonized Latinx become the defenders of white supremacy. White nationalist Christian thought facilitates the mental shackling of Latinx when some of their skinfolk put on holy vestments to guide the faithful through the wide gate and broad way that leads to destruction. Fawning over political opportunities seeking to maintain and sustain white supremacy, they sell out their own communities for thirty pieces of silver. You can spot them as they appear on racist news outlets like Fox News, OANN, and NewsMax or at the White House laying hands upon the one who builds walls to separate Brown bodies from the labor they provide and wealth they produce for others while throwing their children in camps and cages. Whether because of a need to survive or greed to personally benefit, their full-throttled support of white supremacy provides the opportunity to grow rich off the mite of the Latina widow.

There are always members of one's own community who are willing to consciously or naively betray their own people for the trappings of power, be it by speaking during the inauguration of a racist or laying hands on the anti-Christ at the Oval Office. The Trump White House was an administration that launched its quest for the highest office in the land by disparaging Latinx as "bringing . . . problems with them. They're bringing drugs. They're bringing crime. They're rapists."[27] And while Brown people are being targeted by border agents and hate groups, Brown ministers arise to provide political cover. Take Samuel Rodriguez, for example, founder of the National Hispanic Leadership Conference (NHCLC) who delusionally claimed to be a voice for the undocumented. His idolatrous support of the president was based on the presupposition that Trump would be interested in hearing a voice from the Latinx marginalized. Rodriguez embraced a white nationalist Christianity that is, and always will be, detrimental to the community he claims to represent. For example, he preaches that racism is not a hate problem but a heart problem,[28] embracing the hyperindividuality of Eurocentric Christianity by claiming the answer is not political advocacy, but repentance of personal sin by becoming "born again" (code language for embracing white evangelical Christianity). Such pronouncements tickle the fancy of white Christian racists, while asking nothing of them to deal with the systemic racism responsible not only for death-dealing immigration policies but also the disproportionate number of Latinx falling ill to the coronavirus.

Contrary to Rodriguez's embrace of Eurocentric supremacist Christianity, racism is, and always has been, a hate problem. Many slaveholders who professed their love for Jesus and commitment to evangelism had heart, so much heart that they formed their own white nationalist denomination—the Southern Baptists—so that they could reconcile the oppression of Black slave bodies with their born-again love for Jesus. Rodriguez and other Brown-faced ministers who are ontologically white—like Mario Bramnick, Pasqual Urrabazo, and Ramiro Peña—advocate for a kind of heart allowing whites to love Jesus while hating Jesús. Their deep ties to the Trump administration reinforced a white supremacist theology that reduces attempts to bring about racial and ethnic justice to a matter of prayer rather than praxis, conversion rather than confrontation.

The colonized minds of Brown ministers define intelligence through white Christian academic paradigms, the same paradigms that pose an existential threat to Brown bodies seeking the liberation of their minds. They, along with some religion scholars of color, look to their oppressors for the means by which to define and express their thoughts. An unsuccessful attempt is made to liberate dark bodies through white thinking. Instead, what they accomplish is leading Latinx to vote against their own best interests. When 33 percent of Latinx Protestants support a racist president who launched his campaign demonizing Brown bodies, a problem exists within our community. When 11 percent of Latinx Protestants confess that Trump can do nothing to cause their support to waver,[29] then their minds have been so successfully colonized that they worship an idol rather than their God. These Brown apologists for Trump provide cover and consent for white Christians to support anti-Latinx policies with the peace of mind in knowing they aren't really racist because they can point to a Brown face who speaks like they do.

No to Jesus, Sí a Jesús

Brown ministers advocating a Eurocentric Christianity that contributes to death—spiritually and physically—are instrumental in the colonization process of Latinx's minds. A decolonization of our minds begins with the full and total rejection of white Christianity and all those within our community who for monetary rewards or access to power peddle its lies. The task of decolonization of our minds begins with learning to think our own thoughts rooted within our own communities, apart from white Eurocentrism. *"El vino, de plátano; y si sale agrio, ¡Es nuestro vino!"* As long as we look to a white Christian nationalism on which to construct our liberative philosophical paradigms, we are doomed not only to fail but to reinforce white theological supremacy. No person can serve two masters, for they will love one and despise the other. Colonized people who serve and love white Christianity, which was created to spiritually justify their exclusion, or the white Gods and Jesuses bent on their subservience, will learn how to despise the religious and philosophical wisdom embedded within their own community. The task before Latinx communities is to discern how to think thoughts that are less a response, and more an Indigenous radical worldview different from the normative philosophies that have historically justified our subservient place within society.

Echoing Fredrick Douglass's observation concerning the congruency of slavocracy and the Christian church, we today must ask why the white Jesus of the dominant culture has nothing to say about Latinx disproportionately being infected by the coronavirus, or is silent concerning Latinx children being torn from their parents' arms and placed in cages due to the virus of white supremacy. Silence, as James Cone reminds us, is why white Christianity is Satanic. This is a Jesus who masquerades as an angel of light. This Jesus who embraces US nationalism must be rejected not only by Latinx but by all who are left out of justice and domestic tranquility. Saying no to the Eurocentric Jesus becomes the first step toward saying yes to the self and yes to liberation—in short, yes to Jesús.

An attempt is here made to literally *do* Christology with an accent—and not just over the "u," but also the linguistic accent of Latinx attempting to speak against the language of empire. Seeking a liberative spirituality demands putting away the white Jesus advocated by Brown apologists, so as to claim the Jesús congruent with the Latinx context suffering the oppressive structures of white supremacy manifested as disproportionate deaths during COVID-19. This is obviously not the Jesús of conquistadores and caudillos, who are just as satanic as the white Jesus of empire and who tend to justify, legitimize, and normalize oppression, but rather the Jesús of the disenfranchised, the dispossessed, and the disinherited. Christology becomes the task of creating a Jesús congruent with the Latinx context who resonates with the communities' trials and tribulations—a Jesús committed to fulfilling the mission of providing life, and life abundantly (John 10:10).

A Latinx-Base Response for Such a Time as This

Building walls on artificial international lines of demarcation or along neighborhood boundaries constructed to separate whiteness from color ensures domestic tranquility for those whom society privileges. The proliferation of for-profit prisons to house and prosper from the criminalization and containment of the prime of Brown and Black America ensures domestic tranquility for those whom society empowers. The militarization of law enforcement on our nation's borders and our community's streets ensures domestic tranquility for those upon whom society bestows peace. Ensuring domestic tranquility for white Christians early on required the genocide of the land's original inhabitants, so that a chosen people could build a new nation upon scattered Indigenous bones. Ensuring domestic tranquility for white Christians also required the enslavement of those a continent away, so that a so-called exceptional people could monopolize the sweat of another's brow and the strength of another's arm to enrich an emerging Republic. Ensuring domestic tranquility for white Christians required building roads to sovereign nations to the south, so as to steal their raw material and cheap labor in order that a so-called exceptional people could create the most powerful empire ever witnessed on the planet. Ensuring domestic tranquility becomes patriotic code language that masks the domestication of bodies that fall short of the white ideal. We are not "all in this together," because ensuring domestic tranquility has historically been paid for by offering up the lives and bodies of those relegated to the underside of white power, profit, and privilege as living sacrifices to the white God. Communities of color are crucified on the COVID-19 crosses of racism and classism, so that whites can have life and live abundantly. We have indeed achieved a more perfect nation, that is, a more perfect nation for the dominant culture, legitimized by laws, maintained by courts, normalized by schools, and ordained by Christian churches.

For several years, I have been an advocate for what I have been calling an ethics *para joder* as a response to the hopelessness of the moment, an ethics "that screws with" the dominant culture. Before the vastness of institutionalized racism, institutionalized violence, and institutionalized oppression, where resistance is indeed futile and where victory over evil is hopeless, the only ethical response from the margins is an ethics *para joder*. Few alternatives exist for the least of these to demand justice.[30] They can always hope white Christians might have a come-to-Jesus moment in which they renounce racism and crucify their privilege, but until now, such hope has accomplished little to ease or lift the burden of centuries of oppression. Few liberals and progressives are willing to lift a finger, if it entails being stripped of their white affirmative action. Full frontal rebellion often leads to massacres whenever white affirmative action is threatened by upsetting their domestic tranquility. How then can change be brought forth without becoming martyrs?

Screwing with the power structures becomes a badass Christian tactic. If law and order further oppressive structures, then subversion provides opportunities for a more perfect union. When marginalized communities begin to *joder*, the domestic tranquility of whites are threatened and disabled. To *joder* is a subversive praxis that refuses to play by the rules established by those who maintain social order because it protects their privilege, power, and profit. If the goal is to bring forth a more perfect union, which by definition means the current unjust one must be overthrown, then no choice exists but to move beyond established rules designed to further the current Eurocentric system. In order to stop engaging in police brutality, we must stop going to the police department to obtain a permit from the police department in order to obtain permission to protest the police department.

Let Jesús be our example. When he overturned bankers' tables at the Temple, he was *jodiendo*. This badass ethics of *jodiendo* response is not some new concept dreamed up in my ivory tower. This has always been a survival strategy employed by the world's wretched. Coining "an ethics *para joder*" simply puts into words a practice that has existed for centuries among the oppressed and repressed. I am simply taking a page from our cultures of color and embracing the trickster image. Consider the coyote and the spider within the Indigenous community, or Br'er Rabbit within the African American community, or Cantinflas within the Mexican community, or Elegúa within my own Cuban community—all are tricksters who through lies, humor, tricks, and tomfoolery unmasked the hypocrisies of our dominating oppressors who hide behind the rhetoric of ensuring domestic tranquility. How does one ethically lie to discover truth, and morally steal to feed the hungry?

Think of the slaveholder during the antebellum South who hires a preacher to routinely teach his slaves not to steal, to work hard, and to obey their master as unto the Lord. There is no end of irony that one who stole the enslaved person's body in the first place established the laws and rules that define stealing, laziness, or disobedience as illegal or immoral when done by Blacks. An ethics *para joder* would argue that the slave has a moral obligation to steal from the master's coop so as to feed her family, to pretend to work hard while trying to conserve as much energy as possible so as to survive, to disobey, and when possible, to free themselves. Killing the slaveholders might very well be the ethical response to save the lives of the slave community. The laws that reinforced the white Christianity of that time were not only satanic but had to be overcome and overpowered in order to achieve true justice. Unfortunately, those slavocracy norms simply morphed into what we have today. So, if we truly wish for a more perfect union, rather than blindly seek to ensure domestic tranquility, we might be more successful seeking the chaos that subverts and disrupts the perceived peace and superficial societal equilibrium needed for oppression to persist and repression to flourish.

NOTES

1 Frederick Douglass, *Narrative of the Life of Frederick Douglass: An American Slave* (1845; New York: Cosimo Classics, 2008), 72.

2 Kelsey S. Geiser et al., *Racial and Identity Profiling Advisory Board Annual Report 2019* (Sacramento: State of California Department of Justice, 2019), 58, 82.

3 International Organization of Migration, "More Deaths Recorded in the Americas in 2019 Than Previous Years," United Nations press release, January 28, 2020, www.iom.int/news.

4 No More Deaths / No más muertes, *A Culture of Cruelty: Abuse and Impunity in Short-Term U.S. Border Patrol Custody* (Tucson, AZ: No More Deaths, 2011), 11.

5 Daniella Silva, "Migrant Women File Class-Action Lawsuit for Alleged Medical Abuse at ICE Detention Center," NBC News, December 22, 2020.

6 "Coronavirus Map: Tracking the Global Outbreak," *New York Times*, December 28, 2020.

7 Shawn Hubler, Thomas Fuller, Anjali Singhvi and Juliette Love, "Latinos Bearing Heavier Burden in the Outbreak," *New York Times*, June 27, 2020.

8 Donnelle Eller, "Trump Orders Meat Plants to Stay Open during COVID-19 Pandemic," *Des Moines Register*, April 28, 2020; Ana Swanson, David Yaffe-Bellany and Michael Corkey, "At Iowa Meat Plant, It's Worker Safety vs. Food Supply," *New York Times*, May 11, 2020; and Ryan J. Foley, "Another Worker at Tyson Foods' Waterloo Plant Dies after Long Battle with COVID-19," Associated Press, May 25, 2020.

9 Trip Gabriel, "Ohio Lawmaker Asks Racist Question about Black People and Hand-Washing," *New York Times*, June 11, 2020.

10 Katie Weis, "Denver Hispanics Neighborhoods with Higher COVID-19 Hospitalization Rates Also Have Higher Air Pollution Levels Than White Neighborhoods," CBS Denver, August 6, 2020.

11 Xiao Wu et al., *Exposure to Air Pollution and COVID-19 Mortality in the United States: A Nationwide Cross-Section Study* (Boston: Department of Biostatistics, Harvard T.H. Chan School of Public Health, 2020), 1.

12 Erin Donaghue, "800+ Hate Crimes against Asian in California Reported in Past 3 Months," CBS San Francisco Bay Area, July 5, 2020.

13 Caitlin Dickerson and Michael D. Shear, "Revisited Plan Cites Sickness to Seal Border," *New York Times*, May 4, 2020.

14 Kirk Semple, "After Lockdown Lull, Illegal Migration from Mexico Soars," *New York Times*, August 7, 2020.

15 Zolan Kanno-Youngs, Eric Lipton, Stephanie Saul, and Scott Shane, "How Bannon and His Indicted Business Partners Cashed In on Trump," *New York Times*, August 20, 2020.

16 Brad Brooks, "Victims of Anti-Latino Hate Crimes Soar in U.S.: FBI Report," Reuters, November 12, 2019.

17 Katie Rogers, "Watchdog Bares Emails of Trump Aide Pushing White Nationalist Views," *New York Times*, November 11, 2019.

18 Julie Hirschfeld Davis, Sheryl Gay Stolberg, and Thomas Kaplan, "Trump Alarms Lawmakers with Disparaging Words for Haiti and Africa," *New York Times*, January 11, 2018.

19 Adeel Hassan, "Assaults Linked to Hate Crimes Were Up in 2008 According to F.B.I.," *New York Times*, November 13, 2019.

20 Jason Wilson, "US Hate Groups Have Seen Ideas Enter Mainstream in Trump Era, Report Finds," *The Guardian*, February 20, 2019. These statistics are also confirmed by the Southern Poverty Law Center and the Anti-Defamation League.

21 Christopher Mele, "Man Faces Terrorism Charge after Threatening to Kill Michigan's Governor, Officials Say," *New York Times*, May 15, 2020.

22 Sergio Olmos, Mike Baker, and Zolan Kanno-Youngs, "Federal Officers Deployed in Portland Didn't Have Proper Training, D.H.S. Memo Said," *New York Times*, July 18, 2020.

23 Adam Gabbatt, "'Unparalleled Privilege': Why White Evangelicals See Trump as Their Savior," *The Guardian*, January 11, 2020.

24 Richard Luscombe, "'He Was Sent to Us': At Church Rally, Evangelicals Worship God and Trump," *The Guardian*, January 4, 2020.

25 Bianca Padró Ocasio, "'Demonic Spirit:' Miami Pastor Rejects Coronavirus Warning," *Miami Herald*, March 15, 2020.

26 Ed Morales, "What the 2020 Election Reveals about Latino Voters," CNN, November 16, 2020; Ashitha Nagesh, "US Election 2020: Why Trump Gained Support among Minorities," BBC, November 22, 2020.

27 Donald Trump presidential announcement speech, New York, June 16, 2015, time.com.

28 Aaron E. Sanchez, "Who Are the Latino Evangelicals That Support Trump?," *Sojourners*, November 26, 2019.

29 "Fractured Nation: Widening Partisan Polarization and Key Issues in 2020 Presidential Elections," Public Religion Research Institute, October 20, 2019.

30 Miguel A. De La Torre, *Latina/o Social Ethics: Moving beyond Eurocentric Moral Thinking* (Waco, TX: Baylor University Press, 2010), 92–97.

8

Deep in the Heart of Texas

Race, Religion, and Rights in the COVID-19 Era

JUAN M. FLOYD-THOMAS

Texas is a state of mind. Texas is an obsession.
—John Steinbeck, *Travels with Charley: In Search of America*

On March 23, 2020, Texas lieutenant governor Dan Patrick faced a social media maelstrom after he told Fox News analyst Tucker Carlson he would rather "take a chance" and go back to work, even if it meant risking death, rather than see recent coronavirus restrictions, "stay-at-home" orders, and "social distancing" do prolonged damage to the US economy. Patrick's comments directly contradicted the mandates and guidelines established by the Centers for Disease Control and Prevention (CDC) designed to mitigate the spread of this highly transmissible and potentially fatal disease. As a high-ranking elected Republican official in one of the nation's largest and most diverse states, Patrick made his controversial remarks against the backdrop of a rising tide of thousands of infections in Texas and hundreds of deaths due to the COVID-19 pandemic. Patrick's appearance on the program came after President Donald Trump declared earlier the same day that he wanted the nation to get back to business in a matter of weeks rather than months. A month later, Patrick returned to Fox News and doubled down on his earlier comments by saying, "When you start shutting down society and people start losing their paychecks and businesses can't open and governments aren't getting revenues . . . I'm sorry to say that I was right on this." By the end of the interview, host Tucker Carlson repeated his interpretation of Patrick's argument: "You're basically saying that this disease could take your life, but that's not the scariest thing to you, there's something worse than dying?" To which Patrick answered with a definitive "Yeah."[1]

Even as Patrick uttered his controversial comments, the mayors of most of Texas's largest cities were following the instructions from medical doctors, health care professionals, and biomedical researchers by gradually ordering their cities' residents to stay home. Medical experts insisted at the outset of the COVID-19 outbreak that the federal government should implement a wide-ranging, aggressive nationwide response to the looming pandemic in order to contain the disease. Experts say the moves that officials and citizens made in those early weeks of awareness determined the likely trajectory COVID-19 assumed at a national level. In March 2020, public health experts seeking to minimize infections advised as follows: identify and isolate people who are ill; trace those with whom sick people had contact to find others who might have been exposed; quarantine anyone who may have been exposed to the virus; close schools, workplaces, houses of worship, and other communal spaces; and encourage people to avoid crowded spaces by enacting a policy of social distancing. Insisting these strict measures were indispensable to reducing the virus's spread throughout the population, public health experts also sought to prevent skyrocketing infection rates from overwhelming the nation's health care system.

This chapter utilizes a microhistorical approach—an intensive, extremely close-up investigation of a historical event from a relatively small time or space made large—in the hopes of making the best possible use of rich local and state documentary data for the state of Texas in order to discern the universal from the specific.[2] As a methodological approach, microhistory should be considered more akin to a core sample than a case study; it illuminates the density and complexity of localized social dynamics for easy comparison with broader national patterns on both a quantitative and qualitative basis. An effort to understand why conservative elected officials in the Lone Star State would make decisions so inherently detrimental and deadly to their citizenry can appear somewhat murky and muddled if one tries to assess what is going on solely based on observations of nationwide trends. Considering the avalanche of COVID-19 cases and resulting casualties since February 2020, many issues and questions can elude the grasp of a macrohistorical account of COVID-19's impact on the United States during the subsequent twelve months. For that reason, a microhistorical approach is arguably best suited to address complex considerations by reaching into the horizontal and vertical relational networks in a localized context and among various demographic subgroups found within it. As historian David Sabean argues, "Social facts are always conditioned by their positions inside a set of specific relations."[3] Or as novelist Gustave Flaubert succinctly put it, "God is in the details."[4]

As 2020 drew to a close, the United States had surpassed more than 20 million infections and more than 346,000 deaths from COVID-19, while global cases rose to an estimated 83,832,334 infections and 1,824,590 deaths. The vast majority of these infections and deaths occurred after January 21, 2020, the now infamous day when a Chinese scientist, Zhong Nanshan, MD, confirmed the likelihood of COVID-19 human transmission and CDC medical researchers confirmed a Washington state resident as the first US novel coronavirus case.[5] From that date, it took only ninety-six days to reach 1 million cases in the United States. As Table 8.1 indicates, the rate of infected Americans per millions over a given span of days then largely accelerated from mid-March to mid-November 2020.

When looking at national estimates, note that all displayed counts include confirmed COVID-19 cases and deaths as reported by US states, US territories, New York City (NYC), and the District of Columbia from the previous day. Counts for certain jurisdictions also include probable COVID-19 cases and deaths.[6] Figure 8.1 shows the total cumulative rate of COVID-19 cases per 100,000 population in Texas from the date of the first US infection until the end of the year. Figure 8.2 reveals the total

Table 8.1. Rate of Increase in Total COVID-19 US Cases per 1,000,000 Population

1 to 2 million	44 days
2 to 3 million	27 days
3 to 4 million	15 days
4 to 5 million	17 days
5 to 6 million	22 days
6 to 7 million	25 days
7 to 8 million	21 days
8 to 9 million	14 days
9 to 10 million	10 days
10 to 11 million	7 days
11 to 12 million	6 days

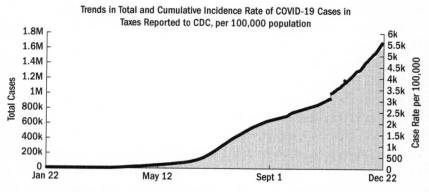

Figure 8.1. Total cumulative rate of COVID-19 cases per 100,000 population in Texas. Source: Graph derived from cdc.gov data from January 20, 2020, to December 31, 2020.

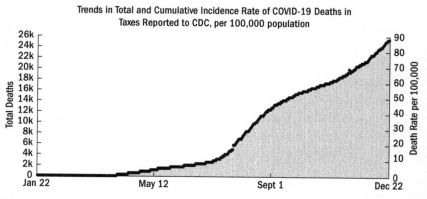

Figure 8.2. Total cumulative COVID-19 deaths per 100,000 population in Texas. Graph derived from cdc.gov data from January 20, 2020, to December 31, 2020.

cumulative incidence rate of COVID-19 deaths per 100,000 population in Texas during that same period.

As outlandish and horrific as these nationwide statistics are, even more resonant data are uncovered by examining Texas more closely. For example, in the wake of the state's Republican leadership's rush to end stay-at-home orders by prematurely reopening every facet of life in the state, Texas suffered the ravages associated with a pandemic raging out of control. By October 2020, the state's public health officials had recorded over

917,000 COVID-19 infections and 18,076 deaths. Texas witnessed a 19 percent positivity rate among those tested and a 43 percent increase among
those infected during a single seven-day period, which is astronomical
compared to just a few months earlier.[7] Infections in Texas surpassed
those found in the whole nation of Mexico, its neighbor to the south,
which had 891,160 at the time. The mindset among the state's leadership
unfortunately resulted in Texas, the second-most-populous state in the
nation, surpassing 1 million cases in early November 2020. Texas held the
dubious distinction of becoming the first US state to record such a high
volume of COVID-19 cases. By the summer of 2020, El Paso County in
Texas ranked among the hardest-hit areas in the country. NPR stated the
matter succinctly: "If Texas was a country instead of a state, it would rank
in the top 10 nations with the most overall coronavirus cases."[8]

While emblematic of the right-wing fervor to reopen the US economy,
Patrick's remarks on the Fox News broadcast also revealed crucial insight
into the innermost workings of Trumpism as a significant, albeit sham-
bolic, theory of politics. The worldview espoused by Patrick and many
of his fellow Republicans in their manic frenzy to "reopen America" reflects what I term the "unholy trinity" at the core of Trumpism: neoliberalism, nihilism, and necropolitics. When contemplating the duty of
human care and concern for others in the face of diametrically opposed,
antagonistic concerns, Augustine of Hippo proves useful. Central to his
writings, Augustine instructed the faithful believer of the responsibility
to discern a hierarchical ordering of people, priorities, and principles,
to "love" them rightly on a metaphysical level, and to attune oneself to
that selfsame love. Augustine defined rightly ordered loves as virtue and
disordered loves as vice. He taught that people are most fundamentally
shaped not as much by what they believe or think or even do, but by
what they love. To invoke even more romantic imagery, those things
people hold most sacred are held deepest in their hearts. The functional
cause of crisis in our season of woe and discontent is that our loves are
out of order. Using another powerful illustration, Augustine coined the
theological phrase *incurvatus in se* (Latin: "curved inward on oneself")
to describe one's worldview bent "inward" toward oneself rather than
reaching "outward" for God and other human beings—a framework for
seeing sinfulness as an intrinsic, idolatrous human inclination to turn
away from others in their time of jeopardy or dire need.[9]

The work of this chapter, therefore, is to gauge the extent to which the core tenets of Trumpism—neoliberalism, nihilism, and necropolitics—burrowed their way deep into the heart of Texas during this very specific moment in history. However, before delving into the specific function of this unholy trinity of Trumpism, we must first inspect the definition of religion. Ritual represents one of the most rudimentary aspects within the scope of religious experience and expression. Possibly the most succinct, germane definition of ritual is offered by Catherine Bell, who refers to it as "particularly thoughtless action—routinized, habitual, obsessive, or mimetic—and therefore the purely formal, secondary, and mere physical expression of logically prior ideas."[10] Part of the argument of this chapter is that if religion is about the routinized enactment of the sacred as well as the ritualistic empowerment of the quotidian that orders attitudes, appetites, and actions, then the scope of what qualifies as "religion" is much broader than we currently envision it.[11]

For example, religion is not just merely proclaiming faith in Jesus Christ, Jehovah, or Allah in a robotic fashion or quoting holy scripture by rote memorization. Instead, it is—or at least ought to be—about how we engage with experiences and expressions of shared sacred beliefs as well as secular values. For instance, religious studies scholars have already done the work of arguing that capitalism is a religion and that the market functions as a serviceable God.[12] In this view, the ritualistic activity of mundane economic exchange that we engage in endlessly every single day functions as a religious system by promising to transform our lives. By making capitalism the natural and normal object of our daily devotion, we make it an indelible and inescapable part of our existence as human beings. This worldview slowly but surely indoctrinates us into lives fixated by the innermost workings of the market, but never quite fixed by our relationship with the market.

Neoliberalism

Police officer Derek Chauvin murdered George Floyd in Minneapolis on Memorial Day 2020 by choking him to death while three of his fellow police officers stood and watched. Floyd thus became one of the most infamous victims of police brutality in the era of #BlackLivesMatter. At the time of his death, he had only recently arrived in Minneapolis from his beloved hometown of Houston. Born in North Carolina in October 1973, his single mother relocated him and his siblings to Houston in his early childhood. Upon their arrival in Texas, his family lived in the Cuney Homes public housing project in Houston's Third Ward. As a young man, he had lofty dreams of growing up one day to become "a Supreme Court Judge [sic]" as he once wrote in a second-grade essay assignment. During his later adolescent and teen years, his interests turned away from scholastics toward sports, and he played in the local YMCA basketball league. As his physique grew to an imposing six feet seven inches tall and 250 pounds, he eventually garnered the nickname "Big Floyd." Many locals fondly recalled Floyd as a stellar athlete at Jack Yates High School, where he played basketball and football. In addition to his athletic prowess and good-natured affability, Big Floyd became a minor local celebrity in his Third Ward community thanks to his rap performances on DJ Screw's legendary 1990s mixtapes, which show-cased Big Floyd and dozens of other local emerging rappers.

Following his graduation from Yates in 1993, the next two decades of Floyd's life were fraught with the perilous struggles of a young Black man trapped between the diminishing job opportunities and the under-ground economy of Houston's Third Ward and Texas's voracious car-ceral state. His dreams of playing in the NBA faded once he ended his collegiate basketball playing career at Florida State College and Texas A&M–Kingsville. He confessed to being homesick for Houston and summarily returned there. However, as Floyd's childhood friend Meshah Hawkins recounts, "He got into trouble. . . . He fell into the things a lot of the guys in the neighborhood were doing." Consequently, in 1998 police arrested Floyd and charged him with theft. In a later instance, he faced charges for drug possession. Convicted in 2009 after pleading guilty to aggravated robbery with a deadly weapon, Floyd went to prison for four years in East Texas. Paroled in 2013 and, a year later, recognizing the lack of job opportunities and social mobility in Texas as far too limiting, Floyd made the trek to the Twin Cities area in search of a better, longer life.[13]

Millions around the nation and worldwide witnessed George Floyd literally being crushed under the knee of a cruel and callous police of-ficer, a heinous yet symbolic act on a number of levels. First, society was already crushing the life out of George Floyd as he struggled to realize his constantly frustrated dreams of a successful, sustainable future for him and his loved ones within a reality defined by a fiercely neoliberal world order. He experienced the structural inequality of this lopsided economy as suffocating. As a formerly incarcerated person in a society that doesn't provide much grace or mercy to those who've been imprisoned, Floyd experienced the crushing weight of the world around him in yet another way. The offense that led to his interaction with the police— allegedly passing a counterfeit twenty-dollar bill that might not have been his at a nearby convenience store—certainly wasn't a crime worthy of death. Even worse, his autopsy revealed that George Floyd tested positive for COVID-19, which leads one to wonder if the cops would have even stepped near him had they had known his possibly contagious state. Although Floyd became a casualty of the equally lethal and loathsome "policeman-demic" sweeping the nation, his lifetime spent in the throes of neoliberalism in Texas acted as the preexisting condition to his inability to grapple with the ravages of the coronavirus pandemic, economic panic, and political pandemonium, well before the police killed him.

In light of these tensions, neoliberalism must be discussed. As a system of macroeconomic policies that have been widely implemented in the United States and globally, philosopher and activist Angela Davis states, "Neoliberalism sees the market as the very paradigm of freedom, and democracy emerges as a synonym for capitalism, which has reemerged as the telos of history."[14] While it has been fashionable in academic and activist contexts to attack the very mention of the term "neoliberalism," the critique has become so ubiquitous that it hovers innocuously on the verge of being either a euphemism or an epithet. Since the 1990s, "neoliberal" has been largely used by the left as a blanket term to condemn contemporary capitalism and social inequality.[15] As historians Andrew J. Diamond and Thomas J. Sugrue contend, "Neoliberalism is sometimes a name for the deregulatory and anti-welfare policies of Margaret Thatcher in Britain and Ronald Reagan in the United States and their successors. It is sometimes a loose description of an orientation toward the market and a faith in market-based solutions to social problems."[16] In his book *A Brief History of Neoliberalism*, David Harvey presents the default account of the neoliberal ascendency by chronicling the global rise of neoliberal regimes, which, among other things, were increasingly oligarchic in nature with commitments to unrestrained movement of capital, imposition of economic austerity on governments, the privatization of public works, and the financialization of the economy.[17] Gradually, the term has become synonymous with any and all right-wing fiscal policies or conservative market-oriented economic programs (most often stated in the harshest, most strident, and pejorative sense possible) without any shred of nuance or distinction.

The rise of neoliberal practices is especially notable in the transformation of the Texan political economy over the past half-century. With the ascendancy of American conservatism since the Reagan-Bush era, we have witnessed every dimension of human activity from industry, education, entertainment, government, and even religion skewed toward the desired effects of the rich getting richer and the poor growing poorer, by prioritizing profitability over the public good. One cannot overstate how much the neoliberal impulse demonstrated by Lieutenant Governor Patrick's statement on Fox News reflects the daunting force that propelled him and many of his ilk in their zealous, reckless frenzy to reopen society, because money is deemed more important than either morality or mortality.

More than hypertension, obesity, diabetes, or any other form of comorbidity, the COVID-19 pandemic has revealed that racial capitalism is the deadliest, most dangerous preexisting condition in the United States. Building upon the work of other earlier Black radical intellectuals such as W. E. B. Du Bois, C. L. R. James, and Oliver C. Cox, among others, political theorist Cedric Robinson's articulation of racial capitalism challenged both traditional and Marxist views of modern political economy. Robinson advanced the argument that capitalism is a reiteration of, instead of a revolution away from, early modes of political economy in the West that always infused class thoroughly with racialism. Capitalism and racism did not break from the old order, but rather evolved seamlessly within it, in order to produce a modern world system anchored by white supremacy, chattel slavery, violence, imperialism, dispossession, and genocide. Robinson's analysis provided a perspectival shift in a critical analysis of race and class, by developing a paradigm that took capitalism from merely describing a specific mode of economic activity to a way of understanding the general history of political economy in the modern world.[18]

To even the most casual observer of American race relations, Texas possesses a pernicious history as a modern racial state that deserves a reckoning. The white Texan power brokers have created a structural regime characterized by racism, robbery, and ruthlessness. The origins of the state in the 1830s were in the westward imperialist expansionism of a white settler society on land watered by the blood of slaughtered Indigenous and Mexican peoples. Settlers made the "Lone Star Republic" a reality by establishing a slaveocracy to drain the life, labor, and liberty of countless Black women, men, and children.[19] Amid all the recent reflection surrounding Juneteenth as a holiday celebrating Black emancipation, we should remember its sad origins: white Texans hoodwinked and bamboozled Black Texans into spending additional time trapped in chattel slavery.[20] We can also consider how, roughly a century after the end of the Civil War, the civil rights movement epitomized by Dr. Martin Luther King Jr.'s life and leadership pretty much missed Texas entirely in ways that left recurring ramifications within the state.[21] Even more recently, Trump spent much of his presidential term obsessively focusing on the Texas borderlands as the site for his bogus Mexican border wall as well as the Immigration and Customs Enforcement concentration camps.

The COVID-19 recession started in February 2020 and arguably may have been the most comprehensive business downturn in the history of economics. As the novel coronavirus began to spread around the globe, whole sectors of the US economy had to be temporarily placed into suspended animation in order to enable public health officials to prevent further spread of the virus. Although substantial job losses occurred for most of 2020, for better or worse, the impact of the recession affected industries and services most highly likely to spread the coronavirus: restaurants, movie theaters, bars, gyms, cruise ships, airlines, sports venues, and the like—all deemed inessential enough to be closed until safer, alternate arrangements could be devised. In a historic moment in which millions of Americans—disproportionately Black and Brown low-wage employees—are being called "essential workers," Angela Davis reminds us the "invisible work of racism not only influences the life chances of millions of people, it helps to nourish a psychic reservoir of racism that often erupts through the utterances and actions of individuals," which have little or no impact on such widespread, massive phenomena because they "can only be answered if we are able to recognize this deep structural life of racism."[22] The most logical goal of economic policy hoped to make this lockdown tolerable and temporary, by limiting economic activities only to a labor force of essential workers while also sustaining the incomes of those unable to work through no fault of their own until everyone could return to business as usual. The most logical approach for the nation to combat COVID-19 seemed simple: if we freeze the virus, then we can free the economy. In his assessment of Trump and the GOP's response to the looming economic crisis, Nobel Prize–winning economist Paul Krugman argues, "Republicans, however, have shown no sign of understanding any of this. The policy proposals being floated by White House aides and advisers are almost surreal in their disconnect from reality. Cutting payroll taxes on workers who can't work? Letting businesspeople deduct the full cost of three-martini lunches they can't eat? . . . Above all, Republicans seem obsessed with the idea that unemployment benefits are making workers lazy and unwilling to accept jobs."[23]

The night before Patrick's appearance on Tucker Carlson's program, Texas comptroller Glenn Hegar briefed Texas House members on the state's overall economic situation. During his report, Hegar told the legislators that, although it was too premature to make specific predictions, he foresaw both the economy and budget were likely to take massive hits in the wake of the coronavirus pandemic. According to the *Texas Tribune*, the members-only call with the comptroller—led by House Speaker Dennis Bonnen (R-Angleton)—represented one of state lawmakers' first glimpses into the devastating financial impact the virus would have on the Texan economy. Hegar warned that the state's economy was already experiencing a recessionary cycle by mid-March 2020—that both the general revenue for the state budget derived from multiple industries and state finances as well as Texas's Economic Stabilization Fund (the savings account known as a rainy-day fund largely fed by revenue by the oil industry) would suffer drastically lower balances, possibly a shortfall of billions of dollars. Driven by this bleak fiscal forecast, the comptroller's office warned the lawmakers that, unless the legislature spent money out of the Economic Stabilization Fund by or before July, the fund's balance would be revised downward by an estimated $1 billion. In October 2019, Hegar estimated that the state's budget would have a nearly $3 billion balance for the fiscal 2020–21 biennium while, during a similar period, the balance of the Economic Stabilization Fund had been projected to reach $9.3 billion by the end of the 2021 fiscal year.[24]

Without question, the virus had already sent devastating shock waves to economies around the nation as well as the farthest reaches of the globe. As the infectious spread of the novel coronavirus grew into a full-blown pandemic, a huge aura of uncertainty accompanied this health crisis about how deep and extensive the repercussions would be after shutting down the world's largest, most robust economies. For instance, when many of the world's industrialized societies imposed strict stay-at-home orders for their inhabitants, this brought a huge proportion of human transportation via car, bus, airplane, and ship to a screeching halt. To offset the corresponding downward spiral of global demand for petroleum, Saudi Arabia waged a price war with Russia that resulted in oil prices plummeting to their lowest levels in decades. As the top oil-producing state in the United States, Texas's economy and budget have always been particularly sensitive to volatility in global oil prices. Additionally, as the virus began creeping onto the nation's shores and across state borders, the fear for public safety led officials to shut down countless industries' operations to limit public interactions and stem the growing tide of new infections. The combination of these twin concerns created a double whammy by slowing two key revenues integral to fueling the state's budget and economy: sales taxes and oil and gas production.

In a rare spirit of unanimity, medical experts and economists agreed that the full extent of economic damage would depend on how society constrained the duration and severity of the public health crisis. For his part, Governor Greg Abbott issued an executive order directing bars, dine-in restaurants, gyms, churches, and schools to close, as he estimated that tens of thousands of Texans could test positive for COVID-19 that spring. During this particularly fraught period, Abbott noted he and the legislature could tap into the state's disaster relief fund immediately in order to help respond to the virus as well as use the Economic Stabilization Fund "at the appropriate time," once state leaders "know the full extent of the challenge we're dealing with." While at a town hall meeting, someone asked Abbott about the likelihood of calling for special emergency measures to access these vast financial resources to help mitigate the burdens wrought by the virus. According to the *Texas Tribune*, the governor replied that "every option remains on the table," but he also emphasized there would not be any need for such an action if every Texan followed guidance to help curb the virus.[25] Unfortunately, his warning went largely unheeded and the governmental dysfunction persisted because too many civil and corporate leaders were more interested in protecting profit margins than marginalized people.

Nihilism

When Greg Abbott became the forty-eighth governor of Texas, he assumed control of the tenth-largest economy in the world with one of the most fragmentary state administrations imaginable. Before the number of COVID-19 cases in Texas spiraled out of control, many in the state widely believed the state's organizing political principle—less government means more money—enabled Texas to reach record low unemployment rates and lead the nation in job creation.[26] With its 254 counties—the most of any state in the nation—the Texan vision of government routinely has meant that local authorities, rather than the elected leaders in Austin and Washington, DC, are more often the ones who are really in charge in Texas. Whether borne of libertarian or contrarian beliefs, this perennial distrust for any level of government runs so deep that the Texas State Legislature meets as infrequently as possible, once every two years, by law. As it so happens, the COVID-19 pandemic took place during 2020, an off-year in which the legislature had no session scheduled and therefore had no input or influence on matters pertaining to the state's brewing public health crisis.

To illustrate why this situation is so troubling, in order for Governor Abbott to have the ability to access and release any monies from the stabilization fund as mentioned earlier, he would have needed to make the extraordinary effort of calling the state lawmakers back to Austin for a special session before the regularly scheduled session in January 2021. Based on Abbott's reluctance to violate this key tenet of Texan political culture, the Texas state government effectively sidelined itself during what arguably was the greatest life-or-death struggle the nation had seen in a century. Faced with a rapidly spreading viral pandemic poised to cripple the entire economy, leadership efforts to guarantee public safety were further frustrated by the state of Texas's long-standing commitment to local control, state sovereignty, and limited government.[27] To use a sports analogy, the inability of the Texas state government to meet the swirling crises confronting its populace with all the means at its disposal was kind of like being in a boxing match against the heavyweight champion with your hands shackled and your feet trapped in a concrete slab.

An internecine battle for prominence within the Texas GOP further compounded the inefficacy of Texas's system of government. There seemed to be a localized battle of wills between a somewhat hapless and beleaguered Abbott and the more Trumpist wing of the state Republicans led by Patrick and Texas attorney general Ken Paxton, both of whom were perfectly willing to take marching orders from the Trump White House as long as it called for governmental inaction. Flummoxed by what policy to pursue, based on the absence of leadership from the Trump White House, coupled with the fierce tenacity and doggedly independent spirit of many in the state (some might call this being stubborn and just plain "ornery"), Governor Abbott tried to persuade his fellow Texans in the early months of the COVID-19 pandemic that so long as the populace complied with directives by public health experts to devote "Fourteen Days to Flatten the Curve," relying on localized rather than statewide mask mandates and shutdowns, they could avert the possible disaster.[28]

As might be imagined, many Texans remained apprehensive on both personal and political levels, due to their knee-jerk reactions to any perceptions of government intrusion even in the midst of a public health crisis. Nonetheless, Houston, Dallas, Fort Worth, Austin, El Paso, and other major metropolitan areas devised what seemed to be reasonable measures to ostensibly "flatten the curve" of the outbreak in their own municipalities. In addition to safeguarding the general public, Texas's widespread compliance with these preventative efforts to slow the virus would provide invaluable data necessary for epidemiologists and other experts in infectious diseases to dictate future actions.

By the time the governor lifted even the nominal restrictions imposed statewide by May 1, 2020, there had been severe issues with how well the CDC guidelines had been enforced, which, in turn, posed considerable problems in the data being reported and collected. More than anything else, the Lone Star State's faltering attempt to flatten the curve made it glaringly apparent that public health measures to combat COVID-19 depended heavily on a viable and enforceable government plan in tandem with general trust and individual responsibility by the public. In the earliest phase of the coronavirus pandemic, Governor Greg Abbott, with his flawed leadership and furtive stewardship, seemed perfectly content to let Texas's 254 county and 1,214 city authorities take the lead. The state's vastness—with its widening contrast between rural reaches and exploding metropolises—argued for local decision making. And the conservative governor had little to gain by organizing an economic lockdown that a minority of Republicans considered tantamount to treason. By late March, however, with Texas still relatively unscathed by the virus, Abbott's political calculus changed. For instance, he struck down an effort to make mask-wearing legally enforceable in Houston. He also issued orders—ahead of almost any other governor—to reopen the bars, restaurants, and other public venues that local officials had shuttered. It must have seemed like good politics as well as economics at the time, but it ended up having disastrous consequences.

In this light, we can explore how what we might mistakenly call white nationalism is actually white nihilism. I am arguing that the central axis of the Trumpian worldview has never been about partisan political views, but actually has been more akin to the Nietzschean vision of nihilism most often characterized as an emptying of human existence—and ultimately the world itself—of any pure meaning, legitimate purpose, comprehensible truth, or essential value. Philosopher and activist Cornel West helps us understand that "nihilism is to be understood here not as a philosophic doctrine that there are no rational grounds for legitimate standards or authority; it is, far more, the lived experience of coping with a life of horrifying meaninglessness, hopelessness, and (most important) lovelessness."[29]

Whatever else Trumpism might be, it and its followers have no connection to a vision of the nation as Lincoln once famously articulated as "government of the people, by the people, and for the people." In an August 2016 op-ed deconstructing the Trump campaign's infamous slogan as a racially coded catchphrase, New York Times columnist Charles Blow insightfully observed, "'Make America Great Again' is in fact an inverted admission of loss—lost primacy, lost privilege, lost prestige."[30] But these losses among many so-called Trump voters have become magnified and take on added force because they generate the perception of uncertainty regarding one's status, and, correspondingly, a fear of falling to a level that would make white Americans merely equal to their nonwhite counterparts. In his classic treatise on the American political tradition, historian Richard Hofstadter argues that this impulse toward nationalistic nostalgia is nothing new:

> A longing to recapture the past . . . has been such a basic ingredient of the recent American past that no history of political thinking is complete which does not attempt to explain it. In American politics the development of a retrospective and nostalgic cast of mind has gone hand in hand with the slow decline of a traditional faith. When competition and enterprise were rising, [people] thought of the future; when they were flourishing, of the present. Now—in an age of concentration, bigness, and corporate monopoly—when competition and opportunity have gone into decline, [some people] look wistfully back toward a golden age.[31]

The existential crisis is especially critical for white American men, because it is largely being defined by a growing sense of deprivation, ambiguity, and insecurity that runs contrary to what whiteness as a collective racial identity and masculinity as a gendered reality once afforded them less than a generation ago. Therefore, confronting the biological descendants and behavioral dependents of white supremacy in all its varieties by means of civil disobedience and constructive political unrest is the desperately necessary work of our present era.

Furthermore, many elected political officials across the left-right political spectrum are absolutely terrified by the prospect of white mainstream backlash based on the creeping suspicion that someone, somewhere, somehow will become livid about the "undeserving" folks— stereotypically read as people of color—reaping any benefits from any public policy and therefore reverse-engineer every government policy or program in the hopes of avoiding it. Of course, the outcome of such thinking has leaders designing bewildering bureaucracies with byzantine policies and obtuse, incomprehensible rules that are practically designed to fail. This results in an increasingly frustrated and outraged citizenry that inevitably doubts the veracity and viability of government at any level of society to do anything to improve the quality of human existence. In many cases, we witness the creation of a vicious cycle wherein we live in a world of precious yet precarious resources based on market values and competition in which everyone is considered unworthy by someone else. In turn, the existing political order is preoccupied with weeding out any comforts to those poor souls based on perceived merit, eventually morphing itself into a government that abnegates its duty of care and ignores its societal responsibility to preserve human lives altogether. When all is said and done, the state cannot even imagine saving lives because it has constrained its own mission and mandate only to focus on its capacity to dole out despair or even exposure to death itself in order to prove a point that never mattered in the first place.[32] This might suggest why so many of our fellow citizens have become so demoralized by the current state of politics to the point where they treat it as either blood sport to be won at all costs or a plague to be avoided altogether.

Necropolitics

Finally, we cannot fully comprehend the dual impact of neoliberalism and nihilism without fully wrestling with Trumpism's wholehearted embrace of necropolitics. Deep in the heart of Texas, in Houston—America's fourth-largest city and home to the nation's biggest hospital network—the intensive-care wards were filled beyond capacity for weeks on end. The coronavirus pandemic revealed the latest battleground in racialized class warfare between the haves and have-nots. For instance, although other Texas cities, most notably Dallas and Austin, extended local eviction moratoriums in the wake of the COVID-19 lockdown, Houston did not, thus making it the largest US city to resume evictions in the midst of the crisis. This situation is further compounded by the fact that, at the peak of the COVID-19 infections in Harris County where Houston is located, most medical facilities had to turn away sick and dying patients due to a lack of available space in their hospitals. This dual dilemma—a loss of housing and a lack of hospitalization—amid a public health crisis that depends on either sheltering in place or seeking medical help—is both obscene and absurd. In this instance alone it is obvious how a genuine yet gruesome blind spot in addressing the needs of "the least of these" potentially left hundreds of thousands of Black and Brown Houstonians struggling as they braced for the combined devastation of disease, despair, dispossession, and disenfranchisement at the worst time imaginable.

Meanwhile, groups such as Texans for Vaccine Choice (TFVC) have been doggedly opposed to many CDC guidelines designed to protect the populace from further spread of the novel coronavirus, especially mask mandates, by invoking claims of "health freedom." TFVC was founded in 2015 by a group of mothers as an antivaccine Facebook group vigorously opposed to proposed state legislation to eliminate conscientious exemptions to vaccination requirements for schoolchildren in the state. Later the group transformed itself into a political action committee based in Texas. TFVC's lobbying efforts have proven highly effective, with the rate of Texas families opting out of at least one vaccine at least doubling since the group's founding five years ago. Current estimates count roughly more than fifty thousand Texas schoolchildren whose families refuse to vaccinate them.[33] Meanwhile, TFVC's political fortunes increased greatly once Trump's avid embrace of discredited antivaccine theories became widely publicized.[34]

Cloaked in a rhetoric of personal responsibility, commitment to our families, and limited government, many of these libertarian activist groups sprang to life as "AstroTurf movements" arose in the early 2010s and coalesced against passage of the Affordable Care Act, more commonly known as Obamacare. TFVC's executive director and founder, Jackie Schlegel, has claimed the TFVC's core principles were "the right to bodily autonomy, to medical privacy, and to making the day-to-day choices necessary to keep ourselves and our families healthy." It is ironic that far-right groups such as TFVC that proudly came into existence nearly a decade ago in order to denounce the possibility for free health care by accusing Democrats of wanting to form "death panels" are now touting "health freedom" that encourages folks to expose themselves and others to a lethal, highly contagious virus. Toward that end, Schlegel defends TFVC's opposition to any statewide or national COVID-19 measures because she argues that the group

is no stranger to judgement and shaming at the hands of those who claim to value science above all else. We have been scolded for our "selfish disregard" for vulnerable populations and accused of spreading diseases we don't have to the community at large. Now, the "party of science," otherwise known as the Democrat Party, is utilizing the same weapons of propaganda against our families to berate Texans who are opposed to the overreaching aspects of the newest COVID policies. Where we have traditionally been labeled "anti-science" and "anti-vaxxers," we now see the term "anti-maskers" making headlines.[35]

In an especially interesting bit of agitprop masquerading as prose, Schlegel proclaims "the majority of Texans—I would say conservative Christians, especially—would argue that they are beyond capable of educating their children, managing their finances, and pursuing their relationship with God in the manner they see fit; and yet somehow, so many of them seem to fall into the trap of believing that they are not competent enough to manage their own health without the intrusion of government."[36] Her effort not only assumes that she is the voice for most Texans, but also makes the leap that all these selfsame Texans she champions are also "conservative Christians" who are completely aware of and at peace with the espousal of views that completely contradict the core teachings of their faith. Whereas Schlegel seemingly only cares about these conservative Christian, patriotic (read: white) Texans as "the right kind of people," it is almost ludicrous to understand the religion she professes as "Christian" except in some strict political sense. For example, given the fact that a considerable portion of the miracles performed in the New Testament involved Jesus Christ and the apostles providing free, unlimited health care to the sick and wounded, why would white Christianity be so vehemently opposed to mask wearing, hospitalization, and vaccination as means of curtailing a deadly disease? By and large, she espouses that any adherence to or compliance with public health guidelines makes people "complicit in the loss of your religious freedoms, your Second Amendment freedom, your freedom to choose how you or your children are educated, your freedom to choose your career path. . . . The American Dream dies."[37] By this token, the stakes for the supporters of the "health freedom" movement in the Trump era are nothing less than the apocalyptic undoing of everything they know and love.

In order to better fathom the extent of the crisis, we need to grasp necropolitics. Philosopher Achille Mbembe describes necropolitics as "the ultimate expression of sovereignty [that] resides . . . in the power to dictate who may live and who must die."[38] He deploys necropolitics as a means of engaging and expanding on Michel Foucault's original formulation of biopower as a concept in his groundbreaking work *Society Must Be Defended*, especially as it grapples with the nexus of racism and power at work in society. In a Foucauldian sense, biopower as a mechanism for the social construction of race hinges on maintaining the critical balance between the living and the dead. Race (and racism, for that matter) becomes so integral to the establishment, expression, and extrapolation of biopower that both can be entirely understandable and yet totally unacceptable. After all, race has perpetually and perniciously haunted the contours of Western political thought and practice since the dawn of modernity, most particularly when it comes to imagining the inhumanity of, and thus the divine mandate to rule over, the racial other.

Delving into the broad scope of this transhistorical problem, sociologist Karen Fields and historian Barbara Fields specifically coin the neologism "racecraft" to describe the "ability of pre- or non-scientific modes of thought to hijack the minds of the scientifically literate."[39] In terms of racecraft, such an exercise of power not only defines itself in relation to race on biological and sociological levels—and imbues itself with meaning—but also situates itself in terms of psychological and theological dimensions in order to take control over the existential concerns of humans. In turn, these dicta of control both presuppose and prejudice the division of the human species into groups, the subdivision of the population into subgroups, and the establishment of a biological lacuna between one another that makes the dispersal of insults, indignities, and injuries entirely justifiable. Yet in his book *Cosmopolitanism*, philosopher Kwame Anthony Appiah contends, "When you do something that harms someone else, you must be able to justify it. . . . It's not that they don't matter; it's that they have *earned* our hatred or contempt. They deserve what we are doing to them."[40] This, one might argue, is a key feature of the phenomenon we most often refer to as racism.[41]

Referring to the phantasmagorical, albeit paradoxical, presence of race as it functions in the modern world, philosopher Hannah Arendt locates the roots of racial otherness within an antagonistic worldview that suggests that the politics of race is invariably and inextricably linked to the politics of death. In her examination into the origins of totalitarian

regimes, Arendt outlines, "Race is, politically speaking, not the beginning of humanity but its end . . . not the natural birth of [human beings]
but [their] unnatural death."[42] Briefly returning once more to Foucault
in this discussion, racism is deemed, above all, a technology of terror
aimed at permitting the exercise of "that old sovereign right of death" to
supersede (or trump, if you will) the possibility of a shared humanity.[43]
Central to this way of thinking, racism functions as a means of making
possible the murderous functionality of the state in order to regulate
the distribution of death among those identified as unworthy of human
freedom and flourishing. Racism also prepares "the condition for the
acceptability of putting to death" within the society at large.[44]

Given Trump's support of white supremacists—most notably neo-
Nazis—and his own (thankfully) unsuccessful attempts to establish his
own autocratic regime in the United States, it might no longer seem so
far-fetched to draw parallels between Trumpism and Nazism. By way of
illustration, the Nazi state, according to Foucault, was the most complete
example of a state exercising the sovereign right to kill as prescribed
in the myriad ways that all modern states function but harnessing said
power in service of white supremacy against those members of society
designated as worthless.[45] Indeed, it can be seen as the peak form of
white supremacist state power in modernity when the state's constitutive
elements made the control, coercion, contempt, and condemnation of
lives coextensive with the sovereign right to kill. By biological extrapolation incumbent to the state's necropolitical objectives against those
considered objectionable while simultaneously exposing those people
to death, Nazi Germany's right to kill can be seen as having opened the
way for a formidable consolidation of white supremacist state power that
culminated in the project known the "Final Solution." As Mbembe argues, the Nazi regime "became the archetype of a power formation that
combined the characteristics of the racist state, the murderous state, and
the suicidal state."[46] In his classic text *The Fire Next Time*, James Baldwin
addresses the matter:

> The terms "civilized" and "Christian" begin to have a very strange ring,
> particularly in the ears of those who have been judged neither civilized
> nor Christian, when a Christian nation surrenders to a foul and violent
> orgy as Germany did during the Third Reich. For the crime of their

ancestry, millions of people in the middle of the twentieth century and in the heart of Europe—God's citadel—were sent to a death so calculated, so hideous, and so prolonged that no age before this enlightened one had been able to imagine it, much less achieve and record it. . . . The fact of the Third Reich alone makes obsolete forever any question of Christian superiority, except in technological terms. White people were, and are, astounded by the holocaust in Germany. They did not know that they could act that way.[47]

Akin to Mbembe's notion of necropolitics, Baldwin's stark condemnation of Nazi Germany as the benchmark of Western civilization's worst xenophobic and genocidal tendencies speaks volumes to the reality that white supremacy quintessentially represents a destabilization of any strides toward human progress. Much like the contemporary turmoil wrought by the most violent and radicalized members of Trump's MAGA movement, Baldwin's critique of the white German populace under Hitler's sway reveals that, rather than assuming it to be an absolute state of being, "civilization" is actually the ongoing struggle of a society to recognize that it is always in a relative state of becoming more humane in orientation and outlook. Taken together, the views of Mbembe, Foucault, Arendt, Baldwin, and the Fieldses help us consider that, although modernity and civilization are frequently treated as interchangeable, the truth is that adherence to racism and white supremacy, its more pernicious cognate, is always on the verge of the savage. It is not the marginalized or subjugated racial-ethnic minorities who own the monopoly on the brutal savagery of this world, but they bear witness to the atrocities of history that happen all too often to them.

Therefore, when thinking about the seemingly illogical stance of the TFVC and like-minded conservatives who use their political activism to exert overwhelming pressure on the public and private sectors alike in order to demonstrate their control over potentially lifesaving measures in Texas, one is further reminded of Mbembe's query: "What is the relationship between politics and death in those systems that can function only in a state of emergency?"[48] To override the administration of lifesaving measures or to make it impossible for society at large and the health care system in particular to meet the needs of the sick and dying is not advocacy for the American way of life. Instead, it is guaranteeing the American way of death. Forcing the most vulnerable and disadvantaged members of society—more often than not people of color and immigrants—to only engage in labor others are either unable or unwilling to do for themselves, while also refashioning the daily operation of society to intentionally undermine the life span of those same people, demonstrates the entrenched desire of whiteness to prioritize the right to kill over the right to coexist. Simply put, to quote *The Atlantic's* Adam Serwer's precise diagnosis of Trumpism's appeal for MAGA supporters: "The cruelty is the point."[49]

This perception of the coexistence of the other only as a manifestation of a nightmarish Hobbesian worldview of being human without the blessings and burdens of common decency is a life that is "solitary, poor, nasty, brutish, and short"—or what Trump himself infamously hailed in his 2017 inaugural address as "American Carnage"—is, to put it mildly, a problem. Recognition of this baseline perception that every other person who is not you is a mortal danger or absolute threat and whose eradication would only serve to strengthen your potential for life, love, and liberty is not the teaching of any of the world's great religious traditions. To the contrary, the best and most meaningful beliefs and practices that humanity has perpetuated throughout its posterity have provided the underpinnings of those values that are most admirable about humanity: namely, freedom, justice, equality, dignity, and hope. Indeed, even as necropolitics in our current time represents a full-blown assault on the lives and livelihoods of millions of our fellow human beings, it can only be countered by the proclamation, protection, and promulgation of the inherent essence of what it truly means to be a human being in ways that rise above the impersonal, the illogical, the irreverent, and even the irredeemable. Hard as it might seem, we must both contest and reject a definition of human existence as a state of being in the world that insists upon the idea—predicated by a fear of scarcity mimicking sheer necessity—that the calculus of life is made possible only through the death of the other. In his acclaimed book *Between the World and Me*, Ta-Nehisi Coates has channeled so much of this desperate sentiment when he argues, "In accepting both the chaos of history and the fact of my total end, I was freed to truly consider how I wished to live—specifically, how do I live free in this black body? It is a profound question because America understands itself as God's handiwork, but the black body is the clearest evidence that America is the work of [humans]."⁵⁰ To state the matter bluntly, if forced to make a choice between the survival of the human species or the sovereignty of white supremacy (which consists of the will, desire, and capacity to kill in order to live), which would you choose? Sadly, the fact this question even has to be posed at all reveals how much work remains to be done.

Conclusion

By shining a glaring spotlight on Trump's sociopathic lack of compassion and empathy for the widespread loss of human lives, especially among so-called essential workers, as well as the grotesque paradox that his ineptitude led to crippling the robust economy he boasted about so often, the COVID-19 pandemic brought this sinister trifecta of Trumpism into the sharpest relief imaginable, especially as it negatively affected the core demographics of our society who are most vulnerable: the working poor, women, people of color, immigrants, and the elderly. The conundrum of being trapped in Trump's America left millions forced to make the dire decision to choose between lives and livelihoods. Trumpism is neither an invention nor an innovation of the crazy, crude, cruel, craven, and criminal man who formerly inhabited the Oval Office; to borrow the language of viral infection, Trumpism is actually a symptom rather than a source of this political pathogen. Meanwhile, so-called white evangelicals who have become desensitized to the plights of others fail to recognize the meaning of every human life as a precious and holy gift from a living and loving God!

One might argue that it is precisely this worshiping of white supremacy, misogyny, xenophobia, homophobia, and class exploitation that reveals the constraints of the nation-state as a concept. Thus, when seeking to confront and demolish the unholy trinity of neoliberalism, nihilism, and necropolitics that stands as the bedrock of Trumpism, we must, as Nietzsche suggests, be driven by the imperative to "philosophize with a hammer" in the hopes of smashing the false idol of white nihilism.⁵¹ Part of this vital work entails that we reject any and all structural frameworks that deem Black lives as the utter negation of what it means to be fully and freely human.⁵² Furthermore, it is urgent to locate actively prophetic movements for social justice as part of a larger ritual praxis that requires that we remain in "the hold," as Christina Sharpe brilliantly inveighs, and argue that the force of this idolatrous negativity is counter-intuitively generative to Black resistance insofar as Black humanity finds the wherewithal to assert the divine right to coexist in God's Creation.[53]

The bulk of this chapter has taken great pains to note how the corrosive and corrupt elements of Trumpism operate within our contemporary political economy. We must nevertheless also strive to demonstrate how the merger of divine and social justice vis-à-vis overcoming daily struggles via mundane acts of resistance by the multitude of frontline health care professionals, essential workers, and average citizens banding together can invoke the numinous—that transcendent concept of the Divine that is fully holy as well as wholly humane—to serve as a moral and spiritual ballast against the Trump administration's mishandling of the COVID-19 public health crisis. It is no small irony that the activism of the #BlackLivesMatter movement, now acknowledged as the largest sustained protest movement in world history, is considered crucial in helping to topple Trumpism's unholy trinity of neoliberalism, nihilism, and necropolitics and its foothold deep in the heart of Texas and elsewhere. This prayerful petition by Rev. Dr. William J. Barber II, leader of the Poor People's Campaign, summarizes this spirit best:

> May we who are merely inconvenienced remember those whose lives are at stake. May we who have no risk factors remember those most vulnerable. May we have the necessary righteous indignation in this moment to fight for transformation. . . . During this time when we cannot physically wrap our arms around each other, let us yet find ways to be the loving embrace of God for our neighbors. And let us recognize that we cannot give up in this moment, and no matter what it takes; let it at least be written down in history that with our last breaths we fought for the world that ought to be.[54]

NOTES

1 Paul J. Weber, "Texas' Lieutenant Governor Says US Should Get 'Back to Work,'" ABC.com, March 23, 2020, https://abcnews.go.com; Abby Livingston, "Texas Lt. Gov. Dan Patrick Says a Failing Economy Is Worse Than Coronavirus," *Texas Tribune*, March 23, 2020, www.texastribune.org.

2 For examples of microhistory, see Carlo Ginzburg, *The Cheese and the Worms: The Cosmos of a Sixteenth-Century Miller*, trans. John and Anne C. Tedeschi

(Baltimore: Johns Hopkins University Press, 2013); David Warren Sabean, *Property, Production, and Family in Neckarhausen, 1700–1870* (Cambridge: Cambridge University Press, 1990); Giovanni Levi, "On Microhistory," in Peter Burke, ed., *New Perspectives on Historical Writing* (Cambridge, MA: Polity, 1991), 93–113; James Sharpe, "History from Below," in Peter Burke, ed., *New Perspectives on Historical Writing* (Cambridge, MA: Polity, 1991), 24–41; Edward Muir, "Observing Trifles." in Edward Muir and Guido Ruggiero, eds., *Microhistory and the Lost Peoples of Europe* (Baltimore: Johns Hopkins University Press, 1991), vii–xviii; Jacques Revel, "Compte rendu: Alf Lüdtke éd., *Histoire du quotidien* (traduit de l'allemand par O. Manoni), (Paris: Éditions de la Maison des Sciences de l'Homme, 1994), xi–341, Annales 50 (1995): 805–8; Juan M. Floyd-Thomas, "The Burning of Rebellious Thoughts: MOVE as an Expression of Black Radical Humanism, 1970–2001," *Black Scholar* 32, no. 1 (Spring 2002): 11–21; Mark Phillips, "Histories, Micro- and Literary: Problems of Genre and Distance," *New Literary History* 34, no. 2 (2003): 211–29, 224; and Jesse Hoffnung-Garskof, *Racial Migrations: New York City and the Revolutionary Politics of the Spanish Caribbean* (Princeton, NJ: Princeton University Press, 2019).

3   David Warren Sabean, *Kinship in Neckarhausen, 1700–1870* (Cambridge: Cambridge University Press, 1998), 399.

4   According to Wikipedia, the phrase "God is in the detail" has been attributed in various iterations to numerous people, but one of the earliest forms, "Le bon Dieu est dans le détail" [the good God is in the detail], is most notably attributed to Gustave Flaubert (1821–1880). See Wikipedia, s.v. "The devil is in the detail," accessed February 1, 2021, https://en.wikipedia.org. Also see Gregory Titelman, *Random House Dictionary of Popular Proverbs and Sayings, Random House Reference* (New York: Random House, 1996); and John Bartlett, *Bartlett's Familiar Quotations: A Collection of Passages, Phrases, and Proverbs Traced to Their Sources in Ancient and Modern Literature*, 17th ed. (New York: Little, Brown and Company, 2002).

5   "A Timeline of COVID-19 Developments in 2020," AJMC.com, updated January 1, 2021, www.ajmc.com.

6   More information on how the CDC collects COVID-19 case surveillance data can be found at CDC's COVID-19 FAQ webpage at www.cdc.gov.

7   "Number of COVID-19 Hospitalizations," Texas Health and Human Services, accessed February 1, 2021, https://txdshs.maps.arcgis.com.

8   Reese Oxner, "Texas Surpasses 1 Million Coronavirus Cases, According to Johns Hopkins University," NPR, November 11, 2020, www.npr.org.

9   Matt Jenson, *The Gravity of Sin: Augustine, Luther, and Barth on 'homo incurvatus in se'* (New York: T&T Clark, 2007).

10 Catherine Bell, *Ritual Theory, Ritual Practice* (New York: Oxford University Press, 1992), 19.

11 See Clifford Geertz, "Religion as a Cultural System," in *The Interpretation of Cultures: Selected Essays* (London: Fontana Press, 1993), 87–125; Bell, *Ritual*

Theory; Juan M. Floyd-Thomas, Stacey M. Floyd-Thomas, and Mark G. Toulouse, *The Altars Where We Worship: The Religious Significance of Popular Culture* (Louisville, KY: Westminster John Knox, 2016).

12 See Harvey Cox, "The Market as God," *The Atlantic*, March 1, 1999, www.theatlan tic.com; Kathryn Tanner, *Economy of Grace* (Minneapolis: Fortress, 2005); Floyd-Thomas, Floyd-Thomas, and Toulouse, *Altars Where We Worship*, 41–67.

13 Michael Hall, "The Houston Years of George Floyd," *Texas Monthly*, May 30, 2020, www.texasmonthly.com.

14 Angela Y. Davis, *The Meaning of Freedom and Other Difficult Dialogues* (San Francisco: City Lights, 2012), 169.

15 To be sure, a heated debate over the term's usage and utility has persisted for more than a decade. For example, Daniel T. Rodgers, arguably one of the leading US intellectual historians of the 1970s and 1980s, only uses the term "neoliberal" twice in his widely influential account *Age of Fracture* (Cambridge, MA: Harvard University Press, 2011). See Scott Spillman, "Splinters," n+1, June 8, 2011, https://nplusonemag.mag. Rodgers has more recently offered a strong critique of neoliberalism as a category of analysis in "The Uses and Abuses of Neoliberalism," *Dissent* (Winter 2018): 78–87. For critical responses to Rodgers's essay, see "Debating the Uses and Abuses of 'Neoliberalism': A Forum," with comments by Julia Ott, Nathan Connolly, Mike Konczal, and Timothy Shenk, and a reply by Daniel Rodgers, *Dissent*, January 2018, www.dissentmagazine.org. See also Angus Burgin, *The Great Persuasion: Reinventing Free Markets since the Depression* (Cambridge, MA: Harvard University Press, 2012); Daniel Stedman Jones, *Masters of the Universe: Hayek, Friedman, and the Birth of Neoliberal Politics* (Princeton, NJ: Princeton University Press, 2012); Nancy MacLean, *Democracy in Chains: The Deep History of the Radical Right's Stealth Plan for America* (New York: Viking, 2017). For critical overviews of the term and the field, see Stephanie Mudge, "The State of the Art: What Is Neoliberalism?" *Socio-Economic Review* 6 (2008): 703–31; James Ferguson, "The Uses of Neoliberalism," *Antipode* 41, no. 1 (2009): 166–84; Terry Flew, "Six Theories of Neoliberalism," *Thesis Eleven* 122, no. 1 (2014): 49–71. Gary Gerstle has recently argued that it is problematic to use "neoliberalism" as synonymous for "right-wing" or "conservative politics." See Gerstle, "The Rise and Fall(?) of America's Neoliberal Order," *Transactions of the Royal Historical Society* 28 (2018): 241–64.

16 Andrew J. Diamond and Thomas J. Sugrue, eds., *Neoliberal Cities: The Remaking of Postwar Urban America* (New York: NYU Press, 2020), 2.

17 David Harvey, *A Brief History of Neoliberalism* (Oxford: Oxford University Press, 2001); see also Gérard Duménil and Dominique Levy, *The Crisis of Neoliberalism* (Cambridge, MA: Harvard University Press, 2011).

18 See Cedric J. Robinson, *Black Marxism: The Making of the Black Radical Tradition* (London: Zed, 1983), chap. 1.

19 See Lester G. Bugbee, "Slavery in Early Texas," *Political Science Quarterly* 13, no. 3 (September 1898): 389–412; Karl E. Ashburn, "Slavery and Cotton Production in

Texas," *Southwestern Social Science Quarterly* 14, no. 3 (1933): 257–71; Randolph B. Campbell, *An Empire for Slavery: The Peculiar Institution in Texas, 1821–1865* (Baton Rouge: Louisiana State University Press, 1989); Andrew J. Torget, *Seeds of Empire: Cotton, Slavery, and the Transformation of the Texas Borderlands, 1800–1850* (Chapel Hill: University of North Carolina Press, 2015); Sean M. Kelley, *Los Brazos de Dios: A Plantation Society in the Texas Borderlands, 1821–1865* (Baton Rouge: Louisiana State University Press, 2010); Alwyn Barr, *Black Texans: A History of African Americans in Texas, 1528–1995*, 2nd ed. (Norman: University of Oklahoma Press, 1996).

20 See Vann R. Newkirk II, "The Quintessential Americanness of Juneteenth," *The Atlantic*, June 19, 2017, www.theatlantic.com; Jameelah Nasheed, "What Is Juneteenth, How Is It Celebrated, and Why Does It Matter? Juneteenth Isn't the 'Other' Independence Day, It Is the Independence Day," *Teen Vogue*, June 19, 2019, www.teenvogue.com; Jamelle Bouie, "Why Juneteenth Matters," *New York Times*, June 18, 2020, www.nytimes.com.

21 Alwyn Barr, *Black Texans: A History of Negroes in Texas, 1528–1971* (Austin, TX: Jenkins, 1973); Michael L. Gillette, "Blacks Challenge the White University," *Southwestern Historical Quarterly* 86 (October 1982): 321–44; Michael L. Gillette, "The Rise of the NAACP in Texas," *Southwestern Historical Quarterly* 81 (April 1978): 393–416; Darlene Clark Hine, *Black Victory: The Rise and Fall of the White Primary in Texas* (Millwood, NY: KTO, 1979); Merline Pitre, *Through Many Dangers, Toils, and Snares: The Black Leadership of Texas, 1868–1900* (Austin, TX: Eakin, 1985). Merline Pitre, *In Struggle against Jim Crow: Lulu B. White and the NAACP, 1900–1957* (College Station: Texas A&M University Press, 2010).

22 Davis, *Meaning of Freedom and Other Difficult Dialogues*, 174.

23 Paul Krugman, "The Unemployed Stare into the Abyss. Republicans Look Away," *New York Times*, August 3, 2020, www.nytimes.com.

24 "'Texas' Budget Could Take Massive Hit as Coronavirus Crisis Continues Unfolding, Lawmakers Learn," *Texas Tribune*, March 22, 2020, www.texastribune.org.

25 Ibid.

26 "Texas Governor Greg Abbott," the State of Texas Governor, accessed February 1, 2021, https://gov.texas.gov/governor-abbott.

27 "Texas Tries to Balance Local Control with the Threat of a Pandemic," *New York Times*, March 24, 2020, www.nytimes.com.

28 Rhea Mahbubani, "The US Has One Week to Enforce Social Distancing and 'Flatten the Curve' as the Coronavirus Outbreak Escalates. Here's Why These Days Are So Critical," *Business Insider*, March 17, 2020, www.businessinsider.com.

29 Cornel West, *Race Matters* (Boston: Beacon, 1993), 14–15.

30 Charles M. Blow, "Trump Reflects White Male Fragility," *New York Times*, August 4, 2016, www.nytimes.com.

31 Richard Hofstadter, *The American Political Tradition and the Men Who Made It* (New York: A. A. Knopf, 1948), xxxiv.

32 Alex Pareene, "The $2,000 Checks and Our Failing Vaccine Rollout Have Something in Common," *New Republic*, January 8, 2021, https://newrepublic.com.

33 Todd Ackerman, "Vaccine Exemptions on the Rise among Texas Students," *Houston Chronicle*, August 15, 2016, www.houstonchronicle.com; Carol Pearson, "US Scientists: Refusing Vaccines Puts Everyone's Health at Risk." Voice of America, February 22, 2017, www.voanews.com; Kai Kupferschmidt, "Why Texas Is Becoming a Major Antivaccine Battlefield," *Science*, November 30, 2016, www.sciencemag.org.

34 Lena H. Sun, "Trump Energizes the Anti-Vaccine Movement in Texas," *Washington Post*, February 20, 2017, www.washingtonpost.com.

35 Jackie Schlegel, "Commentary: COVID Response in Texas Highlights Vicious War for Medical Freedom," *Texas Scoreboard.com*, June 26, 2020, https://texasscorecard.com ; see also the Texans for Vaccine Choice website, www.texansforvaccinechoice.com/online/action-alert-tfvc-proclamation-to-support-texans-right-to-their-livelihood/.

36 Jackie Schlegel, "Commentary: COVID Response in Texas Highlight Vicious War for Medical Freedom."

37 Ibid.

38 Achille Mbembé, "Necropolitics," trans. Libby Meintjes, *Public Culture* 15, no. 1 (Winter 2003): 11.

39 Karen E. Fields and Barbara J. Fields, *Racecraft: The Soul of Inequality in American Life* (London: Verso, 2012), 5–6.

40 Kwame Anthony Appiah, *Cosmopolitanism: Ethics in a World of Strangers* (New York: W. W. Norton, 2007), 151, 152.

41 Michel Foucault, *"Society Must Be Defended": Lectures at the Collège de France, 1975–1976* (New York: Picador, 2003), 57–74.

42 Hannah Arendt, *Origins of Totalitarianism* (New York: Schocken, 1951), 157.

43 Foucault, *"Society Must Be Defended,"* 214.

44 Ibid., 228.

45 Ibid., 227–32.

46 Mbembé, "Necropolitics," 17.

47 James Baldwin, *The Fire Next Time* (1963; New York: Vintage, 1993), 52.

48 Mbembé, "Necropolitics," 16.

49 Adam Serwer, "The Cruelty Is the Point," *The Atlantic*, October 3, 2018, www.theatlantic.com.

50 Ta-Nehisi Coates, *Between the World and Me* (New York: Spiegel & Grau, 2015), 12.

51 Friedrich Nietzsche, *Twilight of the Idols and the Anti-Christ: Or How To Philosophize with a Hammer*, trans. R. J. Hollindale (New York: Penguin Classics, 1990).

52 Calvin Warren, *Ontological Terror: Blackness, Nihilism, and Emancipation* (Durham, NC: Duke University Press, 2018); Fred Moten, "Blackness and

Nothingness (Mysticism in the Flesh)," *South Atlantic Quarterly* 112, no. 4 (2013): 737–80.

53 Christina Sharpe, *In the Wake: On Blackness and Being* (Durham, NC: Duke University Press, 2016).

54 Rev. Dr. William J. Barber II, "A Prayer for Justice and Compassion during the Pandemic," *The Nation*, May 3, 2020, www.thenation.com.

9

Dying Laughing

Comedic Relief and Redemption in the Time of COVID-19

CONÃ S. M. MARSHALL

> This is weird and less than ideal circumstance to do a show, but the only
> way to figure out if the shit would actually work out is to do the show
> so thank you all for coming. . . . Are you all having a good time or is
> this weird? I gotta tell ya, this is actually like the first concert inside of
> North America since all this shit happened so like it or not it's history.
> It's gonna be in the books. At least we tried. There were other comedians
> [inaudible]. . . . Well this is not the first show, but the other shows were
> like in drive-ins. [And if] People like the nigga's jokes, they honked the
> horn. That doesn't sound like any fun at all did it?[1]

In his unrefined Netflix special *8:46*, Dave Chappelle addressed his audience in Ohio on June 6, 2020, to gauge their temperature during this
pandemic. Approaching thirty million views, Chappelle's voice during
the pandemic was poignant and necessary. He knew that humor was
needed in the moment and, as opposed to organizing a filmed production from which he could profit, he encouraged everyone to join him
in supporting the Equal Justice Initiative and the protection of human
rights—contributing to equity in the midst of crisis. Dave Chappelle
understood that, in the moment of so much dying and absurdity,
laughter and, even more so, healing were needed. His Netflix special
represented one of the first public, communal moments; most people
in Beavercreek, Ohio, had not gathered publicly in months. He sat and
spoke with the audience, weaving in prose and laughter, outlining in
detail the deaths made at the hands of law enforcement as well as the
very lethal coronavirus.

The expression "dying laughing" is often used as a statement to signify laughter to the point of one's mortal demise. This chapter utilizes this colloquial phrase as an analytical lens for understanding the nuanced relationship that Black American comedians and their audiences have with laughter as a means of interpreting humanity, injustice, and liberation during this coronavirus pandemic. The liminal space that dying occupies is an active response to the absurd—that which is extremely unreasonable or devoid of meaning. While scholars have debated solutions to the absurd by offering valid responses such as escaping existence,[2] believing in entities beyond the absurd,[3] or accepting the absurd,[4] it is within comedy that I, and many others, grapple with accepting the absurd or "dying" with laughter.

In the midst of the COVID-19 crisis the political and racial climates were hostile at best. Americans witnessed loved ones impacted by the virus without the possibility of in-person check-ins and personal farewells. Moreover, despite having become a technologically driven society that relinquishes many social interactions to social media apps like Facebook, Instagram, and Twitter, the COVID-19 pandemic crisis made us aware just how much we still publicly gather. The doors of churches closed, along with doors to gyms, bars, schools and universities, salons and barbershops, restaurants, and sports arenas. By force of the necessity of crisis, modes and methods of communing were reenvisioned. People were home from work. There was more time to wrestle with thoughts and loved ones. Alcohol sales soared,[5] accompanied by a rise in domestic violence.[6] Our children were educated at home via Zoom and Zearn and Class Dojo. For many, this context led to a state of despair within which depression and anxiety spiked. The pastor was no longer capable of laying hands on the sick; no one could lie at the altar, and there was no holding of hands during the benediction or testimony service. It felt as if everyone was either on the sick or shut-in list. We have longed for answers during this time of depression and faith crisis, and they have come from perhaps an unlikely source: the comedian.

For the sake of this chapter, I recognize the wide scope of comedy in general, but specifically I am interested in comedy that provides social commentary.[7] During the pandemic, comedians worked to devise the meaning-making strategies expected of contemporary religious leaders by assuming their authority, rallying their audiences, and telling their prophetic truths. Comedians surveilled their surroundings as a researcher investigates and analyzes scenarios through a lens of socially and politically learned norms and interactions. They sifted their analysis through a countercultural lens of socialism and equity. Additionally, "comedic relief" rhetoric has dominated conversations on comedy within absurdity. However, I add that comedy may serve differently within the absurd. Historically, comedic relief has been employed to distract or divert attention from a pressing matter—to cause a diversion or foment palatability in order to digest the gravity of particular matters, such as politics and social injustices, and thus create a sense of relief. I posit that we think of comedy in a holistic manner by offering comedic redemption as a viable option in engaging absurdity. *Comedic redemption* does not seek to distract or make serious matters palatable, but rather *names injustice* and *situates humanity*. Womanist ethicist Stacey Floyd-Thomas offers redemptive self-love as an ethical tenet of womanism that asserts humanity, reaffirms Black womanhood, and values Black women's ingenuity.[8] It is within mores such as these that I grapple with the redeeming properties of comedy and the attempts of comedians to make sense of the world.

The kind of comedy that I engage is that which wrestles with the absurd. It is the comedy that offers Richard Pryor the space to state, "I am not addicted to cocaine, I just love the way that it smells."[9] We laugh at the absurdity of the joke: in order to consume the drug of cocaine, one most commonly inhales it through the nose. Therefore, the action of smelling and the sentiment of loving to smell equates to an admittance of substance abuse. Ordinarily, we would not laugh at someone with a substance abuse problem—or hopefully we would not, because we consider this a grave, serious matter. The comedian is able to communicate this public health issue without victimizing himself. He directly engages the absurdity of addiction—its criminalization, conversations around the subject, and the lack of social care and concern. Richard Pryor not only engaged these varied subjects but also had fun every time he was on stage—following his own advice, which he also gave to a teenage Tiffany Haddish, who is known to heed it each time she takes the stage as well.[10]

The last time most adults were able to have unabated fun was in their childhood, a time of life devoid of dependents and much responsibility.

Comedians capture those moments of "fun" by often alluding to obstacles that get in the way of such moments—as we are only promised the "pursuit" of happiness by our government, and not necessarily the *attainment* of happiness. The comedian suspends those moments of happiness for the audience, creating a symbiotic relationship with them. Comedians encapsulate freedom and locate the barriers thereof, whether it is universal freedoms or localized freedom of advertisers, as expressed in an exchange between Jimmy Fallon and Jerry Seinfeld.[11] Fallon is expressing to Seinfeld his disdain for companies that push their latest product on consumers. Fallon displays this frustration when speaking of the "new and improved" Mr. Clean product: "What was the swill of Mr. Clean that we were using before?" Seinfeld interjects and states, "I was happy when I saw the commercial, happy when I bought the product . . . and maybe not so happy with the product, but the situation brought me a lot of happiness overall." While Fallon harps on being swindled into pseudo–product enhancements, as opposed to freely thinking and assessing the heightened efficacy of household cleaning products on his own, Seinfeld quantifies the amounts of happiness evoked by the company offering the promise of it in the first place. Both comedians are drawing on the push-pull relationship of freedom of choice and happiness; in so doing, they compel us to consider perspectives that perhaps we had not considered in relation to the mundanity of cleaning our homes. Yet this brief exchange prompts us to critically engage the influence of advertisers and our constructed realities of life that cause us to focus on the ineffectiveness of the product and not the levels of happiness that it brought throughout the process. The comedians are not campaigning for the audience to buy into their stance, rather to consider the shared aspects of life and perhaps a new way of engaging and navigating it. It is a juxtaposition that many parents attempt to straddle and comedians maneuver often, in order to foster a relaxed atmosphere of fun.

Audiences of comedy come to the comedic moment for intimacy and enjoyment. A vulnerability is shared through narrative, a real reciprocal call-and-response of enjoyment—laughter and even boos—as opposed to the call-and-response affirmations to piety that take place with church congregants. Audiences of comedy also differ from congregants in that the pay they offer up establishes an expectation of humorous enjoyment, whereas the exchange of tithes in churches does not ensure such gratification. There is also immediate feedback given and received by both the comedian and audience member alike. This form of communing is different from posting comments online or waiting for a review to come out. The relationship between the audience and comedian is one of reciprocity. Comics put their experiences out there, inviting the audience to examine the world around them.

Within Black communities, comedians follow the rhetorical lineage of the trickster, griot, and preacher. They hold a particular relationship with the audience, one of trust and reciprocity, not solely entertainment and good feelings. The comedian is situated within the context of the audience; like that of the preacher and griot, a comedian must not only know the audience but also be able to analyze the social, political, and economic climate of the time while also inserting a particular narrativizing lens that may not be popular.

The Black Church is the first autonomous Black institution in America that served as more than a spiritual hub by also providing a sociopolitical space in which Black people could convene and commune.[12] The Black Church wrestles theologically with the Christian God's role in Black life by aiding Black people in response to the oppression faced in America.[13] The shared epicenter of the Black Church and Black comedy is that of suffering and absurdity. I don't postulate that either comedy or Black Christianity offers an answer to these phenomena; rather they offer directional guidance for moving through or about suffering, absurdity, or both.

One goal that neither the Black Church nor any church has been able to accomplish is racial reconciliation. Yet premier stand-up comedian and late-night host Trevor Noah recalls a time during a parade in Johannesburg, South Africa, soon after apartheid ended when the police were mounted on horses and shouting at people to move out of the way.[14] That's when Trevor Noah's grandfather interjected with his personal commentary on a picture of the South African president kissing a horse who had won the South African version of the Kentucky Derby on the front cover of the newspaper and said, "Why is it that your president can kiss a horse, but not my sister?" Bewildered and befuddled, the policeman responded, "Sir, I do not know." At that moment Trevor's grandfather responded, "That's because you haven't seen my sister." The policeman put down his baton and he and Trevor's grandfather erupted together in laughter. That was the first time Trevor witnessed the power of comedy; it had the power to create a positive exchange between Black and white South Africans. And while Rev. Dr. Martin Luther King Jr's observation of Sunday at 11 a.m. being the "most segregated hour of the week" still rings true, comedians have more crossover success among races.[15]

Like pulpit orators, comedians seek to persuade; however, church leaders are bound to specific Christian and cultural doctrinal codes and ways of thinking, whereas the comedian can weave in and out of varying philosophies, religious thoughts, and "secular" understandings of the world in navigating the absurd or the crisis of faith. Comedians are not bound by such religious parameters. Nevertheless, pastors and comedians are both navigating their audiences through absurdity.

Black People and COVID-19

The coronavirus entered the United States from China initially via affluent white suburban areas.[16] All the while, social media misinformation flooded the internet that Black people were immune to the virus—creating an early racial conversation on COVID-19 about susceptibility, contraction, medical care, and death rates among racial groups. Not only would we all soon find out that Black people were by no means immune, but also Black people were about to witness the gravity of racial inequity manifesting itself through the inequality of economics, politics, and health care—all under the auspices of a global health pandemic.

Black Americans disproportionately have preexisting conditions that make them more likely to be unable to ward off the virus.[17] High blood pressure, heart disease, asthma, and diabetes are conditions that manifest in higher percentages in Black communities. A confluence of poor diet and poor health care have led to these catastrophic numbers in Black American health. The food provided to enslaved Africans were the scraps of whatever the white overseer decided to provide. These were not the most nutritious of foods; often they were pig intestines and the like. In addition to making delicacies out of scraps, Black people were not afforded proper health care—and when health care was provided, it often was in a manner that did not privilege the humanity of the patient. Not only are Black people susceptible due to inadequate diet and health care, Black people are more at risk as they constitute a disproportionately large percentage of the essential workers asked to put themselves at risk regularly so that the many can get their groceries and go about their daily existence.[18] Essential workers are fundamental in helping Americans carry out their routine tasks, while also financially having to depend on their continued "essential" employment to provide for themselves and their families. They are also situated precariously and, as such, are more susceptible to COVID-19 exposure. Therefore, Black people, when sick or in poor health, either do not trust the care of physicians or cannot afford to handle their bills.

Black Americans often have a deeply seated distrust of the American health care system, due to various medical abuses. The "Tuskegee Study of Untreated Syphilis in the Negro Male" is an example of medical abuse, whereby the US Public Health System (USPHS) wanted to track the course of untreated syphilis by effectively and unwittingly blocking treatment to four hundred men who had syphilis.[19] The study was to last six months, but it stretched over the course of forty years (1932–1972) and impacted six hundred men—leading the Center for Disease Control (CDC) to take oversight of the program. This horrific history, coupled with the vast, nonconsensual use of the HeLa cell line from Henrietta Lacks, an African American woman who was being treated for cervical cancer, contributes to the mistrust that Black people have with the US health care system.[20] The HeLa cell line is one of the most important in medical research history and is still being produced and utilized today, without Henrietta Lacks or her family having received compensation for her contribution to the advancement of the medical research field.[21] These two catastrophic cases, in addition to several other statistics that reflect the disenfranchisement of Black Americans, have fed the apprehension Black people have with the health care system that has direct consequences on Black people trusting the CDC, actively seeking treatment, and ultimately taking part in a coronavirus vaccine.

Fifty-four percent of Black people live in southern states with Republican governors who minimized the severity of the virus and were slow to institute shelter-in-place orders.[22] The country became divided on the issue of sheltering in place. Southern governors from Georgia,

Alabama, Florida, South Carolina, and Arkansas defied recommenda-
tions regarding sheltering-in-place orders from Dr. Anthony Fauci, one
of the world's leading experts on infectious diseases.[23] Contradicting
President Donald Trump's insistence that nationwide stay-at-home orders were unnecessary and his call for flexibility in this respect between
states, Fauci said in a CNN interview, "I don't understand why that's
not happening. . . . But if you look at what's going on in this country, I
just don't understand why we're not doing that."[24] Considering both the
history and political climate, Black people were never in an ideal position to survive a pandemic. Not surprisingly, then, the data indicate that
Black people are suffering at exorbitantly higher rates than their fellow
White Americans. Cities across the country began pouring in data that
confirmed the vulnerable position of Black Americans. The January 15,
2021, issue of the *Morbidity and Mortality Weekly Report*, compiled by
the CDC, highlighted 534 COVID-19 patients admitted to the hospital.
Of these, 261 (45 percent) were non-Hispanic white and 192 (33.1 percent) were non-Hispanic Black, which is astounding given that Black
citizens make up less than 13 percent of the population.[25] All of these
historic factors create a reality for Black people that impacts their mental and physical health, causing a strained relationship among the very
institutions implemented to heal.

Comedic Redemption: Dave Chappelle, a Case Study

Comedian David Chappelle was called up by Lorne Michaels, the cre-
ator and producer of *Saturday Night Live* (SNL), to host the show on
November 12, 2016—the one immediately following the election of
Donald Trump. Michaels knew that the world needed an explanation
as to what had taken place. For the same reason Michaels called upon
Richard Pryor to host the inaugural episode of SNL, he wanted Dave
Chappelle, because he is a "truth-teller and the funniest man today."[26]
During the read-through of the show, Chappelle read a passage from
American novelist Toni Morrison:

> This is precisely the time when artists go to work. There is no time for
> despair, no place for self-pity, no need for silence, no room for fear. We
> speak, we write, we do language. That is how civilizations heal.[27]

SNL had recordbreaking viewership that night. In a similar moment, in need of healing, on August 23, 2019, in Dayton, Ohio, one hundred feet away from the site of the largest mass shooting in American history, Chappelle assisted in creating a benefit concert. He shared with fellow comedian Jon Stewart, who joined him on stage that night, "This is their memory now."[28] He understood the need to redeem a moment inflicted by hate.

With this history of action coupled with the content of his message, Dave Chappelle can be a conduit for healing during this pandemic. Chappelle even reflects on the question why the audience desires to hear his input during this time in history. He was able to answer his own question: "Because you all trust me. Every institution that we trust lies to us. . . . I don't lie to you."[29] Dave Chappelle has a history of telling a critically engaged truth—one centering the lens of Black people. Americans and Black Americans specifically need that "new memory"; they need to heal, and to echo Morrison, in order to do so, the artists must go to work—and to work Chappelle went, displaying comedic redemptive tenets of fun, happiness, critical engagement, intimacy and enjoyment, and communing.

Returning to the opening quote of this chapter, Chappelle is concerned with the audience's level of fun. While he refers to this performance as a concert, he opens up speaking to the alternative safety precautions implemented due to the coronavirus pandemic. Early on in the special, Chappelle checks the temperature of the audience: "Are you all having a good time or is this weird?" Though the title and content of 8:46 pertain to grave situations, Chappelle simultaneously ensures there is an element of fun. He desires for everyone to understand the severity of racial discrimination, while also ensuring the audience members have fun. Laughter is a good indicator of fun.

Dave Chappelle critically engages the world around him, utilizing as the lens of his analysis his subjectivity of being a Black man in a racist, capitalist world. Dave Chappelle was honored with the Kennedy Center's *Mark Twain Prize for American Humor* in 2019, during which his colleagues spoke to Chappelle's ability to engage critically. Sarah Silverman, a fellow comedian who came up with Chappelle as a teen circulating in the comedy clubs in New York City, shared, "His critical thinking is his art."[30] Aziz Ansari, a fan and fellow comedian, stated,

"He's even unique as a genius as most geniuses are aloof." And one of the greatest stand-up comedians alive, Eddie Murphy, confessed, "Dave is so much smarter than everyone. He is probably the most intellectual comedian of all time."[31] They all marvel at Chappelle's uncanny ability to critically engage the world, filtered through his own experiences, and present the result back to the world. Silverman recalled Chappelle's first time in Compton. The reputation of Compton had made an indelible impression upon his imagination; however, Chappelle was taken aback by people mowing their lawns—an image not represented in music, media, and film. Even his sketch comedy show, *The Dave Chappelle Show*, served as a microcosm for what it might have been like for a Black man in America.

In *8:46* he narrates the culminating events of police brutality that led to mass protests surrounding the death of George Floyd during the pandemic. Chappelle studiously used the absurdity of George Floyd's death as the thesis of his twenty-seven-minute-long special, supporting it with the unjust deaths of John Crawford, Mike Brown, Tamir Rice, Philando Castile, Eric Garner, and Trayvon Martin. He included John Crawford, who was a local of Beavercreek, Ohio, where he was performing, in order to connect the epidemic of police brutality locally with what takes place countrywide. Chappelle even interjected a narrative of Christopher Dorner, a former African American officer of the Los Angeles Police Department (LAPD), who, after being fired for reporting a fellow white woman police officer for using excessive force, went on a killing spree of officers and their families.[32] This story serves as an example of what happens when officers intervene on behalf of civilians—circling back to why fellow officers stood around failing to intercede in the murder of George Floyd (and others). Concluding, Chappelle continued to highlight the absurdity of Black lives not mattering in this country by not offering solutions, but rather observations—"the streets are talking."[33] This is in reference to protests taking place during the coronavirus pandemic. Chappelle did not speak prior to this special and he declares that he will not speak after, because civilians and activists alike are doing an excellent job speaking truth to power and advocating for those disenfranchised. He leaves the audience to consider that this moment in time is one of dialogue, and if this dialogue is not engaged, chaos and perhaps anarchy will follow, as Chappelle discloses, "This is the last stronghold for civil discourse. After this, it's just rat-a-tat-tat!"[34]

Chappelle, like most stand-up comedians, cultivates intimacy. Chappelle donned that stage as he always does, with relaxed clothing and a cigarette. Sitting on a stool and speaking to the audience in an informal manner, he displayed the comfortability of speaking with a friend or family member. He shared that he didn't watch the video footage of George Floyd's death for a week because the number was burned into his brain. Chappelle connected the story of the fear experienced during his first earthquake, the desperation of his dying father calling out to his (Chappelle's father) dead mother, an anecdote of Christopher Dorner, culminating with the time of his own birth at 8:46 a.m., to articulate the constellating moments that brought us to this moment of George Floyd crying out for his dead mother with the officer's knee on his neck. Chappelle shared intimate details of his familial history as well as the time of his birth so that the audience could understand his connection to this murder. He shared his intimate relationship with the event, because, as for many Americans, it was hard to watch and process—Chappelle takes us through his process and showcases the pain and hurt accompanied by the footage. This vulnerability creates an intimate space for the audience to also explore their emotions surrounding the death of George Floyd. At the end of the special Chappelle shared, "I trust you guys, I love you guys"—ending on the intimate nature in which he began.[35]

According to comedian Tiffany Haddish, "Dave brings people together like no one in the world can," capturing his communing nature.[36] In the summer of 2004, after turning down $50 million offered to him by Comedy Central for another season of his sketch comedy show, Chappelle threw a block party in Brooklyn with headliners such as Common, Kanye West, Jill Scott, Lauryn Hill, Fugees, the Roots, and Mos Def, to honor the death of music producer J Dilla. The concert was free to the public and is archived in the documentary *Dave Chappelle's Block Party*.[37] Chappelle was called on to aid the nation after the 2016 election. He set out to heal a community again in 2019, when he held a benefit concert held in Dayton, Ohio, honoring Dayton shooting victims. For these reasons, the *8:46* Netflix special garnered close to thirty million views. Communities were longing to commune with someone who would aid in their healing during this time of sheltering in place.

Growing up, Chappelle's mother, Yvonne Seon, an African and African American studies professor, taught him about the definition and function of the word *griot*. The term is of West African origins and is one among the community who maintains a tradition of oral histories.[38] Chappelle's mother suggested that Chappelle be a griot, filing the stories and histories of all those around him at a young age. She explained to him that he was living in a hostile world that needed to be tamed. Chappelle, like a griot, collects stories and arranges them to make a salient point. The function of the griot is to preserve genealogies, histories, and oral traditions. Chappelle provided an American genealogical history of Black men murdered at the hands of police officers in *8:46*, recounting the context for each victim. One does not suddenly and simply become a griot; one becomes a griot through a sort of apprenticeship, collecting and memorizing stories. Under the tutelage of his mother, who not only served as a professor but also was an administrative officer in the government of Patrice Lumumba, the first prime minister of the Independent Democratic Republic of the Congo, Chappelle digested pan-African ideologies.[39] Chappelle's mother was also the first African American woman ordained in the Unitarian Universalist Church in 1981, while his great-grandfather was a bishop of the African Methodist Episcopal Church who led a delegate to the White House to discuss with Woodrow Wilson lynchings taking place at that time. Not only does Dave Chappelle have this rich history in his family background, he calls it to memory and uses these personal histories to inform the world about the impacts of the institution of slavery.

Chappelle recalls and re-members many stories, and the content always engages the absurd—or suffering. The entire special was named after and centered on absurdity—an officer sworn to protect and serve kneeled on the neck of another human being for eight minutes and forty-six seconds while fellow officers stood by watching with their hands in their pockets. A man lies lamenting for his mother, who is no longer living. It is unconscionable that one human could do that to another human. What is most egregious, however, is that the American judicial system is predominantly orchestrated in incidents such as these to support the officers and not the George Floyd's of the country, because of the color of their skin. Chappelle always engages absurdity as opposed to escaping it or believing solely on a figure beyond the absurd. He often does this by posing a question to the audience before interjecting his opinion as he wants them to wrestle with the absurdity of the query. Much like my earlier outline on the impacts of COVID-19, Chappelle succinctly communicates the government's involvement with HIV/AIDS:

> Isn't it weird how there's a disease that just starts in 1980 and it doesn't kill anybody but niggas, fags and junkies? Isn't that a fucking amazing coincidence that this disease hates everybody that old white people hate? I think either god is white, or the government hid that shit in disco balls.[40]

Dave Chappelle communicates that even diseases can be used on Black people and other marginalized communities as weapons of terror—a foreshadowing of our current pandemic whereby Black people again are the most vulnerable population to disease and lack of treatment. While he directs his focus on the government often, Chappelle confesses, "I don't even necessarily believe in politics, but I think trust in politics is something that the country really needs."[41] He is dedicating his entire career to using comedy as a way to engage and process the absurd—redeeming those most vulnerable and locating the source. Dave Chappelle offers guidance on how to make comedy and humor serve as necessary agents for change. And while he does not believe in or trust politics, he understands the importance of understanding politics and its impact on communities. Chappelle shares his interpretations of politics with his audience in order to name absurdity.

Chappelle closes his set speaking of a mass shooting killing nine cops that took place during the same time that Kobe Bryant was playing his final game against the Utah Jazz. He situated the context by stating that the world seemed as if it would crumble after the shooting of the nine cops, but like Chappelle and myself, many other Americans were tuned in to see Kobe Bryant's final performance. "I watched this nigga dribble and save this country from itself. I love Kobe."[42] Kobe Bryant distracted US citizens from hate, yet we could still turn the channel and live the horrors of a nation that has its armed services personnel fighting acts of terror against their own police service. Dave

Chappelle's comedy aids in processing the pandemic and police brutality as opposed to distracting us with comical asides. He navigates us through emotions, utilizing history and humor to heal. The day before Chappelle received his Mark Twain Prize for American Humor he spoke to a select group of people in DC and made a bold revelation: "Humor was our mode of survival."[43] The following day upon receiving the award, he emphasized that statement by further elaborating on the role of comedy: "This might be America's last safe place to say what you feel like saying. . . . This [comedy] is sacred ground."[44] For Chappelle and many other comedians, the function of comedy is to survive while the genre itself is sacred. What might we make of this? Chappelle learned at a young age that he lived in a hostile world not designed for everyone to survive.

Chappelle, a Muslim, lauds comedy as sacred ground because he uses comedy as the space for transformation. The comedy stage as a sacred space is not unlike an altar or pulpit, with the rhetor parsing out means of redemption. Congregants respect the space in order that they may hear a prophetic word, which is what comedians provide—as Chappelle did when he stated, "This is the last stronghold for civil discourse,"[45] in relation to nationwide protests of police brutality. We cannot separate the unjust killings of Black people at the hands of law enforcement from disproportionate COVID-19 cases and deaths in Black communities at this moment, because it is the same justice system governing these Black lives and it is evident they don't matter. Black people are dying at the hands of police and COVID-19. In the midst of the deaths—those funerals that we cannot attend or loved ones that we cannot touch—we must laugh. Laughter is more than the extension of the mouth, the rising of cheeks, shoulders rising and falling with chuckles escaping the mouth; rather laughter engages the absurd and redeems power. Chappelle does not seek to entertain or distract from serious matters, nor does he falter to directly engage the time that we are in; rather, he leans into it. For instance, he took all precautions to still commune, marking out chairs and maintaining the appropriate distance. While he knew that we were experiencing a pandemic, he also knew that we needed someone to make sense of the world with truth and clarity. He rose to the occasion once again, helping Americans to make sense of the absurdity of the world by redeeming and valuing the work of protesters and activists and also making us laugh in the midst of many deaths—both at the hands of law enforcement and the coronavirus.

NOTES

1 Dave Chappelle, *8:46*, June 12, 2020, Netflix.

2 Søren Kierkegaard, *The Sickness unto Death* (London: Penguin, 2008).

3 Albert Camus and Justin O'Brien, *The Myth of Sisyphus: And Other Essays* (New York: Vintage, 1959).

4 Frantz Fanon, *The Wretched of the Earth*, preface by Jean-Paul Sartre (New York: Grove, 1968).

5 Brian Mann, "Hangover from Alcohol Boom Could Last Long after Pandemic Ends," *Morning Edition*, NPR, September 11, 2020, www.npr.org.

6 Caroline Bradbury-Jones and Louise Isham, "The Pandemic Paradox: The Consequences of COVID-19 on Domestic Violence," *Journal of Clinical Nursing* 29, no. 13–14 (April 12, 2020), https://onlinelibrary.wiley.com.

7 Matthew R. Meier and Casey R. Schmitt, *Standing Up, Speaking Out: Stand-Up Comedy and the Rhetoric of Social Change* (New York: Routledge, Taylor & Francis, 2017).

8 Stacey M. Floyd-Thomas, ed., *Deeper Shades of Purple: Womanism in Religion and Society* (New York: NYU , 2006), 142.

9 Richard Pryor, "Cocaine," *The Anthology: 1968–1992*, accessed May 31, 2020, https://www.youtube.com/watch?v=Ad6fJy8aOuw.

10 *My Next Guest Needs No Introduction with David Letterman*, May 31, 2019, season 3, episode 10, Netflix.

11 Jerry Seinfield, "Jimmy Fallon: The Unsinkable Legend—Part I and II," *Comedians in Cars Getting Coffee*, season 5, episode 8, Netflix.

12 Stacey M. Floyd-Thomas, Juan Floyd-Thomas, et al., *Black Church Studies: An Introduction* (Nashville: Abingdon, 2007).

13 James Cone, *A Black Theology of Liberation* (Maryknoll, NY: Orbis, 1989).

14 Jerry Seinfeld, "Trevor Noah: That's the Whole Point of Apartheid Jerry," *Comedians in Cars Getting Coffee*, season 6, episode 5, Netflix.

15 "The Most Segregated Hour in America – Martin Luther King Jr.," www.youtube.com/watch?v=1q881g1L_d8.

16 "About COVID-19," Centers for Disease Control and Prevention, updated September 1 2020, www.cdc.gov.

17 Chris Horn, "COVID-19 Highlights Underlying Racial Health Disparities," University of South Carolina, June 8, 2020, www.sc.edu

18 Jeff Lagasse, "COVID-19 Deaths among Black Essential Workers Linked to Racial Disparities," *Healthcare Finance News*, September 11, 2020, www.healthcarefinancenews.com.

19 Brandt, Allan M., "Racism and Research: The Case of the Tuskegee Syphilis Study," *Hastings Center Report* 8, no. 6 (December 1978): 21–29, www.jstor.org.

20 Benjamin Butanis, "The Immortal Life of Henrietta Lacks," *Johns Hopkins Medicine*, April 12, 2017, www.hopkinsmedicine.org.

21 Ibid.
22 US Census Bureau Public Information Office, "Majority of African Americans Live in 10 States; New York City and Chicago Are Cities with Largest Black Populations," *Census 2000–Newsroom*, US Census Bureau, May 19, 2016, www .census.gov.
23 Sergei Klebnikov, "Here Are the 9 State Governors Who Have Refused to Issue Stay-at-Home Orders," *Forbes*, April 6, 2020, www.forbes.com.
24 Paul LeBlanc, "Fauci: 'I Don't Understand Why' Every State Hasn't Issued Stay-at-Home Orders," CNN, April 3, 2020, www.cnn.com.
25 *Morbidity and Mortality Weekly Report (MMWR)*, Centers for Disease Control and Prevention, January 15, 2021, www.cdc.gov.
26 Lorne Michaels, "Dave Chappelle: The Kennedy Center—Mark Twain Prize for American Humor," Washington, DC, October 27, 2019, Netflix.
27 Toni Morrison, "No Place for Self-Pity, No Room for Fear," *The Nation*, December 23, 2019, www.thenation.com.
28 Michaels, "Dave Chappelle," 2019.
29 Chappelle, *8:46*.
30 Michaels, "Dave Chappelle," 2019.
31 Ibid.
32 "Why Do People Sympathize With Christopher Dorner?" NPR, February 15, 2013, www.npr.org.
33 Chappelle, *8:46*.
34 Ibid.
35 Ibid.
36 Michaels, "Dave Chappelle," 2019.
37 *Dave Chappelle's Block Party* (dir. Michel Gondry), Rogue Pictures, 2005.
38 Adam Banks, *Digital Griots: African American Rhetoric in a Multimedia Age* (Carbondale: Southern Illinois University Press, 2011).
39 "Yvonne Seon's Biography," *The HistoryMakers*, January 16, 2021, www.thehistory makers.org.
40 Michaels, "Dave Chappelle," 2019.
41 Ibid.
42 Chappelle, *8:46*.
43 Michaels, "Dave Chappelle," 2019.
44 Ibid.
45 Chappelle, *8:46*.

10

Toxic Religion, Toxic Churches, and Toxic Policies

Evangelicals, "White Blessing," and COVID-19

DAVID P. GUSHEE

COVID-19 is a ferocious enemy to human life and was going to be a difficult challenge to every religion, government, and people. But it found the United States desperately vulnerable, in part because of built-in problems in the large and influential white fundamentalist-evangelical subculture and in its relation to the broader culture. While serious debates need to take place at the intersection of religion, ethics, and COVID-19, the big story here has been the sustained difficulty of white fundamentalists and evangelicals in dealing with COVID-19 on the terms required for the social good. This chapter focuses on that dilemma.

The Worst Pandemic in a Century

This is my first effort to write at any length about the COVID-19 pandemic. As I attempt to do so, I find I must wring every word out of myself. This project feels much more like writing a funeral eulogy than like writing another academic essay, a reminder that COVID-19 has been a mass death experience, one that has come home personally to many of us. I am only now beginning to try to put some words to this experience, moving beyond day-to-day survival mode and my own barely acknowledged, barely processed trauma and grief, to try to make some meaning out of this catastrophe.

In recent human history, pandemics of this magnitude have been exceedingly rare. It has been one hundred years since the world has suffered an epidemic anything like COVID-19. That epidemic, most commonly known as the Spanish flu, lasted over two years, infected 500 million people, and took 50 million lives, including 675,000 in the United States.[1]

In any case, COVID-19 is a once-in-a-century experience. That itself is testimony, at least in part, to advances in public health and preventive medicine. But the downside is that only the specialists were acutely aware of how perennial the threat of pandemics is and how destructive such pandemics can be. As evolutionary virologist Edward Holmes has said, "People keep using the term *unprecedented*. . . . Biologically, there is nothing unprecedented about this virus. . . . It's behaving exactly as I would expect a respiratory virus to behave."[2]

The rest of us, however, were lulled into a false sense of complacency. We didn't think about pandemics. Or if we did, we thought about them as belonging in the long-ago human past, or only in scary science fiction movies. We were not ready.

The United States: The Worst Response in the Developed World

I just said that "we" were not ready. At one level, I speak of all humankind. China, where COVID-19 began, was not ready—it wasn't ready for the virus, and it wasn't quite ready to share the news with the rest of the world before the virus began its global spread.[3] Europe was not ready. Italy and Spain especially staggered under massive early COVID-19 deaths.[4] India was not ready. Brazil was not ready. Russia was not ready.

But the United States, our proud land, won the gold medal this time. We had over one-fourth of the world's entire caseload (4.4 million out of 17 million) and nearly one-fourth of global COVID fatalities.[5] By comparison, with the Spanish flu we had 10 percent of the world's cases and 1.3 percent of its fatalities. Our peers looked on with astonishment at our staggering failure. As *Washington Post* reporter Dan Balz wrote, "The rest of the world sees the United States not as a leader in dealing with the coronavirus but as the country with the highest number of coronavirus infections and COVID-19 deaths, and with the disease far from under control."[6] Americans were banned from travel to Europe and Canada. Canada's sole Major League Baseball team, the Toronto Blue Jays, was banned from playing any games in Canada to prevent cross-border US-Canada traffic of baseball players and staff. Basically, Americans were not welcome anywhere. It is a deadly, staggering, embarrassing failure.

We must try to understand what has gone so very wrong here.

Why the United States Failed So Badly

There are many reasons for our nation's especially catastrophic failure to contain COVID-19. The postmortems will continue for a long time. Here are a few of the most important conclusions.

It was always going to be difficult to fight the spread of this pandemic. Forty percent or more of people infected with COVID-19 show no symptoms.[7] Infected people who become symptomatic do not immediately develop such symptoms—the average lag time is five days.[8] If asymptomatic or not-yet-symptomatic infected people are out and about, especially if they are not wearing masks and keeping apart from others, they are prime candidates to infect others. And that is not to speak of infection paths for those who are visibly sick but being cared for by others, including dedicated medical professionals who sometimes are not spared being infected themselves, despite every precaution. If one infected person spreads it to two others, then two to four, then four to eight, the virus is on a path to spread geometrically, which will ravage a population within weeks. That is precisely what happened.

To combat such a threat successfully once it jumped to the United States would have required immediate recognition of the severity of the disease, extremely rapid response to its first appearances, tracing of contacts among those who were initially sickened, and draconian lockdowns to keep people from spreading the disease while its first cases were treated and isolated. But all this would have required a highly alert government, led by people who trust the expertise of skilled public health and pandemic experts, with such experts making the right judgments in a timely manner, and with government officials able to entice or coerce their citizens to cooperate with emergency measures.

The United States, it turned out, did not have any of this in place as of January 2020, and the situation never really improved during the Trump presidency. It turns out that we have a relatively weak public health system, for a variety of reasons, including financial underinvestment and a lack of glamour attached to this kind of medical work compared to others. Our public health infrastructure was not ready for this assault.[9] Experts, especially academics, are quite mistrusted by significant portions of the population. Public health officials are almost always experts with academic degrees, training, and manner. American antielitism triggers negative reactions to such experts.[10] Scientific and medical experts are especially distrusted by portions of the population who believe they have reasons not to respect or accept their convictions or advice. Consider the strength of the antivaccination movement, long before COVID-19, as well as the long history of mistrust of science in such matters as evolution and sexuality.[11]

We lack agreed-upon, trusted information sources. If one major media ecosystem, in this case Fox News and the right-wing media, casts doubt for a sustained period of time on the significance or truthfulness of mainstream health information and warnings, then those doubts will hinder cooperation with public health concerns and mandates for a significant minority of Americans.[12]

A long tradition of "Don't tread on me" American libertarianism makes defiance the default response of some Americans when they are told what to do. COVID-19 has fed on that libertarianism.[13] This is the same country that so resisted seat belts, motorcycle safety helmets, and health warnings on cigarettes—aided and abetted by industry money, of course.

America's federalist system generally failed us. In a situation where a disease advances geometrically and (of course) does not respect local, state, and regional borders, we needed a coherent response led by the federal government and health officials the entire nation would support. But in our country, public health responsibilities are decentralized, not just to the states but down to the county and local levels, and awkwardly shared between politicians and medical authorities. This hampered a coordinated national response when one was needed.[14] It is impossible to be certain about how much better our federalized system would have worked with stronger US government leadership. Public health decentralization would have been a challenge regardless.

Political divisions and lack of agreed-upon leaders hurt us badly. Our red-blue divisions are more than matters of opinion. They are more tribal than that. Red (conservative) team distrusts blue (liberal) team. Blue team distrusts red team. Red team leaders are therefore distrusted by blue team members, and vice versa. Concretely, this meant Democratic mayors and governors were distrusted by Republican citizens, and Republican mayors, governors, and the president were distrusted by Democratic citizens. A lack of social trust across red-blue divisions wounded us badly here.[15] The situation was made far worse because the US president chose to downplay the virus and the primary public health responses.

President Trump needed to be the head of government and coordinator or delegator of a swift and authoritative national pandemic response guided by medical experts already situated in government for this purpose. He also needed to offer inspiring and reliable guidance and a good example to his fellow citizens. Instead, he could not get beyond being a skeptical internet troll rather than US president. He did not lead a properly coordinated whole-of-government response; he acted as if just keeping foreigners out would stop the disease; he practiced magical thinking that the disease would just suddenly disappear; he cast doubt on experts and their warnings and gave aid and comfort to stupid conspiracy theories; he trashed Democratic-led government responses; he pooh-poohed information sources he did not like; he encouraged libertarian defiance of public health mandates; he demonstrated almost no empathy for COVID victims and their families; he never attended to the disproportionate impact of COVID on people of color; and for months he made social distancing and mask-wearing a partisan or even masculinity issue.[16] He did this for his own reasons, not just political self-interest, apparently, but also an in-built temperamental bias to respond to most of life's situations in precisely this same way. As Washington Post reporters Ashley Parker and Philip Rucker reported,

> People close to Trump . . . say the president's inability to wholly address the crisis is due to his almost pathological unwillingness to admit error; a positive feedback loop of overly rosy assessments and data from advisers and Fox News; and a penchant for magical thinking that prevented him from fully engaging with the pandemic.[17]

COVID-19 is a fierce enemy to human life. All it needed was a bit of an opening to grow geometrically in even a partially locked-down country. We gave it much more than that, and COVID-19 had its way with us.

Now what does any of this have to do with American religion? My thesis is that pretty much everything I just said about Donald Trump can be said about a large section of the American religious community. I speak especially of America's white fundamentalists and evangelicals. Even though Donald Trump is not an evangelical in terms of his churchgoing, personal behavior, or stated religious beliefs, he is the consummate evangelical in terms of certain pernicious characteristics that have developed in this movement over its history.

Who Are the US Fundamentalists-Evangelicals?

To support this claim, I need to step back for a moment and offer my account of US white fundamentalism and evangelicalism.[18] The modern American evangelicalism that so many (including me) have now abandoned was a brilliant social construction, an invented religious *identity*, that over decades yielded something like an actual religious *community*. The modern evangelical *identity* was invented through a historical retrieval and rebranding move undertaken by an ambitious group of reformers within the white US Protestant fundamentalist community of the 1940s. These men were frustrated with the failures of a reactionary and angry fundamentalism and believed a third way between fundamentalism and mainline Protestantism was needed. The modern evangelical community was the eventual product of their entrepreneurial efforts, with an assist over several decades from journalists, historians, pollsters, marketers, consumers, congregations, denominations, parachurch organizations, and regular Christians who all decided to accept the existence of evangelicalism or to identify as evangelical.

The term "evangelical" was by no means created out of whole cloth when the National Association of Evangelicals was created in 1942 by a group of semimoderate white fundamentalists. The word does have a long, traceable history.[19] It once had distinguished Protestants from Catholics in Europe, Puritans and Methodists from Anglicans in England, and revivalists and Pietists from formalist Protestants everywhere. Still, I side with the skeptics on the question of whether there was anything that could fairly be described as "evangelicalism" or an "evangelical community" before the term was reinvented by the "new evangelicals" in the 1940s. What happened in the 1940s was the purposeful creation within white US fundamentalism of a new religious identity and community.[20] Those using the term deployed it to describe themselves as theologically orthodox, spiritually vital, intellectually sharp, and morally serious Christians.

The Greek etymological origin of the term "evangelical" offers a clue to why the reformist fundamentalists of the 1940s turned to it for self-definition. Derived from the New Testament term *evangelion*, meaning "gospel" or "good news," "evangelical" was an appealingly laudatory self-description. To be evangelical was to be a gospel Christian, a good news Christian, a New Testament Christian. It has almost always been deployed as a contrast term against other versions of Christianity viewed as less than ideal.

There were certainly appealing qualities to many of the Christian groups that were identified as evangelical in the past. Especially because the groups claimed as evangelicals were so diverse, one could reach back into history for any number of examples matching one's preference in launching a new movement while claiming to be retrieving the best of the past.

Both the etymological and the historical appeal of the term help explain why the terms "neo-evangelical" and "evangelical"[21] were deployed by that determined group of Protestant fundamentalists in the early 1940s to advance what amounted to a new religious identity. These men had profound ambitions for rescuing Christian witness in a world, and a church, in crisis. They wanted to contribute to renewing American, Western, and human civilization.

There was no intrinsic reason why Christians of color could not qualify as evangelicals, but the new evangelicals almost entirely overlooked nonwhite Christians when they began their movement in the 1940s. These were white Christian men in the habit of segregation—and in the grip of the four-hundred-year-old white supremacist assumption that white Christians are the ones called to lead America. But it went deeper than this—the new evangelicals quickly demonstrated that they were not interested in raising challenges to Jim Crow or white domination of America.

As the twentieth century progressed and evangelicalism coalesced as a recognized religious community, it seemed to become more difficult to define its center and boundaries. It was much easier to know who was a Catholic, Methodist, or Lutheran than it was to know who was an evangelical. Every effort to define evangelicals failed to convince somebody else who was doing their own defining.[22] Constant power struggles erupted over who counted as a real evangelical, who should make evangelical doctrinal decisions, and what boundary lines they were drawing. Judgments by "important" voices within the evangelical world that an individual or group had drifted into heresy gained the power to ruin people's careers. Perceived doctrinal slippage within the big evangelical tent played a key role in the high evangelical anxiety about definitions. When conflicts emerged, old fundamentalist tendencies often surfaced, both in tactics and in theology. Crush dissenters, circle the wagons, and defend the fundamentals. This was the standard fundamentalist-evangelical approach, and it left many out of so-called evangelicalism who really wanted to be, or stay, within the fold.

Beginning in the late 1960s, American politics intervened and, in a sense, solved the evangelical identity problem—at grievous cost. The emergence of a highly visible partisan evangelicalism, especially accentuated by the birth of what was originally called the New Christian Right, turned the focus of many evangelicals, and the understanding of US evangelicals from outside the community, away from evangelism and theology toward politics. White evangelicals gradually became identified as, and with, socially conservative Republicans—and eventually with any old kind of Republican, in a process that can be described as *identity fusion* between "white evangelical" and "Republican." Supposedly Christian politics now included support for Cold War policies, opposition to most civil rights legislation and enforcement, laissez-faire economic policies, and restrictive attitudes toward women's roles, sex, and abortion.

This move may have provided a welcome shared identity and purpose for most white US evangelicals, but it shattered the earlier big-tent coalition, at least insofar as it had included (in a small way) nonwhite and politically progressive evangelicals. It also deeply compromised the religious identity and mission of evangelical Christianity. Incidentally, it also erased any meaningful distinction between evangelicalism and fundamentalism.[23]

The partisan politicizing of the evangelical label in this way did not cohere with the original plan of evangelical strategists in the 1940s. They wanted to move fundamentalists out of their bunkers and into "biblical," effective, social-ethical-political engagement. Their agenda was generally conservative but not partisan. It was a different era in any case. There were liberal Republicans and conservative Democrats then. America had not sundered into totalistic left-right tribalism.

Still, the signs were there. The political statements and involvements of postwar American evangelical leaders were consistently conservative from the beginning, as earlier fundamentalism had been when it attempted to engage the politics of its time, and this pattern carried forward right through the 1960s.[24] And when, after that, American politics turned sharply binary—left-right, Democratic-Republican—white evangelicals were easily persuaded to turn right. They had been there all along. Long before the Moral Majority existed, authoritative white evangelical leaders were already anticommunist, nationalist, antiliberal, antifeminist, antigay, anti–civil rights movement (or at best lukewarm), Goldwater/Nixon/Reagan Republicans.[25]

In the election of 2016, evangelical politics took a disastrous turn in its overwhelming support for Donald Trump—including 81 percent of the voters who identified as evangelical, with considerable cover from highly visible "evangelical leaders" like Franklin Graham, Paula White, and then-powerful but now-disgraced Jerry Falwell Jr. With Trumpism, American evangelical politics reached its nadir. Any level of corruption was fine as long as evangelicals could advance in political access and power.[26] With COVID-19, the true cost of this misbegotten alliance has become all too visible.

White US Fundamentalists-Evangelicals and COVID-19

US white fundamentalists and evangelicals bear disproportionate responsibility for the disastrous national response to COVID-19, in two distinct but related ways: through the conduct of some of their churches and leaders, and through their support for Donald Trump not just in 2016 but throughout his presidency. Indeed, support is not quite strong enough a word—he is more like the embodiment of their worst tendencies. He is *their* president, and his weaknesses and theirs are entirely intertwined.

Throughout the spring of 2020, reports emerged from various parts of the country of churches that were meeting despite temporary government bans on gatherings of more than ten people, or were meeting without following current social distancing mandates, or were sending young adults on trips and to camps despite the manifest danger of such events becoming "superspreaders."[27] Every church that I saw in such news accounts can fairly be described as fundamentalist, Pentecostal, or evangelical; almost all were white churches.

These churches sometimes defended their actions based on religious liberty. They did not seem to understand that religious liberty, while a major moral value and constitutional right, is not absolute.[28] Our religious liberty, like other freedoms, must be constrained by the well-being of our own members and of others in our communities. Just as religious people are not free to sacrifice children on their altars in the name of religious liberty, we are also not free to sacrifice community health in the name of our religion.

Fundamentalist and evangelical churches often had difficulty taking the science (and the scientists) related to COVID-19 seriously, and thus they were far too likely to disregard precisely such community health considerations. It is not a coincidence that these same churches have struggled mightily to take evolutionary biology seriously since the dawn of Darwin's theory in the mid-nineteenth century. COVID-19 is a real-time case study in evolutionary biology. It is no surprise that the anti-science part of the Christian community would struggle here as on other scientific issues.

Especially during the early days of the crisis, magical thinking surfaced among some of these same Christians. Especially on the Pentecostal side of American Christianity, occasional examples surfaced of ministers claiming some kind of supernatural immunity, divine healing power, or miraculously pure HVAC systems in relation to COVID-19.[29] This is not the first nor will it be the last such example of this kind of magical thinking in the wilder quadrants of American Christianity. Normally, such excesses affect only members and their families, but in this case, given the geometric spread of this virus, every church that encouraged reckless behavior and magical thinking risked the health of their entire community.[30]

It should be noted that Pentecostalism is not solely a white phenomenon. But the long-standing and tragic split between white and Black US Pentecostalism surfaced in striking ways during this crisis.

White Pentecostals often joined President Trump and their white co-religionists in his politicized and magical-thinking downplaying of the virus. I did not spot any news accounts in the spring or summer of 2020 in which Black- or Hispanic-led Pentecostal (or any other) churches were making magical immunity claims. The fact that COVID-19 was ravaging communities of color became clear early in the pandemic.[31] Most Black Church leaders responded by rapidly closing their doors and if possible moving online. One wonders if some misbegotten sense of white immunity or even "white blessing"[32] affected the behavior of some of the most irresponsible white fundamentalist and evangelical church leaders. This COVID thing—it can't happen to us. Right? It makes one wonder if one aspect of the "faith" of white Christians is faith in white health supremacy even over the facts of a deadly virus.

Still, the broader fundamentalist-evangelical symbiosis with Trump strikes me as most important and most lamentable. As noted in the sketch of white fundamentalism above, for one hundred years or more this subculture at its worst has tended toward an insular, antiscience, antielite, anti–mainstream media, antiliberal, conspiracy-oriented, racist or racially oblivious, paranoid-populist way of engaging the world. Such a posture also characterizes Donald Trump, the president whom this community embraced (and apparently will always embrace) with around 80 percent approval. In a sense, Trump is their embodiment, just without (what's left of) the piety. His tendencies are theirs. Even as he may be gone from the scene, they will still be there, with these same tendencies, the same morally corrupt quest for power, tinged with a nauseating religiosity. The disastrous response of President Trump to COVID-19 seems inextricably connected to the tendencies of his most strident followers. Indeed, it may not be possible to draw a meaningful distinction between at least the Trumpist version of the GOP and the most visible version of white US fundamentalism-evangelicalism.

To conclude, COVID-19 is a fierce enemy to human life. Limiting its deadly spread required an effectiveness in government and a responsiveness in the public that many nations have not been able to quite muster. The reasons vary, but in the case of the United States the toxicity of the disease is directly related to the toxicity of the political and intellectual proclivities of now-Trumpified white fundamentalists and evangelicals. Their votes supported Donald Trump to the end and their loyalty followed him over the COVID cliff. Their churches sometimes became superspreader sites. Their sense of "white blessing" created the illusion of imperviousness to the virus. Their unique power in US society contributed to the disaster in ways seldom seen anywhere else in the world.

NOTES

1 "1918 Pandemic (H1N1 virus)," Centers for Disease Control and Prevention, accessed February 1, 2021, www.cdc.gov/flu/pandemic-resources/1918-pandemic -h1n1.html.

2 Quoted in Charlie Campbell and Alice Park, "Anatomy of a Pandemic," *Time*, August 3–10, 2020, 85.

3 "China's Response to COVID-19: The Good, the Bad, and the Ugly," *TrialSite News*, March 30, 2020, www.trialsitenews.com.

4 "New COVID-19 Forecasts for Europe: Italy and Spain Have Passed the Peak of Their Epidemics; UK, Early in Its Epidemic, Faces a Fast-Mounting Death Toll," IHME, April 6, 2020, www.healthdata.org.

5 Data drawn from the invaluable research offered by Johns Hopkins University, as of July 30, 2020, https://coronavirus.jhu.edu/map.html.

6 Dan Balz, "America's Global Standing Is at a Low Point. The Pandemic Made It Worse," *Washington Post*, July 26, 2020.

7 "Up to 45 percent of SARS-CoV-2 Infections May Be Asymptomatic," Scripps Research Institute, Science Daily, June 12, 2020, www.sciencedaily.com.

8 Erica Hersh, "How Long Is the Incubation Period for the Coronavirus?," Healthline, March 13, 2020, www.healthline.com.

9 Jeneen Interlandi, "Why We're Losing the Battle with COVID-19," *New York Times Magazine*, July 14, 2020, www.nytimes.com.

10 Ron Pruessen, "Trump's Crude Anti-Elitism Is Nothing New in the American Story," LSE US Centre, January 15, 2020, https://blogs.lse.ac.uk.

11 Philip Ball, "Anti-Vaccine Movement Could Undermine Efforts to End Pandemic, Researchers Warn," *Nature*, May 13, 2020, www.nature.com.

12 Christopher Ingraham, "New Research Explores How Conservative Media Misinformation May Have Intensified the Severity of the Pandemic," *Washington Post*, June 25, 2020, www.washingtonpost.com.

13 Sean Illing, "Is America Too Libertarian to Deal with the Coronavirus?" *Vox*, May 24, 2020, www.vox.com.

14 Sarah Gordon, "What Federalism Means for the US Response to Coronavirus 2019," *JAMANetwork*, May 15, 2020, https://jamanetwork.com.

15 "Coronavirus Response Highlights Deepening Partisan Divide," *USNews*, March 30, 2020, www.usnews.com.

16 For one account of the early failures, see Cameron Peters, "A Detailed Timeline of All the Ways Trump Failed to Respond to the Coronavirus," *Vox*, June 8, 2020, www.vox.com.

17 Ashley Parker and Philip Rucker, "One Question Still Dogs Trump: Why Not Try Harder to Solve the Coronavirus Crisis?" *Washington Post*, July 27, 2020, www .washingtonpost.com.

18 This section is drawn from my recent book, *After Evangelicalism: The Path to a New Christianity* (Louisville, KY: Westminster John Knox, 2020), chapter 1.

19 Alister McGrath, *Evangelicalism and the Future of Christianity* (Downers Grove, IL: InterVarsity, 1995), 19–23. McGrath spots uses beginning in the late fifteenth century, and traces its appearances in German, French, and English.

20 See D. G. Hart, *Deconstructing Evangelicalism* (Grand Rapids: Baker Academic, 2004). On the pivotal role of pollsters, see also Robert Wuthnow, *Inventing American Religion: Polls, Surveys, and the Tenuous Quest for a Nation's Faith* (New York: Oxford University Press, 2015), 95–128.

21 The same people called themselves, or were called, variously, in stages, "fundamentalist," "neo-fundamentalist," "neo-evangelical," and then finally "evangelical," the term that stuck. That linguistic development itself is fascinating.

22 David W. Bebbington, *Evangelicalism in Modern Britain: A History from the 1730's to the 1980's* (London and New York: Routledge, 1989), 2–17; George M. Marsden, *Understanding Fundamentalism and Evangelicalism* (Grand Rapids, Michigan: Wm. B. Eerdsman Publishing Co., 1991), 4–5.

23 A thorough recent treatment of the politics of white evangelicalism is found in Frances Fitzgerald, *The Evangelicals: The Struggle to Shape America* (New York: Simon & Schuster, 2017). Fitzgerald, a nonevangelical and a journalist, perhaps succumbs to reducing evangelicalism to its politics. But evangelicalism has earned that misreading to a very large extent.

24 Kevin Kruse, *One Nation under God: How Corporate America Invented Christian America* (New York: Basic, 2016).

25 Justin Randall Phillips, "Lord, When Did We See You? The Ethical Vision of White, Progressive Baptists in the South during the Civil Rights Movement" (PhD diss., Fuller Theological Seminary, 2013).

26 Elizabeth Dias, "'Christianity Will Have Power,'" *New York Times*, August 9, 2020, www.nytimes.com.

27 Aylin Woodward, "Trump Declared Houses of Worship Essential. Mounting Evidence Shows That They're Super-Spreader Hotspots," *Business Insider*, May 28, 2020, www.businessinsider.com.

28 David L. Hudson Jr., "A Right to Gather? Balancing Health Risks and Religious Liberties during the COVID-19 Crisis," *ABA Journal*, June 10, 2020, www.abajour nal.com.

29 Jason Lemon, "Conservative Pastor Claims He 'Healed' Viewers of Coronavirus through Their TV Screens," *Newsweek*, March 12, 2020, www.newsweek.com.

30 "Over 40 Infected with Coronavirus after Church Revival Event in Alabama: 'We knew what we were getting into,'" CBS News, July 27, 2020, www.cbsnews.com.

31 Maria Godoy and Daniel Wood, "What Do Coronavirus Racial Disparities Look Like State by State?" NPR, May 30, 2020, www.npr.org.

32 This awful term was used by Atlanta megachurch pastor Louie Giglio in talking about the history of slavery. He apologized. The term still reverberates, however. I deploy it here to describe the possibility that perhaps some white people have considered themselves to be divinely blessed with a (relative or absolute) exemption from COVID-19. Sarah Pulliam Bailey, "Atlanta Megachurch Pastor Louie Giglio Sets Off Firestorm by Calling Slavery a 'Blessing' to Whites," *Washington Post*, June 16, 2020, www.washingtonpost.com.

11

I Know Why the Culture War Stings

Racial Realities and Political Realignment in the "Religious Freedom" Debate

MARLA F. FREDERICK

In the midst of a country ravaged by the coronavirus and upended by protests for justice after the murder of George Floyd, the one loud, resonating cry heard throughout the summer of 2020 was the cry for "freedom." From the White House to evangelical pulpits to grocery store aisles to the streets of St. Louis—the consistent invocation of "freedom" resounded. Strangely enough, the petitions fell largely along lines demarcated by decades'-long culture wars informed by predominantly white cries for individual and religious freedom on the one side and a growing multiracial alliance demanding justice and freedom for Black people under the "Black Lives Matter" banner on the other. As the petitions grew, so did the acrimony.

In the heat of these debates, then-president Donald Trump sent out three tweets on April 17: "Liberate Minnesota!"; "LIBERATE MICHIGAN!"; and, "LIBERATE VIRGINIA, and save your great 2nd Amendment. It is under siege!" Upset by state and government officials who initiated restrictive measures to stem the tide of the coronavirus, Trump and his supporters called for "freedom" from what they viewed as the overzealous, business-killing restrictions of Democratic governors and elected officials. Thirteen days after Trump's tweet, in Michigan, where Governor Gretchen Whitmer issued an executive order extending their state of emergency that curtailed the opening of businesses and extended stay-at-home restrictions, armed militia showed up at the state capital demanding entrance to the floor of the assembly as lawmakers debated the measures.[1] The display of arms, captured in pictures by news media and made viral on social media, showed angry white men with military-style rifles facing off with capitol police.[2] The demonstrations marked some of the most aggressive protests to date against the efforts of legislators to institute measures to alter the course of the coronavirus.

Yet none of these protests was more surprising to some than those issued by pastors, who declared the restrictions an infringement upon their religious liberty. In addition to closing businesses to prevent the spread of the virus, elected officials in states like California also issued ordinances mandating that churches close, pointing to instances of mass religious gatherings as super-spreader events. In March, for example, fifty-three members of a choir were infected with the virus and two members died after attending choir rehearsal at a church in Mount Vernon, Washington.[3] And from April 10 to May 10, twelve Felician sisters at the Presentation of the Blessed Virgin Mary in Livonia, Michigan, died of coronavirus, with a thirteenth sister dying in June.[4] By April 3, seven leaders of the Church of God in Christ—bishops and superintendents of the Michigan district—died of COVID-19 after attending an annual religious convocation in March. A viral social media post captioned "The Historic First Jurisdiction of Michigan Mourns the Loss of So Great a Cloud of Witnesses" showed pictures of the seven men who all died from coronavirus—Superintendent Leon R. McPherson Sr., Superintendent Myron E. Left, Bishop Robert L. Harris, Bishop Robert E. Smith Sr., Superintendent Kevelin B. Jones Sr., Superintendent Paul E. Hester Sr., and Superintendent John D. Beverly.[5] By April 20 the report had grown more ominous. A story posted in *Charisma News* led with a simple title: "Up to 30 COGIC Bishops, Leaders Die from COVID-19."[6] Death hovered over the church—a tragedy of epic proportions unfolded in one of the most storied Black religious institutions in the country, the nation's first incorporated Pentecostal denomination.[7] The March services were conducted before there was universal consensus from the government or other agencies that sizable gatherings, like church worship services, presented dangerous hotspots for the virus to spread.

The national debate over church services, however, devolved almost immediately into a political battle over religious freedom, making the possibility of ordering the closure of churches even more complicated. Nevertheless, the passing of leaders like those in the Church of God in Christ, along with the death of pastors and worshipers from other religious communities, brought into sharp relief the need for immediate change in how religious communities gathered during COVID-19.[8] While most churches subsequently canceled in-person events and went completely online, numerous evangelical churches continued to worship indoors, citing the president's injunction that churches are "essential" institutions and insisting that any mandate to close was just another example of government overreach.

These debates have taken place within a larger US context wherein white evangelicals often see themselves as victims, losing ground as a cultural majority to a perceived non-Christian, multicultural mass of noncitizen socialists. The pandemic's capacity to amplify these fears through necessary limitations on cross-border travel and public gatherings, including worship services, raises important questions about how "religious freedom" operates as a weapon in a larger historical culture war tool kit that is both raced and classed. How have evangelical leaders framed the debate around religious freedom in relationship to this global pandemic? Also, do black religionists feel their religious freedoms are equally under assault? In what ways might black religionists' attention to the disproportionate number of blacks dying from COVID-19 and extrajudicial violence resonate with historic interpretations around the freedoms most under threat from the government and in need of defending? Through reviews of religious media—sermons, news stories, and viral videos—this chapter explores the racial parameters of religionists' understanding of religious freedom in relationship to COVID-19.

I argue that contemporary Christian arguments focused on religious freedom align with a long-standing history of white Christian grievance politics that prioritize white grievance with government engagement in their affairs over concerns largely voiced by African American churches about basic survival and racial justice. The long history of religious freedom arguments, as explored in Tisa Winger's *Religious Freedom: The Contested History of an American Ideal*, illustrates the protracted ways in which religious freedom debates obscure long-held quests for freedom sought by people of color in the United States.[9] During the COVID-19 pandemic, the case for religious freedom was more extraordinary, given the disproportionate rate at which Black and Brown Americans were affected by the virus and the ways in which white evangelicals castigated racial protest rallies as indicative of why the church should remain open.

White Christians Making the Case for Religious Freedom

News stories as early as March 2020 showed pastors resisting the protective orders put in place by local officials. Rodney Howard-Browne, a megachurch pastor in Florida, was arrested after violating state "safer-at-home" regulations by holding two worship services with hundreds of parishioners in attendance. According to news reports, the pastor turned himself in after being charged with "unlawful assembly and violation of a public health emergency order."[10] Released on bail, the pastor's attorney argued that Howard-Browne put in place distancing protocols such that "contrary to Sheriff Chronister's allegation . . . the actions of Hillsborough County and the Hernando County Sheriff are discriminatory against religion and church gatherings."[11] The charge of discrimination against churches was levied by a number of white evangelical pastors who strongly resisted orders for churches to remain closed.

Throughout the summer, numerous other church leaders also claimed religious discrimination when called to follow state orders. Some filed lawsuits to rescind the injunctions. In August 2020, churches in California and Minnesota filed law suits arguing that their religious freedoms were hindered by government mandates.[12] The Minnesota church challenged Governor Tim Walz's mandate to remain six feet apart and to wear masks inside houses of worship. Erick Kaardal, lead counsel for the plaintiff, declared that Walz "gets an F in religious liberties."[13] In addition, Roman Catholic and Lutheran Church–Missouri Synod congregations challenged the governor's limit on ten-person worship services and were able to force the governor to increase the limit to 25 percent capacity.[14] In Florida, Rev. Joel Tillis, pastor of Suncoast Baptist Church, challenged the Manatee County's mask mandate, arguing that it shouldn't extend to houses of worship because masks hindered prayers.[15] In California, the Thomas More Society filed a lawsuit against Governor Gavin Newsom and other officials arguing that their restrictions targeted churches, calling them "unconstitutional and onerous coronavirus pandemic regulations."[16] Orthodox Jewish rabbis and Catholic priests from upstate New York also filed suit, stating that the limit of 25 percent on religious gatherings compared to 50 percent building capacity on all other gatherings was unconstitutional. They prevailed.[17]

Despite the shock and outrage of many at these religious leaders' refusals to comply with COVID-19 restrictions, their movement to remain open persisted throughout the summer and fall. Arguably the most consequential dispute arose with John MacArthur's refusal to close his church doors. With an international television ministry, *Grace to You*, and over one million copies of his *John MacArthur Study Bible*[18] and another one million of his New Testament Bible commentaries sold, John MacArthur is a towering figure in the evangelical movement. On July 29, 2020, Los Angeles County issued a cease-and-desist letter to MacArthur, who also pastors Grace Community Church, a congregation in Los Angeles with more than eight thousand members:[19]

> The County of Los Angeles (the "County") has been advised that Grace Community Church held indoor in-person worship services on July 26, 2020. . . . As of July 13, 2020, indoor worship services are prohibited within the County. The County requests that you immediately cease holding indoor worship services or other indoor gatherings, and adhere to the Health Officer Order directives governing activities at houses of worship. If you or Grace Community Church continue to hold indoor services in violation of the law, you are subject to criminal and civil liability.[20]

After outlining the measures that the government has taken and the ordinances it has issued since March in order to combat the virus that had killed more than forty-four hundred in the county, the notice further stated,

> While having the ability to conduct outdoor and virtual services, Grace Community Church conducted indoor in-person services on July 26, 2020, violating the State and County health orders. Violating these orders is a crime punishable by a fine of up to $1,000 and imprisonment of up to 90 days. . . . Each day that you conduct indoor services is a separate offense. Pursuant to the State and County health orders, Grace Community Church must immediately cease holding indoor worship services. . . . The County again requests Grace Community Church's assistance and adherence to the health and safety protocols listed above as we collectively continue trying to close the spread of COVID-19 in Los Angeles County.[21]

While numerous evangelical pastors have led efforts decrying what they considered government overreach during the most crucial summer months of the pandemic, virtually none is more well known and forthright in their opposition than John MacArthur. Days before the injunction was issued, MacArthur wrote a long treatise titled "Christ, Not Caesar, Is Head of the Church: A Biblical Case for the Church's Duty to Remain Open," explaining for his vast audience the significance of religious freedom and why his congregation would not adhere to government mandates to close.[22] Articulating his belief that God has established three forms of authority on earth, "the family, the state, and the church," he declared that "it has never been the prerogative of civil government to order, modify, forbid, or mandate worship. When, how, and how often the church worships is not subject to Caesar. Caesar himself is subject to God. Jesus affirmed that principle when He told Pilate, 'You would have no authority over Me, unless it had been given you from above' (John 19:11)."[23] By August a local judge rendered a decision allowing the megachurch pastor to continue holding indoor services, a disappointment to county officials. In his first comments to his congregation after the judge's ruling on August 16, McArthur said, "The good news is, you're here, you're not distancing, and you're not wearing masks. . . . And it's also good news that you're not outside because it's very hot out there, so the Lord knew you needed to be inside and unmasked, so he did us that gracious favor."[24]

These instances of public legal dissent represent the formal, litigious side of a culture war at work. Not only, however, were pastors raising concerns at the highest reaches of government, but everyday preachers, some turned internet celebrities, also took to social media to protest what they saw as the overreach of government. These pastor-provocateurs even railed loudly against the wearing of masks in *public* spaces, believing that these requirements as well were an example of government overreach. In one post after the nation topped over 230,000 deaths, outspoken internet preacher and lead pastor of Global Vision Bible Church in Tennessee, Greg Locke, railed against Dunkin Donuts and an employee's request that he wear a mask when he enters the establishment. In his YouTube post he admits to the confrontation, which might have caused other pastors embarrassment, and doubles down on his defiance:

I said, "If you call me a liar one more time, I'm going to take these work boots and I'm going to kick your teeth down your throat." Yes, I said it. And in the moment, I meant it.

I said, "Sir, listen to me very closely, I will be back at 5 o'clock tonight to get my two medium coffees, seven creams, and five sugars and I will be back tonight and I will not be wearing a mask."

I'll go to jail over this. It is the golden calf. I'm sick of Christians saying things like this: "Well, it's just a mask." You know what they used to say? "Oh, it's just a baby, it's just a zygote, it's just a growth in the mother's womb so let's kill it."

No, it's not just a mask, it's a compliance device. This is not about safety, this is about surrendering of our rights.

Can I remind you? This is still the United States of America. This is not communism. This is not China, this ain't North Korea, I don't live in Haiti. Trump 2020! I'm a pastor and I approve this message.[25]

In response to widely circulated media stories asking people to curtail their November 2020 Thanksgiving plans because the nation experienced a fall surge in coronavirus cases, which had pushed some hospitals to their limits, the "redneck theology" preacher (in his own words) posted a taunting message to the public, including his eighty thousand Twitter followers:

Dear Left, I'm celebrating multiple Thanksgiving meals with lots of people at every gathering. We will meet as long as we want without your permission. Y'all need to sit down and seriously stop railroading Americans with your STUPID COMMUNISM.[26]

The politicizing of the virus led a number of pastors and legislators to denounce government safety protocols as evidence of "communism" and a denial of their First Amendment right to freedom. The coalescence of these issues fell amid a broader national campaign for the presidency of the United States. With critiques raging in the news over then-president Donald Trump's handling of the coronavirus and dismay at his determination that the virus was "over" during the 2020 Republican National Convention in August ahead of the November 3, 2020, election, a number of his supporters argued that continuous appeals for safety measures—like mask wearing, social distancing, or temporary closings—were emblematic of Democrats exaggerating the extent and danger of the virus in order to hurt Trump politically. Despite Trump's eventual contraction of the virus along with dozens of his associates, the politically based conspiracy theories continued. These pastors' rejection of the safety measures is, thus, also a rejection of what they see as Democratic politics. As staunch Republican Christians, their response attends both to their religious convictions as well as their political leanings, two passions seamlessly woven together.

Despite the lawsuits filed by white evangelical leaders, according to Pew Research, everyday Republicans and Democrats think restrictions on churches make sense, but more Democrats than Republicans agree.[27] While two-thirds of Republicans believe that houses of worship should be held to the same standards regarding closure as other organizations and businesses, 93 percent of Democrats maintain that stance. These numbers help illustrate why the majority of churches that refused to close during the government shutdown were white and evangelical. While some Black churches remained open and some reopened in limited capacity, by and large they have not made a legal issue out of the restraints implemented by government officials. This reserved response reflects the long history of black Christian engagement with the religious freedom debate as well as the fact that a disproportionate number of African Americans have been affected by the pandemic.

Black Religion and Religious Freedom

From the start of the nation the provision for religious freedom was written into the Constitution with the promise that "Congress shall make no law respecting an establishment of religion, or prohibiting the free exercise thereof; or abridging the freedom of speech, or of the press; or the right of the people peaceably to assemble, and to petition the Government for a redress of grievances." This seemingly clear exhortation to allow the uninhibited, peaceable practice of religion in the United States has led to centuries of disputes. Most glaringly for African Americans, the debate over religious freedom prior to the Civil War framed arguments both in support of and in opposition to the institution of slavery. Pro-slavery ministers and laypeople argued that slavery

was a divine right and that any attempt to amend or eliminate the institution was an infringement upon their religious freedom. According to
historian Tisa Wenger,

> Before the Civil War, the dominant logics of religious freedom had served
> to ward off any challenges to the institution of slavery. In the North as
> well as in the South, many white Protestants sought to silence abolitionist
> agitation and to avoid denominational conflicts by insisting that the slav-
> ery issue must be resolved at the level of individual conscience. . . . They
> denounced abolitionists as radicals who threatened not only the consti-
> tutional rights of private property and state sovereignty but religious free-
> dom as well, . . . These proslavery southerners increasingly defended the
> "sacred right" of slavery as a divinely ordained institution. Alongside the
> principles of states' rights and property rights, they used religious free-
> dom talk to name the abolitionists of the North as the true oppressors.[28]

The wielding of religious freedom to support the institution of slavery did not stop with the debate over black freedom from slavery, but
continued well into the twentieth century with debates over Jim Crow
segregation. "Through the 1940s and 1950s," according to Wenger, "seg-
regationists regularly invoked religious freedom alongside the freedom
of choice and the freedom of association to defend racially exclusive
schools, neighborhoods, and workplaces."[29] This alliance between the
right of white Christians to deny Black rights based upon their religious
freedom made religious freedom a less salient and attractive argument
for Black religionists. "African Americans had good reason to be suspicious of religious freedom talk because those who claimed the mantle of
whiteness had most often employed it to bolster rather than to challenge
the institutionalized hierarchies of race."[30] Instead, Black religionists
argued for civil and voting rights, with the presumption of religious freedom already active in their petitions.

Wenger suggests that nonmainstream African American religious
practitioners, like those associated with the Black Muslim movement
and various supporters of the Black Gods of the Metropolis, made
greater, though limited, use of religious freedom arguments. Given their
marginal status in the Black religious community and even more marginal status in the nation as a whole, they sought to garner greater rights

by arguing their status as religious minorities as opposed to racial minorities. "For the vast majority of African Americans," however, "religious freedom provided little escape from the confines of a racialized oppression."³¹ The terms of the debate had already been set for religious freedom to benefit by and large the white Protestant majority. As Wenger makes clear in her own assessment of religious freedom, however, "I do not mean to suggest that religious freedom talk has always or necessarily worked in the service of whiteness. Like any other ideal—and like the principle of freedom more generally—religious freedom has been invoked and (re)configured in any number of ways. Nevertheless, the cultural and legal stature of this ideal made it a prominent feature of the racial-religious assemblages that worked more often than not to protect the privileges of whiteness."³²

Although Blacks did not formally invoke the religious freedom argument, according to sociologist Jacqueline Rivers, African Americans have utilized the idea of religious freedom, even if not articulating their advocacy in such terms. Explaining why Blacks should be more concerned about religious freedom, despite the history of white abuses of religious freedom to ensure their subordination, Rivers asserts, "Many actions motivated by religious beliefs are carried out without any reference to religious freedom; rather there is an unquestioning presumption of the right to exercise that freedom, to act as one's faith convictions dictate without the expectation that such an action might be prohibited or otherwise constrained."³³ "For African Americans," Rivers contends that this means that "their assumptions regarding their freedom to act on religious beliefs has had an enormous impact on their lives."³⁴

Drawing on the lives of Christian abolitionists whose vehement opposition to slavery led to the splitting of the Baptist, Methodist, and Presbyterian Churches in the United States, as well as the Christian convictions of Black abolitionists like Frederick Douglass, Harriet Tubman, Sojourner Truth, David Walker, and James McCune Smith, Rivers contends that the *enactment* of religious freedom through their repudiation of slavery demonstrates the emblematic relationship between religious freedom and the fight for racial justice in America.³⁵ "The theological ideas of Arminianism, perfectionism, and beneficence that flowed from the Second Great Awakening transformed religious views and convinced many Christians that slavery was a sin that had to be repented of immediately."[36] Rivers further explores the civil rights movement and the work of contemporary urban ministries in meeting the needs of the poor as evidence of religious freedom enacted. These three moments in history for her narrate the significance of religious freedom to the struggles of Black Americans, yet she contends that given the racial animus motivating white Christian usage of religious freedom along with the growing public rejection of religious freedom arguments in the denial of LGBTQ rights, Black Christians have been largely absent from contemporary debates about religious freedom.

Instead, black Christians have invoked civil rights as a means of voicing their concerns about the adjudication of freedom. As Rev. William H. Lamar IV, pastor of Metropolitan African Methodist Episcopal Church in Washington, DC, explains, even today, religious freedom has a "dubious pedigree. . . . It means nothing. It means everything. Under most circumstances, I want nothing to do with this term. There are other rhetorical choices, choices not rooted in the language of American imperial sloganeering."[37] With the rise of the global pandemic of 2020 and the international Movement for Black Lives, nationally known black ministers along with local pastors have embraced a call for justice. Although the Movement for Black Lives is more diffuse and egalitarian and less explicitly Christian in its organizational structure than the civil rights movement, Black Church leaders have consistently voiced support for the campaign for racial justice in America. National leaders such as Otis Moss, Cynthia Hale, E. Dewey Smith, and Frederick D. Haynes III have been outspoken supporters of this movement, preaching sermons and serving on public panels to help discuss the issues that have animated the nation during the coronavirus pandemic. In addition, from some of the most notable Black megachurches in the country to some of the smallest rural congregations, Black churches have largely remained closed throughout the pandemic, innovating their worship services and media ministries (if they have them) to accommodate congregations with uncertain futures. In large part, they recognize that those most affected by the virus, like essential workers, are in their congregations or in congregations like theirs.

In one online discussion between a social media influencer and comedian, KevinOnStage, and the pastor of a large Chicago-based church, the comedian asked the pastor about a video of his that had gone viral.

In the video the pastor is heard proclaiming to his now online congregation that they would not return to church until city hall reopened. When the governor and the mayor felt as though it was safe for them to be in close proximity with others, then, and only then, the pastor concluded, would he advise his congregants to be in close proximity with one another. With KevinOnStage laughing and talking with the pastor about his dogged determination *not* to reopen, the clip received hundreds of thousands of views. The video itself not only highlighted the ways in which Black religious leaders are innovating their worship service to accommodate an online community, but it also exposed the deep and driving concern that Black pastors have for the physical health of their congregants over and against a demand for what some have described as religious freedom. As Black pastors called for racial justice and white evangelical pastors called for religious freedom, the reality of the culture wars came into sharp focus.

When Race and Religion Collide

The insistence upon one's right to gather in the midst of a pandemic and to disregard health officials' consistent pleas for the suspension of large enclosed gatherings for the sake of the community and its health care workers reflects not only religio/political leanings but also speaks to deeply embedded issues of race. The hyperindividualism motivating much of American evangelicalism has historically played itself out in measures that undermine attention to systemic or collective grievance, particularly as it relates to African Americans. Evangelicalism's individualism has been a tool to champion a certain vision of America, while also limiting the ability of BIPOC (Black, Indigenous, and People of Color) to make claims about the systemic nature of fundamental historic and contemporary harms.

In her work *Mississippi Praying*, Carolyn DuPont argues that white supremacy doesn't exist in spite of American evangelicalism, but rather because of it. The innate belief in the individual supersedes all arguments made by the socially disadvantaged for redress of social ills. With a focus on white evangelical resistance to the civil rights movement and with it a religious rejection to integrating white churches and schools, Dupont points to the historic ways in which a belief in individual rights and freedoms fueled white evangelical support for Jim Crow. In accordance with this belief, the claims made by civil rights activists regarding the systemic nature of harms done to the Black community were discarded by white evangelicals. They insisted that any harm felt in the Black community was self-inflicted and could be addressed by spiritual conversion and, thus, was not a result of structural inequality. She contends, however,

> Contrary to evangelicals' assertions, the conversion of every Mississippian in the state would never correct the sufferings caused by an exclusionary political system, a deficient educational system, a discriminatory economic system, and an unfair judicial system. Yet this individualistic notion of social change allowed Mississippians, among other southern evangelicals, "to decry government initiatives as ineffective and unwarranted intrusions."[38]

This same resistance to "government intrusion" correlates with contemporary white evangelicals' inability to acknowledge the coronavirus as a harm that needs to be addressed by systemic government intervention. Any attempt at a national and comprehensive government response has been rejected by Republican leadership and the white evangelicals. As a result, their unwillingness to intervene and to simply allow the system to operate as it has, to "conserve" the status quo, renders communities of color particularly harmed.

As the effects of the coronavirus began to mushroom, reports emerged indicating that black communities experienced the greater burden of loss from the virus. The US surgeon general, Dr. Jerome Adams, issued a report in April that received high criticism from African Americans.[39] Although he brought attention to the disproportionate harm caused to African Americans by the coronavirus, he laid blame for it solely at their own feet. Citing poor diet and bad personal habits, he suggested that black Americans' preexisting comorbidities were the sole reason for their disproportionate death due to the coronavirus. Research studies, however, suggested that Black Americans were also largely affected because of their socioeconomic status and labor as essential workers, many of whom were without adequate health care. The systemic nature of poverty that rendered Blacks disproportionately reliant upon public transportation, unable to shelter in place from work assignments, and living in confined quarters with others, made them and poorer Americans more vulnerable to the ravages of the virus. Furthermore, Blacks were at the mercy of a health care system that had long been criticized for the differential treatment it offers to African Americans.

To address these types of concerns would take seismic shifts in the American social and economic structure, but in lieu of such changes, addressing the specific spread of the virus, leading scientists argued, would require a nationally coordinated response. Resistance to that, as evidenced by the lawsuits and refusal to wear masks by white evangelicals, makes their response not only insensitive to the health care providers who must take care of the sick, but also to those communities that are disproportionately affected by the virus, particularly African Americans. In this way, as sociologist Bonilla Silva argues, in a post–civil rights era, "color-blind racism" does not require overt and cantankerous racists, it simply requires people, white or nonwhite, who wish to perpetuate a system that ultimately brings harm to disadvantaged others. "Racism without racists" exists to retain the status quo.[40] It requires people who are content to adjust to the status quo, despite the systemic harm such arrangements bring to others.

Conclusion

Over the summer, Sean Feucht, a popular CCM (Christian Contemporary Music) worship leader known in the IHOP (International House of Prayer) Bethel evangelical communities held worship services in protest of the government mandated lockdowns. He called his gatherings "Let Us Worship" and insisted that they were "worship protests," comparing them to the protests that sprung up across the nation in response to the murders of George Floyd, Ahmaud Arberry, and Breonna Taylor. In an op-ed about his movement written for the conservative blog The Federalist he proclaimed,

> Something is happening in America, and it should sound the alarm for every confessing Christian. Simply put, hostile efforts in many cities now threaten to suppress the First Amendment rights of all people to exercise

our faith freely. In unprecedented acts of government-authorized injustice, Christians are being told they cannot gather for worship, they cannot sing songs of praise, and they cannot observe church ordinances.[41]

Feucht insisted that if the left could go out and protest in the streets, then Christians should be allowed to gather together and worship. He intimated the holiness of his movement and railed against what he defined as the destruction endemic to the racial justice movement.

While followers of Jesus are being told we cannot worship in public spaces, violent paid rioters are taking over our streets and being given license to occupy and destroy entire sections of our cities. Churches are being covered in graffiti and even burned while civic leaders call for defunding the police.[42]

Lacing together a string of criticisms to deter from the work of the Black Lives Matter protests that galvanized entire communities, he saw in the protests only destruction, never addressing the fundamental critique at the heart of the nation's discontent. Like other white evangelicals, he obscured the message of the racial justice movement, collapsing it into a simple riotous revolt, while promoting the sanctity of his movement and his individual right to worship.

In the midst of the Floyd protests, Feucht organized a worship service at the site of Floyd's murder and invited people to worship. Apparently in an attempt to drown out the DJ and the mourners who had gathered, Feucht led those gathered around him in what one participant described as "baptisms, healings and conversions." Instead of adhering to the concerns of the protesters, he attempted to redirect their grievance from the systemic murder of unarmed black people by the police to a revival issuing calls for personal salvation.[43] No doubt for Feucht, the officer's murder of Floyd was a result of the officer's personal failing and not a system-wide problem. The solution for Feucht was personal prayer and salvation. And so he continued to invite people to personal worship. In a post emblazoned with over a dozen weeping emojis on June 13, he declared, "I HAVE NO WORDS FOR WHAT GOD IS DOING TONIGHT IN MINNEAPOLIS!!! The valley of anchor," he declared, "has become a door of hope!!!!"[44]

Despite his expression of emotion over what he thought God was doing, others present saw something different. One respondent, Lisa Pierce, retorted, "Wow, way to center yourself. Jesus would have grieved alongside the people, not shown up with a stage and a microphone."[45] The response to Feucht among critics on Twitter told a different story than the one he narrated.[46] Not only had he not embraced the community's sorrow and call for justice, but he, in their eyes, usurped the moment to redirect attention to what *he* deemed the community needed. Furthermore, he offered little by way of support of the community's problem with the police.[47]

For many white evangelicals Feucht's response reflects their primary concern. With a desire to see individual souls saved, and a desire to see individual, personal transformation, they are often unwilling to acknowledge the role of the collective in sin and destruction. In this way religious freedom acts as a foil for individual engagement in the world.

The coronavirus has laid bare the economic fissures that constrain the country, at the same time as it has laid bare the culture wars that continue to animate public life. Instead of science leading the discussion of how we should all respond, the public discussion of the virus and efforts to contain and restrain it have become political talking points and culture war dividing lines. After three months denying the severity of the pandemic and the fact that it travels via air, former president Trump only started wearing a mask in public in April (ultimately doing so very rarely, however), finally signaling to his followers that masks are important and beneficial in the mediation of the virus. With just 4 percent of the world's population, the United States accounted for well over 26 percent of its deaths by the end of the summer. Nevertheless, he continued to emphasize that masks were optional and not required, the call for "freedom" not far from his lips. White evangelicals' alliance with Trump and their calls for "freedom" have privileged only one type of freedom: their personal and individual right to worship and do as they please. This call, however, has come at the expense of another type of freedom for their fellow citizens, the freedom literally to "*LIFE*, liberty and the pursuit of happiness."

As religion scholar Corey D. B. Walker, arguing for a more capacious view of religious freedom, opines in an edited "provocation" about the study of African Americans and religious freedom,

Our current battles over religious freedom are not just about a politics of God, Gods or no God. They are about the norms and rules that will authorize and govern our social and political lives. We need to formulate and embrace an understanding of religious freedom that moves from conceptual closure to democratic openness in ways that are not narrowly tailored, preconfigured ends. In this manner, the discourse of religious freedom will give voice to a new expression of democracy for an ever-widening circle of "We the people."[48]

NOTES

1 Craig Mauger, "Protesters, Some Armed, Enter Michigan Capitol in Rally Against COVID-19 Limits," *Detroit News*, April 30, 2020, www.detroitnews.com.

2 "Armed Protesters Demonstrate against COVID-19 Lockdown at Michigan Capitol," *Guardian*, April 30, 2020, www.theguardian.com.

3 David Waldstein, "Coronavirus Ravaged a Choir. But Isolation Helped Contain It," *New York Times*, May 12, 2020, www.nytimes.com.

4 Allyson Waller and Christine Hauser, "Convent in Michigan Loses 13 Sisters to COVID-19," *New York Times*, July 23, 2020, www.nytimes.com.

5 Marlon Millner, "The Historic First Jurisdiction of Michigan," Facebook, April 2, 2020, www.facebook.com/marlon.millner.9/posts/10221814267207913.

6 Jenny Rose Spaudo, "Up to 30 COGIC Bishops, Leaders Die from COVID-19," *Charisma Magazine*, April 2020, www.charismamag.com.

7 The Church of God in Christ (COGIC) is the largest Black Pentecostal denomination in the country. Formed in the late 1800s through the leadership of Charles Mason, the church emerged as a critique of Baptist and Methodist denominations, which they believed rejected the call to holiness. It grew to incorporate teachings on the supernatural power of the Holy Spirit after Mason attended what came to be known as the Azusa Street revival in 1906 in Los Angeles, California. The revival, led by William Seymour, a black itinerate preacher, emphasized the importance of speaking in tongues as a manifestation of the Holy Spirit. A multiracial event, the revival was pivotal to the spread of global Pentecostalism as we know it today. COGIC reorganized after the revival, with an emphasis on the supernatural gifts of God, and became the first incorporated Pentecostal denomination in the country.

8 Several other stories have emerged about the tragic deaths of religious leaders since the pandemic began. For example, in Virginia, a pastor who defied warnings about the severity of the virus passed away. His daughter later issued a call for people to take the virus seriously. See Neil Vigdor, "Pastor Who Defied Social Distancing Dies after Contracting COVID-19, Church Says," *New York Times* April 14, 2020, www.nytimes.com. Also, a pastor and his wife died within hours of one another in Morrero, Louisiana. See Sherman Desselle, "77-Year-Old Westbank Pastor, Wife Both Die after Testing Positive to COVID-19, Family Says,"

WDSU News, April 11, 2020, www.wdsu.com. Numerous other stories across the country captured the tragedy and concern raised by religious leaders contracting the virus.

9   Tisa Winger, *Religious Freedom: The Contested History of an American Ideal* (Chapel Hill: University of North Carolina Press, 2017).

10 Tamara Lush and Chris O'Meara, "Florida Megachurch Pastor Arrested for Holding Services, Defying Social Distancing Orders," *USA Today*, March 31, 2020, www.usatoday.com.

11 Ibid.

12 David Crary, "More US Churches Sue to Challenge COVID-19 Restrictions," AP News, August 13, 2020, https://apnews.com.

13 Ibid.

14 Ibid.

15 Ibid.

16 Ibid.

17 Ibid.

18 "The Bestselling MacArthur Study Bible Added to Thomas Nelson's Premier Collection," March 2019, https://rushtopress.org.

19 Leah MarieAnn Klett, "Judge Bans Indoor Services at John MacArthur's Grace Community Church," *Christian Post*, September 11, 2020, www.christianpost.com.

20 Jason H. Tokoro, "RE: Notice of Violation of Public Health Orders," letter sent to John MacArthur, dated July 29, 2020, last accessed 11/20/20, www.thomasmore society.org/wp-content/uploads/2020/08/MacArthur-Ex.-5-1_Cease-and-Desist -Letter.pdf.

21 Ibid.

22 John MacArthur, "Christ, Not Caesar, Is Head of the Church: A Biblical Case for the Church's Duty to Remain Open," July 24, 2020, *Grace to You*, www.gty.org.

23 Ibid.

24 Jaclyn Cosgrove, "Judge denies L.A. County's Request to Stop Grace Community Church from Gathering," August 25, 2020, www.latimes.com.

25 www.youtube.com/watch?v=_K1v-Ep6i18, last accessed 11/12/20.

26 Greg Locke on Twitter, November 13, 2020.

27 Justin Nortey, "Republicans More Open to In-Person Worship, but Most Oppose Religious Exemptions from COVID Restrictions," Pew Research Center, August 11, 2020, www.pewresearch.org. See also "Americans Oppose Religious Exemptions From Coronavirus-Related Restrictions," Pew Research Center, August 7, 2020, www.pewforum.org.

28 Tisa Winger, *Religious Freedom: The Contested History of an American Ideal* (Chapel Hill: University of North Carolina Press, 2017), 192.

29 Ibid., 194.

30 Ibid., 192.

31 Ibid., 191.

32 Ibid., 196.

33 Jacqueline Rivers, "The Paradox of the Black Church and Religious Freedom," *Religious Freedom and the Common Good* 15, no. 3 (2019): 680.

34 Ibid.

35 Ibid., 684.

36 Ibid., 685.

37 William H. Lamar IV, "Religious Freedom and the Black Church Today," in Sabrina E. Dent and Corey D. B. Walker, eds., *African Americans and Religious Freedom: New Perspectives for Congregations and Communities* (Washington, DC: Freedom Forum, 2021), 46.

38 Carolyn Renee Dupont, *Mississippi Praying: Southern Evangelicals and the Civil Rights Movement, 1945–1975* (New York: NYU Press, 2013), 9.

39 Curtis Bunn, "Black Health Experts Say Surgeon General's Comments Reflect Lack of Awareness of Black Community," ABC News, April 15, 2020, www.nbc news.com.

40 Eduardo Bonilla Silva, *Racism without Racists: Color-Blind Racism and the Persistence of Racial Inequality*, 5th ed. (Lanham, MD: Rowman and Littlefield, 2018).

41 Sean Feucht, "'Worship Protests' Are Bringing Revival to America's Cities," The Federalist (Blog), September 17, 2020, https://thefederalist.com.

42 Ibid.

43 Several articles narrate this concern, including one opinion piece by a writer who says that she ceased identifying as an evangelical after attending one of Feucht's events held in response to the Black Lives Matter protests. See Ruth Graham, "The Street Corner Where George Floyd Was Killed Has Become a Christian Revivalist Site," *Slate*, June 29, 2020, https://slate.com. See also, D. L. Mayfield, "How a Sean Feucht Worship Service Convinced Me I Am No Longer an Evangelical," Religion News, September 23, 2020, https://religionnews.com/.

44 Sean Feucht @seanfeucht on Twitter, June 20, 2020: https://twitter.com/seanfeucht/status/1271981803264520192.

45 Lisa Pierce @creek_n_canyon on Twitter, June 15, 2020: https:twitter.com/creek_n_canyon/status/1272483707547312128.

46 Melissa Turtinen, "California Christian Musician Criticized for 'Co-opting' George Floyd Memorial," bringmethenews.com, June 15, 2020, https://bringmeth enews.com.

47 Graham, "Street Corner," 2020.

48 Sabrina E. Dent and Corey D. B. Walker, eds., *African Americans and Religious Freedom: New Perspectives for Communities and Congregations* (Washington, D.C.: Freedom Forum, 2021), 71.

ACKNOWLEDGMENTS

A personal and purposeful hindsight for me is to be mindful of those prized people with whom we claim solidarity, for they are the ties that bind us when all else seems to be falling away into nothingness. More than that, they are the ones who breathe life into us and hold us in the grip of our faith. They are the ones who steer us through the journey of a harrowing, hard-won past and keep us living for the future.

There have been many who formed the cloud of witnesses for this work in the valley, who have been human manifestations of divine presence in my thinking, being, and doing of this work. My pillar of clouds by day have been my maternal grandparents, Mary Elizabeth and Sidney Underwood, whose sharecropping history was transformed into a harvest for their fourteen children and thirty-five grandchildren, so that we may, in their estimation, "live as long as we want and not want for as long as we live." Their eldest daughter and her navy sweetheart, Lillian and Charles Floyd, were my parents. It was their constant love and every indulgence that provided me with the fortitude and faith to set my own standard upon the foundation of my faith while forging the biggest room for improvement, rather than seeing myself through normative gaze and the dimly lit perspectives of small minds and petty people.

I am eternally grateful to those colleagues who have contributed to this volume, behind its pages and in the trenches, as they have been my very present help in the time of storm. Particularly and foremost is W. David Nelson, whose insight and commitment have been incomparable—but also the labor of love and generosity offered by Lorraine and Arthur Capers, Clay and Vicki Jones, Sidney Underwood, Amy Martin-Nelson, Mark Toulouse, Lincoln Galloway, Philip Cooke, Cheryl Lowe, Shataia Gresham Howard, Debra Peek Haynes, Amelia Ward, Marvilieu Hall, Sha'Tika Brown, Duane Belgrave, and the Underwood Family Call.

None of this would have been possible without the foresight of Jennifer Hammer, an erstwhile editor and chief advocate of religion and social change with one of the nation's best presses, NYU. I am equally grateful to Anthony Pinn, the co-editor of the NYU Religion and Social Transformation series, whose hard work and guiding hand has furthered the field of religious studies and African American thought. I offer gratitude as well to my erstwhile research assistant, Taqiyyah Elliot, whose tireless efforts and precision illustrate that the future of womanist scholarship is in good and capable hands.

I am very grateful to the institutions that have sheltered and enabled me to live into the integrity of my being, as they have fortified the bridge where there would otherwise be gaps between the academy and the church, faith and reason, and scholarship and activism. To Vanderbilt Divinity School, the Black Religious Scholars Group, Friendship West Baptist Church, Temple Baptist Church, the Society of Race, Ethnicity and Religion, and the Sisters of the Sabbath Book Club, I am forever in your debt.

Lastly, it is befitting that I write this acknowledgment on February 14, 2021, for God's faithfulness has manifested no greater love than the loving faithfulness of my family. My sister, Janet Floyd, has been my daily 5 a.m. prayer partner and midnight cheerleader ever since I can remember. As my last living sibling and the immediate enfleshing of our beloved mother, who is now our angel, she has been my lifeline. My most unique privilege as a scholar and spouse is that I have a soulmate with whom I share a life of head, heart, and hand. Juan Floyd-Thomas is a husband without rival and a colleague without comparison. His genius is only matched by his generosity of love, labor, and laughter. Much of my academic work would be both unimaginable and impossible without his ability to be in step and rhythm with my every stride and thought. "A life of the mind" is easily lost when you are joined to someone who might lose you in translation or someone who cannot fathom how thoughts take time, tenderness, and energy to develop. It is with his unfailing love and co-labor that our sweetest fruit, our greatest work produced, our greatest treasure found, and our wildest dream has come true—our daughter Lillian Makeda Floyd-Thomas, whom I lovingly call "Books." I endlessly delight in every chapter of the wondrous book of love that is her life.

S.M.F.T.
Nashville, Tennessee
February 14, 2021

ABOUT THE EDITOR

STACEY M. FLOYD-THOMAS is E. Rhodes and Leona B. Carpenter Chair and Associate Professor of Ethics and Society at Vanderbilt University. She has published eight books and numerous articles that focus on liberation theology and ethics, critical race theory, critical pedagogy, and postcolonial studies, including *Deeper Shades of Purple: Womanism in Religion and Society, Black Church Studies: An Introduction*, and *The Altars Where We Worship: The Religious Significance of American Popular Culture.*

ABOUT THE CONTRIBUTORS

BLANCHE BONG COOK is Associate Professor at the University of Kentucky Rosenberg College of Law. She graduated from Vassar College and the University of Michigan Law School. She teaches Criminal Law, Criminal Procedure, Evidence, and a Sex Trafficking Seminar. She was formerly a federal prosecutor with the Department of Justice, where she specialized in large-scale drug and sex-trafficking prosecutions. She is a leading expert on race and police violence and sex trafficking. Her publications are available on SSRN.

CHRISTOPHER M. DRISCOLL is Assistant Professor of Religious Studies at Lehigh University in Bethlehem, Pennsylvania. A scholar of race, religion, and culture, specifically historical and contemporary U.S. and European religious, philosophical, and theological thought and traditions, hip hop culture, and existentialism/humanisms, Driscoll is author of *White Lies* (Routledge, 2015), co-author of *Method as Identity* (Lexington, 2018), co-editor of a Special Issue of *Culture and Religion—Mountaineering Religion* (Taylor and Francis, 2021), among other writings.

JUAN M. FLOYD-THOMAS is Associate Professor of African American Religious History at Vanderbilt University Divinity School and the Graduate Department of Religion at Vanderbilt University in Nashville, Tennessee. Floyd-Thomas is author of *Liberating Black Church History: Making It Plain*, and *The Origins of Black Humanism: Reverend Ethelred Brown and the Unitarian Church*; co-author of *The Altars Where We Worship: The Religious Significance of American Popular Culture*, and *Black Church Studies: An Introduction*; and co-editor of *Religion in the Age of Obama*, in addition to other publications.

MARLA F. FREDERICK is the Asa Griggs Candler Professor of Religion and Culture at Emory University's Candler School of Theology. An anthropologist by training, she examines the overlapping spheres of religion, race, gender, media, and politics. She is the author and/or co-author of four books and several articles, including *Between Sundays: Black Women and Everyday Struggles of Faith*; *Colored Television: American Religion Gone Global*; and *Televised Redemption: Black Religious Media and Racial Empowerment*.

DAVID P. GUSHEE is Distinguished University Professor of Christian Ethics and Director of the Center for Theology and Public Life at Mercer University. He is the elected Past-President of both the American Academy of Religion and Society of Christian Ethics, and author and/or editor of 26 books, which have been translated into a dozen languages. He is seen globally as one of this generation's leading Christian ethicists.

MELANIE C. JONES is a womanist ethicist, millennial preacher, and intellectual activist. Melanie joined the Union Presbyterian Seminary faculty as Instructor of Ethics, Theology and Culture and Inaugural Director of the Katie Geneva Cannon Center for Womanist Leadership in fall 2019. Melanie's research engages womanist theological ethics and sacred texts, millennials and faith, and Black aesthetics and popular culture. A third-generation ordained Baptist preacher and sought-after lecturer, Melanie is an emerging millennial voice with noted academic and popular publications as well as features on television, radio, and news outlets.

CONĀ S. M. MARSHALL is an Assistant Professor of American Religion in the Department of Religion and Classics at the University of Rochester. Her forthcoming book, *Ain't I a Preacher?: Black Women's Homiletic Rhetoric* (Lexington Books: Rowman & Littlefield) examines the sermonic rhetoric of four leading contemporary preacher-scholars— Teresa Fry Brown, Vashti McKenzie, Eboni Marshall Turman and Melanie C. Jones—in efforts to describe womanist preaching tenets and prescribe a womanist preaching method.

ANTHONY B. PINN is the Agnes Cullen Arnold Professor of Humanities and professor of religion at Rice University. He is also Professor Extraordinarius at the University of South Africa. He has published more than 30 books, including *Terror and Triumph: The Nature of Black Religion*, *Oxford University Press Handbook of Humanism*, and the forthcoming *The Interplay of Things*. Pinn is the founding director of the Center for Engaged Research and Collaborative Learning, and the inaugural director of the Center for African and African American Studies. Pinn's research interests include Black moralism, religion, and culture; humanism; constructive theologies; and hip-hop culture.

TINK TINKER is a citizen of the Osage Nation (*wazhazhe*) and Emeritus Professor of American Indian Studies at Iliff School of Theology where he spent 33 active teaching years. For nearly three decades he volunteered both administratively and as a traditional spiritual leader at Four Winds American Indian Council in Denver and worked closely with the American Indian Movement of Colorado. He has written extensively, both books and nearly 100 journal articles.

MIGUEL A. DE LA TORRE is Professor of Social Ethics and Latinx Studies at the Iliff School of Theology in Denver. He has published 43 books (five of which won national awards). A Fulbright scholar, he served as the 2012 President of the Society of Christian Ethics and was the co-founder / first executive director of the Society of Race, Ethnicity, and Religion. He also wrote the screenplay for the documentary *Trails of Hope and Terror* (https://www.trailsofhopeandterrorthemovie.com/).

INDEX

Abbott, Greg, 196, 198
abolitionists, 254
Abraham, 108
Abrams, Stacey, xvii, 88
absurdity: in Black Church tradition, 219; Chappelle using, 226–27
Adams, Jerome, 257
advertisements, 218
Affordable Care Act, 202
African Americans. *See* Black people
African Methodist Episcopal Church, 226
Afrocentrism, 34
Afrofuturism, 34
Afro-pessimism, 143
Agamben, Georgio: on bare life, 83; on white defiance, 84–85
Age of Fracture (Rodgers), 211n15
Alexander, Michelle, 157
Algeria, 115–16
American Indians, 8–9; colonialism and genocide of, 123–24; COVID-19 impacting, 126–36; infectious disease and conquest of, 125–26; lands of, 126–29; religion understood by, 140n31; smallpox pandemic impacting, 80; worldview of, 134
Amherst, Jeffrey, 80
Angelou, Maya, 21
Anglicans, 236
Ansari, Aziz, 223–24
anthropocentrism, 135–36
anthropodicy, 105
anti-Blackness, xvii
antielitism, 234

antimaskers, 106, 250–51, 260
anti-vaccination movement, 202–3
apartheid, 219
apology fatigue, 155
Appiah, Kwame Anthony, 204
Arbery, Ahmaud, 58, 88, 159, 258
Arendt, Hannah, on race, 204–5
art, religion and, 111–12
Ase Ire, 34
Asian Americans, 151, 152–54
AstroTurf movements, 202
Augustine of Hippo, on love, 189
Austin, 201
Ayala, Jose, 170, 174

Baby Boomers, 57
Baldwin, James, 110; on Christianity, 205–6
Balz, Dan, 232
Banks, Ingrid, 45
Bannon, Steve, 173
Barber, William J., 209
bare life, 83
Barry, Steve, 94
Beckett, Samuel, 78
Bell, Catherine, 190
Benbow, Candice, 72
Berger, Peter, 18
Bethel Church, 94
Between the World and Me (Coates), 207
Beverly, John D., 246
biblical interpretation, 123; white supremacy and, 48n10
biopolitics, of race, 84–85
biopower, 50n26; defining, 204

273

Lightning Source UK Ltd.
Milton Keynes UK
UKHW011957040122
396612UK00005B/269